DAMN
THE VALLEY

1st Platoon, Bravo Company, 2/508 PIR,
82nd Airborne in the Arghandab River Valley, Afghanistan

WILLIAM YESKE

CASEMATE
Philadelphia & Oxford

Published in the United States of America and Great Britain in 2023 by
CASEMATE PUBLISHERS
1950 Lawrence Road, Havertown, PA 19083, USA
and
The Old Music Hall, 106–108 Cowley Road, Oxford OX4 1JE, UK

Hardcover Edition: ISBN 978-1-63624-365-8
Digital Edition: ISBN 978-1-63624-366-5

Library of Congress Control Number: 2023915407

A CIP record for this book is available from the British Library

Printed and bound in the United States of America by Integrated Books International

Typeset in India by Lapiz Digital Services, Chennai.

For a complete list of Casemate titles, please contact:

CASEMATE PUBLISHERS (US)
Telephone (610) 853-9131
Fax (610) 853-9146
Email: casemate@casematepublishers.com
www.casematepublishers.com

CASEMATE PUBLISHERS (UK)
Telephone (0)1226 734350
Email: casemate-uk@casematepublishers.co.uk
www.casematepublishers.co.uk

The views expressed in this publication are those of the author and do not necessarily reflect the official policy or position of the Department of Defense or the U.S. government. The public release clearance of this publication by the Department of Defense does not imply Department of Defense endorsement or factual accuracy of the material.

Front cover image: Sgt Rodney Garcia

Contents

DEDICATION

"It is foolish and wrong to mourn the men who died.
Rather, we should thank God that such men lived."

— GEORGE S. PATTON JR.

KIA

SPC Jason Johnston—December 26, 2009

Sgt Scott Brunkhorst—March 30, 2010

SPC Joseph Caron—April 11, 2010

SPC Christopher Moon—July 13, 2010

Sgt Allen Thomas—September 28, 2013

Sgt Derek Hill – September 11, 2018

Sgt Jason Spottedhorse—May 29, 2019

Foreword

In 2010, I was the Director of Operations for Regional Command-South, based in Kandahar. William Yeske and I never met, but he remembers me stopping by when Bravo Company, 2/508 PIR, was operating out of Lashkar Gah. Little did we know that our paths would unknowingly cross again after their unit was re-assigned missions and moved into the Arghandab River Valley. It was a rough area in which I was personally affected by a mass casualty situation during a complex attack involving 1-508 at one of the ANCOP facilities within Kandahar that summer.

The challenges faced within the region were many and arduous. At that time, we were the main effort to clean out the region of Taliban from southern Afghanistan. But at the same time, we were dealing with our own internal challenges. This was also when we were hearing echoes of mistakes made during Vietnam as Congress and Presidential Administrations and other factors weighed in on operations conducted on the battlefield. With no real, clearly defined end state in mind, we dealt with constantly shifting sentiments of what our next step in the country should be. It's very difficult to implement policies when there is no clear strategic objective or strategy to guide those policies. This is in large part what ultimately led to our failure in Afghanistan.

As has happened so often in our history, especially since the end of the Second World War, American soldiers are expected to be successful and somehow figure it all out, even when we don't provide them with the best strategic plans or enabling the policies they need to win. Even contending with mistakes at the strategic and political level in Afghanistan, our soldiers fought with courage and honor. The junior officers, the sergeants, and the enlisted soldiers on the ground never failed to amaze me. They bore the brunt of everything and continued to bring the fight to the enemy in increasing efficiency as the fight slogged on. The Paratroopers in Bravo Company were terrific young men from all over America who exceeded the standard in the face of a difficult situation.

I feel, as an officer, now retired, that we owe them our appreciation and respect and a commitment to do all we can to avoid making the same mistake of sending them into combat without a clear objective in mind and an intention to win.

The men that served with Bravo Company were some of the best I ever saw... real All-Americans that fought relentlessly to deny the enemy movement through or establish a stronghold within the Arghandab Valley. None of them were perfect... but each of them did their best. I wish that could be said of all of us who sent them there.

This is their story.

Ben Hodges
LTG, US Army, Retired

Author's Note

I guess it's only fitting that I am writing this on Memorial Day weekend in 2023. The author's note has been written three times already, yet somehow, here I am writing it again. Much like the quality of the story, it still won't do justice to the guys who served throughout the events that transpired within the written story.

The story is something I never wanted to put down on paper, but here we are because of something that was jokingly mentioned on a dusty hill in Afghanistan all those years ago. Sergeant Robert Musil laughed and said we would see the book about our actions 10 years later with my name on the cover of it. I had always thought it would be him or "Doc" Shultz that would be the first to write their memoirs down as they seemed to be much more reflective about everything happening around them than I ever was.

I also knew how much this portion of history meant to the guys who were there. I didn't want to be the one challenging their memories, bringing old wounds to the surface, and possibly getting some of the facts wrong. If 125 people witness a traumatic event, there will be 125 different viewpoints on what really happened… and all of them are correct.

Not 100% accurate but *correct*, because this is how that particular person experienced the event. The mind works in strange ways on what it retains or how it shapes one's beliefs based on one's environment. I have even had my own recollections reshaped during the multiple interviews I had with the guys to solidify the best possible picture that I could get from those who would be willing to talk about it. Keep in mind, these events had happened 13 years ago at this point, but most of them could talk about it like it was yesterday.

Some were happy to hear from me; some answered the call and I could sense the dread in the tone of their voice when I mentioned that I was bringing out a book about the time in the Arghandab; some left threatening messages and various sentiments of "fuck you" for my efforts; but writing this book was worth every bit of the long nights, unsure moments, household strain, and mental load that the project brought with it. I'm not trying to pat myself on the back here, only inspire more of you to do the same. One person keeps stating that "You're not the 'keeper of the story'" and he's right. We all are and I want the various guys that were there to bring it forward. Hell, I'll help you with bringing what you have to a publisher. That's the whole point of this anyway.

That was my reasoning for leaving out portions of the story that didn't fall under the direct involvement of 1st Platoon while in the Arghandab. Even now, the publisher had to tell me to stop adding content to the story. There were so many instances and good material that it was easy to fill the pages of this book. The hard part was whittling down what to submit as content to be included. There is still a lot left uncovered and instances where I thought it more fitting to be told by someone from that particular platoon in depth.

I am not a writer. So I hope you read this note before reading the main body of the book. Just a forewarning. However, I think that the story that was written will resonate with the audience it was intended for as some of you will just never be able to grasp what's held in the pages here. The process involved many of the people mentioned here and attempts were made to reach all of them. Not many, but some, declined to be mentioned as they are in a place in life that they don't want these memories brought back up to haunt them again. Please be aware of and respect their wishes as a lot of what was experienced would have an effect on anyone.

Some of this came through in the writing and I didn't realize it until it was pointed out by a professional writer by trade as he was reviewing the book. He noticed that during some of the most action-packed and traumatic moments, the tense of the words written changed from past tense to present. To some of these guys, this is their every day. They are constantly reliving the trauma of what happened to and around them overseas, but don't even realize that's what's happening to them at the moment.

Another important aspect to remember is that this was the US military during the height of a lengthy, sustained war. The airborne timeline is even more compressed due to the need to stay current in everything a standard unit needs to be trained in with the addition of paratrooper duties to go along with it. This workload provided additional stressors that squeezes the members of a unit such as the 82nd Airborne and makes life for the undisciplined absolute hell. The pace was breakneck and the exposure to such a demand ultimately improved our chances within the Arghandab River Valley, even if it wasn't seen by some of the men at the time.

The best part of writing the book was reconnecting and hearing some of the angles that I never noticed while patrolling in the Arghandab from the other guys who were there. For example, I never stayed on OP165 and had only experienced the views from the mountaintop once during an early patrol that brought up an initial packing of sustainment materials for the posting on the high mountain outcrop.

Someone would see a picture or a snippet on the social media thread that I had created and it would unlock a memory that they needed to share with me. These conversations were invaluable and I really hope to keep in touch to hear more of the stories about where life ends up taking some of them. The sheer willpower and resilience that has been instilled in the men who served in Two Fury has been unmatched during the rest of my time in the service.

The one certainty is that anyone who spent any amount of time within that valley during those years was affected in one way or another. It's my hope that I have been able to convey a story that can be useful to others as well as serve as something to look at and be proud of for having been part of or having gotten through. Not everything about the duty was glorious—hell, none of it was—but somewhere in the world, you made a positive difference in someone's life, whether they will admit to it or not.

That's where I hope to leave this. There are negative instances along with occurrences that happened that some would most likely soon forget, but that's war. Everything needed to be included and some of the embarrassing parts are no exception. It's why I felt the need to include all of mine within the pages, because if I couldn't turn the lens on myself, then what right do I have to do it to others? In most instances, the names were eliminated but in the few where they remain, the subjects were talked to about it prior to publication and asked that it be left in there for record.

I was asked to examine my own thoughts. What did all of it mean to me? Honestly, I thought I knew. I had been so "gung ho" up until now, regurgitating the line that I needed to "honor those in moving forward that didn't get the chance" and "live life double because there are those that were cut down before they even really started".

My answer is a little different now and a whole lot more complicated. I don't think that it's a "me" picture any more. I would say it's more relevant to ask "what did it mean to us?" I don't think I've slowed down enough yet to have a clear picture of what it's personally meant. My views of our success have changed over time. This project and book would have been never completed if it wasn't for the rest of the people that contributed to make it happen. When the publisher asked about content and pictures, I just said yes, even though I didn't have a plan. I knew that if I asked, the guys would come through. If anything, that's the closest I've come to anything resembling a picture of what it's all meant. I have a family that I can reach out to, talk to, ask advice from, and commiserate with along the way.

Instead of the journey of life being a singular path, it's been a convergence of multiple paths to form a bonded cable of those forever intertwined. I feel fortunate to have met these guys even if the context in which we met was less than ideal. I feel grateful and thankful for everything you've done along the way so far and I only hope to be able to give back. For those that sent in the pictures and helped with the content, thank you again.

To my wife and kids, thank you for believing in me to get this done and the sacrifices you made for me to be able to put this down on paper instead of just hearing me occasionally relate various instances throughout the years. I hope you can use some of these lessons in the future so that you don't have to experience the negative side, but if you do, I hope you can draw on the fact that there is always the positive that follows.

To the rest of you, I hope that this story brings laugher, tears, and all of the range of emotions in between. Most importantly, I hope the memories and stories live on through these pages and are told within our circles and beyond.

CHAPTER I

Enlistment

Attitude is Everything

I joined the Army a little later in life than most, but not as late as some that I saw come through the doors when I went through basic training. I always had a sense that I wanted to join the service and had even previously taken the ASVAB (Armed Services Vocational Aptitude Battery) to join the Marines right out of high school. Like most kids, I was unsure of the direction I wanted to head with my life.

Life in general has always been a bit off for me. I've been looking over and examining my younger years to figure out why, but there is never any real answer. I joined the service at the age of 26 knowing that I needed to instill some sort of discipline in my life or I would end up being what I call a "floater." This is basically just a piece of shit floating along, just happy existing in everyone else's life. I had good ASVAB score results and the Marines had told me they wanted me in a slot as a "high speed" satellite technician. Back in 1999, that sounded like some high-level cutting edge technological stuff. Of course, knowing what I know now, it was probably just an infantryman RTO (radio telephone operator) setting up the portable satellite communications antenna while under fire.

My mother will go up and down on how my love for the Army came from an observation of a war games demonstration when I was around 10 years old. My cousins had been living with us at that point for a short stint of time. Their father, my uncle Allen, was a veteran who had served in the Air Force somewhere around the Korean conflict era. I think it was post war but prior to Vietnam... that's where his brothers got sucked into the service. Allen was trying to get his situation straightened out in California as a truck driver, so his two boys were staying with us back in Connecticut.

Either way, maybe the demonstration did leave a lasting impression on both me and my older cousin, Jeremy, who later joined the Marines in an attempt to be a badass not to be messed with in his father's eyes because he felt abandoned and bullied by him at a young age. Maybe it was a bit of that or maybe my uncle was trying to inject some adversity into the kid's life to toughen him up for the challenges later on. Whatever the case, Jeremy made his father proud in the long run.

It was a joint exercise with the National Guard and some Reserves units that hosted the event but it was a good-size production that involved vehicles, troops moving to contact, mortars, a tank or two, and some helicopters that did a few flyovers. They had a machine-gun emplacement and were allowing kids to fire the M60 from inside the fighting position emplacement that was dug out. Even as a little boy, I went full cyclic and was removed from the firing position rather quickly while the barrel was left smoking in the background. The best part for us was being allowed to collect the brass and links to fashion some gun belts out of them. I now know the guys on the detail just didn't want to pick up all the spent shells after a day of firing like that. These days, the range shack won't allow that type of nonsense as every round needs to be accounted for and the expended brass turn-in has to be within a certain weight to pass inspection. It's all turned in to be melted down and recycled into what will probably be end up as just more shell casings to support the never-ending war machine once again.

I ended up being talked out of joining the military at the time because my parents dangled college in front of me with a promise to pay for it. I could go into the service later as an officer with full support from them if I still wanted to serve at the time of graduation. I should have followed my gut instinct. Let that be a lesson to you. If you are passionate about something and truly feel that is the right direction, jump as hard and far as you can right into it. The military at that point in my life would have been an absolute godsend for me looking back. I could have bypassed a ton of problems in a section of my life that was more than just a roller-coaster ride. Yeah, college was never finished at that point. I had watched on a cafeteria TV at the University of Connecticut as the news showed the towers being struck by the planes over and over that day. The administration had pulled everyone out of classes and a bunch of us were trying to understand what exactly this meant for all of us as a nation. I missed my first ride into hell that time around, but what is life without second chances?

When your inner voice tells you something, listen to it. It'll save you a lot of heartache and run around. I eventually ended up in the ranks, but after dropping out of college, a whole lot of money spent, having my heart broken, and the limbo of futile attempts to move forward in a depressed funk, I finally conceded that now might be the time to hit the reset button.

There were other characters of influence in my life that fit into the puzzle, such as a particularly wild old gentleman by the name of Calvin who lived in my neighborhood in Torrington, Connecticut. He had tried telling me up and down and every which way that I was going to hate my time in the Army. He had been in the Army at one point during Vietnam. I had made his acquaintance after one of my friends who was the man's pharmacist asked me to look in on him. He was worried about Cal because his wife had recently passed. I have always liked to talk to the older generation and hear their stories of life lived, so we became friendly rather quickly.

I wasn't sure of Cal's full background, but I quickly dismissed his grumpy ramblings about the Army to be part of the Vietnam schtick that you hear about. Whenever anything surrounding the military would come up, he would state, "You would hate it there." But he would still probe about the status of me signing on the line. Eventually, I signed up for the delayed entry program so I could close up shop back home and the next time we were talking, I told him the date I was headed out. The man's eyes twinkled in a way that I now recognize was his remembering of his own time in service. "You're going to fucking love it!" he stated.

I quickly found out that my little old gentlemanly (mostly) neighbor's background was far more extensive and badass than I would ever know or he would ever fully tell me. He had served with MACV-SOG (Studies and Observations Group) during Vietnam and was one of the few that made it out alive to never talk about it. He gave me some tidbits of advice that I didn't understand at the time, but I get it now. One that proved invaluable is one that I will pass on: "Attitude is everything."

Benning—It's Just a Body

In March 2008, I finally left for Fort Benning Georgia to attend the US Army Infantry School with the goal of getting into Special Forces by way of the fast-track 18X contract. The School of Infantry on Sand Hill in Fort Benning was a particularly fun slice of ridiculousness. Part of the training there was waiting to finally in-process for our class rotation to start. It was one of the worst places to be… 30th AG. There were a bunch of oddballs in our barracks and between watching the games that privates play, I wondered if this was the lot that I would eventually end up next to in combat someday. I can't remember the number starting out, but I know that we were caught up in some unofficial competition between the training companies to drop/recycle as many candidates as possible.

There was Drill Sergeant "O" who had a regimental Ranger scroll on his shoulder. That 75th patch should mean something to anyone that is in combat arms: never get in between the Rangers and their objective. He was there for the first weeks and you didn't want to be on his radar in a bad way, or you were destined for a recycle. He left a few weeks after we started. Some of the guys whispered that it was because he was unstable, and his smoke sessions were too over the top. It was bullshit because he was probably the most capable warfighter there and everyone knew it. He just always drove the point home a bit harder… it was what we needed. However, as we move into the "kinder" and more "gentler" military, the antics of old are no longer tolerated, no matter the value in what they teach. We still train up the best military in the world, but I question if the troops will be able to face the horrors of what future warzones might bring.

One such lesson was taught at the end of the day after being drenched in sweat from whatever particular exercise we were currently doing. He called for everyone to "toe the line." That means to drop whatever the hell it is you are doing and get to the position of attention with your toes at a line that had been created via tape that wrapped around the room. The number one rule in the bay was that no trainees were allowed into the taped-off center section that dominated the room... that was his. He called for shower time in two minutes, so we scrambled to drop our clothing as fast as we could and prepare for the icy blast that was to come.

No warm showers were to be had in basic training... well, not conventional showers exactly. The en masse shower room that held about 20 shower heads in it. There were no "stalls" though, just faucet heads coming out from every angle you could imagine. Cold water would all be turned on and you would essentially walk through the cross blast of the icy water as you lathered some soap onto your armpits and crotch. Hopefully had it rinsed off by the time you hit the 20th shower head because there was no going back for more.

It didn't matter if most of us made the time hack, because there was always someone that had screwed up in one way or another. "Half right face," Sergeant "O" belted out and we all knew what was next. That is almost always the command to get a formation in the position to begin physical punishment for whatever infraction they've just made. "THE SIDE STRADDLE HOP." "The side straddle hop?" we echoed as we sort of looked at each other like. "What the fuck... is he serious?"

You are wondering why this concern if you didn't attend the military at some point during your lifetime. Well, let me fill you in. When you are lined up for the shower, everyone has towels around their waist with one hand holding the towel in place and soap and toiletries in the other. There is no way to do the side straddle hop, or jumping jack as you may know it, without dropping everything to do so. About a quarter of us understood as we just dropped our stuff, including our towels, on the ground. The rest made the futile attempt to keep a hand on their towel to keep it around their waist.

The hilariousness of the scene was unforgettable as 60+ young men were consumed in shame as naked bodies and male genitalia slapped around that room while other exercises were belted out by this barrel-chested Army Ranger, who was dead serious in the moment. It didn't let up until every damn person in the bay completely gave in to the fact that he wasn't fucking around, and the humiliation would continue in mass form until you bent to his will of accepting your nakedness. You had to put your own notions aside and join the rest of the naked bodies engaged in a battle of their own doing within the confines of preconceived societal rules. It took somewhere around three to five minutes for everyone to get on the same page.

"THERE IS NO FUCKING SHAME ON THE BATTLEFIELD," he belted in the middle of the bay floor. "You think that you're not going to face your buddies' naked ass at other points in your career? You think you aren't going to have to stay in some desert shithole in a tent spaced nut to butt? You think you aren't going to have to strip someone down or cut their shit off when you have to treat them after they get blown the fuck up? The fact you have to realize is that you are just in a bag of meat that keeps you alive. This is just the vehicle to get you to the fight. There is no shame in this… it's just another body."

And with that, he left us to shower and bed down on our own that night, thinking our own thoughts on what he had just said. This guy had just taught something that will stick with me always in dealing with any situation that involves patching someone up. It might seem callous and cold, but at the end of the day, it's just a body.

Airborne—How to Fall Out of a Perfectly Good Airplane

After graduation from the School of Infantry, there were about three weeks of hold over time to wait for Airborne School because someone in planning had messed up on the class rotations. We had hardly left Sand Hill in those three weeks except for a handful of times which led to another five or so guys getting dropped from the program and cycled into the needs of the Army. Never leave soldiers without anything to do for too long… they will gravitate towards mischief. I'm not saying we didn't all get into our own little dicey situations, but they were the ones who got caught.

Airborne School is fun. It has its own suck in some aspects, but it was a great experience that could have been a much better time if I had known the ins and outs at the time. But I was just a dipshit E3 at the time that was trying to not fall behind the youth that easily bested me in athletic ability. I was strong, but I was slow. A lot of jogging around the Airborne School area was good practice for how they run the show over at Camp Mackall.

Throughout the training, you can boil its purpose down to just two basic things, but they do it over the course of three weeks to really drive in that repetition. To get the balls together to make the jump from a real plane when the time came and to fall in the right body position that wouldn't snap your legs when you hit the ground at around 24 feet per second (roughly 16½ mph). Who would have thought that you needed a whole solid month to learn how to jump out of a perfectly good airplane?

It's not so much the act of jumping or the thousands of falls you'll experience, but it's the mental game you are facing. You are constantly exposing yourself to adrenaline spikes over the course of the school which will translate over to your body being used to the extreme rushes of adrenaline you'll get when the bullets start flying. It was Lieutenant General James M. Gavin who stated, "Show me a man who will jump out of an airplane, and I'll show you a man who'll fight," and I believe that this is the exact phenomenon that he was referring to.

This also follows a lot of the modern holistic medicine techniques of exposure to spikes in cortisol levels in order to teach to body how to deal with stress and adrenal gland dumps that happen during risky situations. It's your body telling you, no, this is dangerous, but you learn to deal with what your body is telling you and do it anyway. Probably another reinforcing factor in why paratroopers like to push the envelope so much. It's also probably the reason that many of the airborne units out there come off as a collective cult in their job as well as other aspects woven into their life.

You learn to face your fears in one way or another during jump school. It's not exactly natural to be jumping out of a plane in the first place, much less with about 100 extra pounds strapped to you. I have personally been terrified of heights ever since my mother took me on a ski lift in Lake Placid, New York to see the high jumper ski jump in Olympic Village. I'm not even sure how high that lift was, but I felt like it was easily 100+ ft up at some points. So, day after day, I faced the inevitable fear of heights as we fell again, and again, and again.

The worst part for me was jumping out of the towers at that school. It's about the most unnatural thing to be jumping off of a tower that is the height of a three-story window. I didn't mind the plane jumps nearly as much, but those towers had me worried every time. Still… it was just a means to an end. At the end of jump week, we had our jump wings pinned on us. Even though they were starting to crack down on getting them punched into your chest, they still proceeded to do a light version of "blood wings" to us. It was like they practiced using Bruce Lee movies as a guide to the "ultimate punch," when he hits some guy with only an inch to gain momentum and yet he flies across the room due to the force behind the punch.

This is the American airborne tradition of taking the safety backing off the pin on jump wings and placing them on the graduate's chest. They fix them into place by punching the "pin on" wings into the chest of the candidate. It's uncomfortable as hell and if you get someone who places it a bit too high, the pins can catch your collarbone for an exceptionally excruciating experience. The initiation to the cult solidified with the pain of the recollection of tradition being performed at its finest and highest levels.

CHAPTER 2

Fury

If You Want to be Airborne...

The arrival at 4th Brigade, 82nd Airborne was disappointing after the let down from being dropped from the Special Forces program that I had signed up for on my initial enlistment. Big Army determined that I needed time to heal up before attending the rest of the selection process. I was supposed to arrive on crutches due to my profile, but I had too much ego and pride for that. I had been in the medical hold area for a week when the sergeant major over the program at the Special Warfare Center and School decided to drop everyone they had in the medical section regardless of when and why they were there, because they had malingerers hiding in the mixture of troops. My thought in showing up at the 82nd Airborne was that I was healed up enough to suck up anything that these guys could throw at me. They were just part of the regular conventional army. Yeah... they gave me a run for my money on that one. I didn't know that they would break out into six-and-a-half-minute mile run pace occasionally during our regularly scheduled PT.

It wasn't quite Christmas yet, but our group had gotten to the battalion, just as luck would have it, on the day of the big Christmas party. It was about 10pm as we were sitting in the company area after being shuffled around all day when the first sergeant (1SG) finally came in to meet the new members of the company. I couldn't verify, but I'm pretty sure I smelled some whiskey on First Sergeant Donald Mcalister's breath. We were on the other side of the desk, so who really knows.

Up until now, I'd been exposed to just about every asshole the army has to dish out at you and then some, or so one thought, but we all know the professional assholes are the first sergeants. Honestly, Mac was hard on us, but he was always fair from where he came from. The interpretation of what he put out to his team wasn't always professionally followed through with though. He expected discipline and his men to follow the orders put out to the letter, but things could be hidden from the boss's eyes if needed. Mac was originally from the old guard, which explained why he could pick out a uniform issue from a mile away. It may have had part in earning him the nickname of "brass balls" around the company, but there were reasons why he demanded discipline. Reasons we would find out soon enough.

Here I am, assigned to a company in a unit that was rumored on PNN (Private News Network) to lead the Army in two things: AWOL and re-enlistment. In the army, you can use a re-enlistment to get a duty station of choice which would dangle the hope in front of you of getting out of the particular hell you were currently in for the trade of a "better" hell somewhere else within the multiple globally based military duty stations. The ones that went AWOL just felt as though extending the existence within hell wasn't worth their time and effort and they would take their chances becoming a felon due to the paperwork being produced to convict a deserter. Re-enlistment was just a bargaining chip to get out of the unit you were in and on orders to anywhere else other than here.

On top of that, the humorous side of the universe decided to put me (the oldest new member in the company) with a Private 1st Class as a roommate. He wasn't a bad kid; he was just an idiot. This little scrapper was 18 years old, from backwoods Louisiana, with the IQ of a cereal box, and about as much of a nightmare that anyone could have if they were responsible for them.

He would trash his room nightly. I didn't even know how he did it. It was like it was on the damn chore list or something. I tried to be a mentor by showing him what right looked like, but he just didn't get it. I wasn't a stellar soldier either, but anything was better than the shit show that this kid was. Constant soup sandwich due to him. A lot of the time, if he was hemmed up, I was hemmed up right alongside of him. I didn't mind the physical part, but damn, that was mentally taxing. The one thing the kid had going for him was that he was a pretty good shot. So, we tried everything we could do to square him away. One of us ended taking his credit cards at one point and giving him a weekly ATM allowance because of how badly he would make decisions.

Ultimately, he had too many strikes that it could no longer be hidden from 1SG Mac. The final straw came when he was found by the brigade staff duty passed out drunk in front of the Hall of Heroes with puke and shit all down the front of him. That finally got him cut from Bravo Company. I was honestly surprised we were able to keep him there as long as we did because of how little trouble you could stir up within Bravo Company before you were given the axe. Mac didn't mess around with dead weight. He knew better. He was hard but he was fair. Some of the best guys in the military are found after they screw up but then correct their course and find the path of hard right over the easy wrong. Mac knew that, but there was the point of no return where you knew you were gone if you didn't toe the line. If you wanted to stay in Bravo Company, you had to be squared away and have friends there. If you didn't, it could be a very brutal place to be.

It was the night after signing in that I had my first encounter with Sergeant Robert Musil. My first encounter with anyone from the unit and I'm bringing stuff into my room at about midnight on a Friday. Musil is coming back to his barracks room drunk as hell and carrying a bottle of Jameson. He stops down the hall and looks at me. "Who the fuck are you?" he slurs in an aggressive tone. You know the type of tone because it usually accompanies a knife hand. I just smiled and said I was private Yeske and just assigned to Bravo Company. It was probably the most futile attempt to try to be friendly to a drunken Irish airborne sergeant that had ever been seen. In my eyes, he was just a neighbor down the hall and I needed to find out who the allies were around me. The result was that I got told to shut the fuck up and know who you are talking to before you open your mouth. That's basically the nice version.

I have always had trouble meshing with people owing to my social awkwardness. I'm pretty sure it was due to my isolated childhood. To a point, I was the bubble boy. I had a mother that was an ex-alcoholic who took her addiction and turned it over to Jesus... yeah, that type. It wasn't just going to church on Sundays. It was twice on Sunday, Wednesday nights, Friday night youth group, and sometimes a function on Saturday. No public school until my senior year and up until freshman year we went to a private Christian school that was about 30 minutes from our house. So, no really close friends other than a few of the kids whose families were churchgoers and my cousins that took up the rest of the time we had. My father ran a small manufacturing business with two other partners and it was something that required him to be constantly running the shop. We didn't see much of him as kids.

Maybe that is why I never really fit in. I feel like I'm an outsider more times than not. However, it was through going to war with these guys that I saw what combat can do to bring people together as well as tear individuals apart. It's always been a quest of mine to "find myself" and with that search, the journey has brought me to both incredible highs and the lowest of the lows. I tell people that I am on lifetime four or five at this point just due to the sheer volume of life I've been fortunate enough to have experienced.

So... what about this 4th Brigade Combat Team that I was just assigned to? I swear that it was all of the misfits and crazies that had been diverted to fill the ranks in this version of a bastardized airborne brigade. They were a great bunch, but they were definitely always handed the shit end of the stick when it came to possible missions with the 82nd Airborne. However, this seemed to have shaped them into the mean ass sons of bitches that they were. They were definitely effective at war and it was trouble trying to keep them on the leash back home. These were the type you wanted to have your back when things hit the fan, but not exactly the polished type you put in the parade.

Back in 2006 or 2007, someone had uploaded a video to YouTube of the barracks they had these guys in. The Korean War-era barracks were a group bunk set up with a fire team per room and zero privacy. I had stayed at these types of buildings during my initial entry into the SF program. They were livable... but damn, they were disgusting and plagued with issues. They were disgusting enough for President George Bush to take notice and issue orders to get these guys new quarters immediately.

They had just come off a deployment where that unit specifically had been awarded a Valorous Unit Citation… and this was where they were dropped to live.

Fortunately, I showed up just as we were getting to take a temporary residence in the Taj Mahal barracks that 3rd Brigade had left behind as they were in Iraq currently. Our rotation was next anyway and the official word was that we were headed to Iraq as well. This being the case, they didn't see the conflict and played the barracks shuffle while they demolished the other facilities that were the black stain on Bragg for a while because of the negative publicity.

The First jump

In the 82nd Airborne, you are considered a "cherry" for quite some time when you get there. They were trying to get rid of the traditional slur toward the lower enlisted as I was leaving, but I'm sure all of the old troopers will continue to cling to the nostalgia, just as it will always be Fort Bragg and not Fort Liberty for those that served during those times.

It was a fitting reference and the 82nd Airborne is one of those units that has a long history of such references and traditions that they hold near and dear to their hearts. Its these practices that reinforce the membership in the airborne cult. This tradition would have the team leader of the new trooper place a Hostess cherry pie package in the cargo pocket of the jumper so that it would burst with the force of landing when they hit the ground. If they did a proper parachute landing fall (PLF), that action would leave a red stain in the pocket of the now useless pants that would appear to have been bled through by the wearer. Hence… "cherry."

The part about "cherries" in Bravo Company is that they were considered the great unwashed and the bath you required was one that consisted of a torrent of blood, sweat, and probably tears for most as well. Two Fury Battalion alone was a bit on the rougher side of this mentality, but that's due to how it was run by the commander and sergeant major.

Lieutenant Colonel Frank (The Tank) Jenio was considered one of the brightest commanders in the division and was coupled with the formidable Command Sergeant Major Bert Puckett who had grown up within the Army and served within Ranger battalion along the way. They made a hell of a team and stood out among the rest of the brigade as well as the division. Everyone knew that Two Fury was the place to be at the time if you wanted to get into some action.

Along with that came a sense of callousness too. It's not malicious or some sort of sociopathic defense mechanism, but more the definite structure of command coupled with the discipline to do what is asked of you, no matter what, when the command comes. You didn't fall in line or fit the peg, then you either fell out of your position or were hammered into that peg board with the full force of everything your NCO structure could muster behind it.

Some of the leadership were just trying to instill a sense of discipline and trust so they knew that there would be no hesitation when the door breach needed the stack to flow into a room full of bad guys. Others were just downright malicious and got a kick out of smoking the absolute dog shit out of some of the guys. They were professionals at breaking someone's spirit to mold them into the hatred-spewing warfighter capable of going leaps and bounds beyond what the standard-issue human could take. This was the embodiment of the saying attributed to George Orwell—"Rough men stand ready to do violence on their behalf"—in reference to defending the general public that sleeps peaceably in their beds at night. Well… this is how they become rough.

If you were new in Bravo Company, your life was hell until you at least got a combat patch or some kind of rank that came with experience. If you didn't have that, you would be at the mercy of whoever you were farmed out to that particular day and you better hope they were in a good mood… they usually weren't.

Life and the feelings surrounding death had a different meaning on that particular slice of Bragg. Quite honestly, the airborne commanders didn't have the time to be dealing with the immaturity you would get in some of the new privates. With everything that needed to be accomplished within the training cycles they would put us through prior to the year-on, year-off deployments, the men would find themselves scrambling having anything left for their families at the end of the day. Life in the airborne was akin to that of a cult because the lifestyle needed to saturate you being in order to be successful in the task. This is the line of intensity that separated the men from the boys.

ITC

Following Christmas 2008, the company went into a bitter cold intensive training cycle (ITC) for weeks at a time in the field. David Rogler from second squad went down from hypothermia at one point. We were just walking through the woods, practicing a patrol off the sidelines of a range, and he starts taking off his kit, talking loud as hell, and laughing hysterically about something. We made fun of his misfortune (needing his core temp taken via rectal thermometer) because the laughter kept us warm for the time being. CSM Puckett was out there with us, freezing his ass off all the same as us. That was one of my first personal impressions of our higher command team. It reassured me that we weren't just out there flapping while the higher echelon sat up on the ridgeline sipping their morning coffee while discussing tactical possibilities over breakfast. He was in some of the crappy parts of it all, right alongside us.

It was part of the command mantra that the direction of the "Arrow of Responsibility" should always point down. The meaning was that the leadership had a charge to be always looking after the men. Yes, there will be hardships and pain to endure, but rest assured, you will be taken care of by your leadership no matter what kind of conflict you were in. It was built into everything we did, down to the fact that the higher the rank, the further back in the chow line you would be. The lower enlisted would always come first with their instilled doctrine.

We all knew they had paid their dues already from the dress uniforms we would see on that one Friday of the month when Division would pull a payday activities uniform inspection on us. CSM Puckett had jumped into Panama with the Rangers and had a damn mustard stain on his jump wings. That doesn't mean just anything on a soldier that is alive these days. That means that he was a paratrooper and jumped into a combat operation. He fell through the sky while a hail of bullets were being hurled at him while prepping himself to land without breaking his legs and then bring the fight to the enemy. Paratroopers' actions immediately on landing are to snap out of your harness and get your weapon into action as quickly as possible. Assuming they dropped you in the right spot and you aren't too far off course, you then essentially follow whoever the hell you recognize to your semi-designated link-up areas, if able to do so, and then hit your designated attack points while destroying anything in your path.

That's a hell of a thing to have been through and combat changes the way an infantryman soldier sees everything in training and in life. Maybe it's because you realize the true severity of living in moments that define or test your actual existence in reality on this planet. It's no longer just a game or practice… you screw up, it could very well be your final mistake. Shit, you might even just be unlucky and end up dead because you went left instead of right. You never know… but that's what makes it all so beautiful. I do know one thing, I respected the hell out of the man and I have been fortunate enough to get to gawk at pictures of him as a joe inside of the Noriega compound.

There were some "unauthorized" (but really nicely warm as well as tactical) gloves that weren't on the packing list that I had taken out to the field with me. These would help out in the cold better than issued equipment along with fitting the trigger well of my rifle better. Sergeant Allen Thomas, being my squared-away squad leader, saw fit that I didn't wear the unauthorized gear that week or two out there in the cold. I fared OK to a point, but between being yelled at left and right if you were caught with your hands in your pockets and having to grip a cold ass M16 or SAW (Squad Automatic Weapon) at all times, I finally caved. I told Sgt Thomas that the whole thing was bullshit and my hands were pretty much damn frozen at that moment. At which time he looked me right in the eye and calmly said "Yeah" and handed me a set of "authorized" handwear he had stashed in his pocket all along.

Me and Thomas didn't really get along, but I know he wasn't trying to single me out. He was just trying to get me to toe the line. The problem was I had this issue of seeing a better solution or way of doing things. Minor uniform enhancements, like an updated night vision helmet mount that kept my nods from swinging this way and that when walking through the night. During one of the room inspections, my team leader, Sergeant Tyler Anderson, proclaimed, "Damn, Yeske. It's like a friggin' Tactical Tailor Store back there!" in regard to my closet. It's not like I was trying to cause trouble in the matter, I was just a firm believer in the "shooter's preference" principle. I also didn't understand that there was a "dog and pony" back in garrison and the rules flexed when you got overseas. The instances got me labeled as a "gear queer" early on in the company.

Why would you train with one set of gear and then completely change everything once you hit the suck? You preach to "train as you fight" but do you really? I was always looking at ways to improve my equipment and knowledge, so this led to my never-ending hobby of hitting all the cool guy tactical stores around Bragg in search of an RTO bag before we deployed. I did my research and picked up an amazing Mystery Ranch three-day assault pack that had provision for way more than anything that I could ever hope to carry at that time within service. This pack was overbuilt to the gills!

It was also part of the new wave of tactical designs that flooded into the market when there was a new war to fight. There have been some incredible innovations over the years and it's wild to use some of the Vietnam-era stuff in a training capacity while being able to switch over to the modern-era warfighter-built packs and kit that is scrutinized and thought over from every angle possible. I have had packs or webbing gear that I will find a new feature on or realize why a particular piece is the way it is a year or so after I have used it.

I had initially purchased the bag in a multicam pattern but was pulled aside and sternly told by 1SG Mac to return it for an authorized pattern because it was "multicam pattern and only the cool guys get to wear multicam." It wasn't even worn during training on garrison, but I went back to the shop and they graciously allowed me to swap it out for a coyote tan version. About two months later, each squad was being handed the same pack as a new piece of squad equipment for the RTOs within the battalion. Well, isn't that something… I had to pay for mine. At least mine wasn't that godawful ACU (Army Combat Uniform) camouflage they made everyone wear back then.

The installation of that upgraded helmet mount for night vision proved to be a bit of an attention-getter for me as well. The unit in question was a triangle mount that prevented the night vision assembly from swinging around during the night and changing position. For those who don't know just how critical this can be, it can mean life or death. You lose your ability to see at night, you lose a huge advantage. Gone are the days of having to stay in a RON (remain overnight) site and move out after sunrise because of zero to little nighttime operational capability.

I drilled the necessary holes in the carbon fiber helmet, taking care not to damage the structural integrity. Well, it turns out the modification bought me the pleasure of finding another helmet to use for our operations because that one was now considered useless by the platoon sergeant. How dare I have better ability to see than anyone else on the platoon?! $150 later and a tongue lashing from Staff Sergeant Matthew Hill, I had to settle for something that was found off of one of the drop zones and deemed fit for wear on duty. The discovery of the modified helmet was followed by the usual smoke session of an hour or two by Sgt Thomas for my ridiculous attempts to improve anything that Uncle Sam had issued us. I couldn't know any better... I was just PFC Yeske.

Another training mission involved what was supposed to be a tactical road march onto a follow-on mission of a village night raid. Our platoon element took tactical in a different interpretation and decided to break brush for miles until we got to the hit point. It was a good night for it, but I remember it being a long ruck march before we arrived at the patrol base outside of the mock village. I was used to the heavy weight and long rucks because of SOPC (the Special Operations Preparatory Class) but even some of the more experienced guys were sucking that night.

Sergeant Justin Kornegay talked about how he started hallucinating at some point and saw Big Bird out in the woods with us. Not just a "big bird," but the damn *Sesame Street* version that would show up with his buddy Snuffleupagus on our TV during the weekend sometimes. I have no reason to doubt him because everyone was exhausted by the time we got to our assault rally point. The hike had been an arduous one and our bodies were putting off steam that you was visible over the long grass in the fields surrounding the objective.

It went well for us as Battalion had been questioning where we were, but then we materialized out of the wood line not abnormally far off of our specified time to ambush the objective. Command was pissed off at first until they realized that we hadn't taken any of the roads as the other platoons had. The instructions had been vague and our platoon stayed with the full tactical assault approach instead of breaking it off after getting word halfway into our movement. It was a good experience and I remember shivering on the backside of the hillside that overlooked the target compound as we got ready for the simulated fight. I never forgot to have a woobie with me after that one.

We got ready to clear the site by clearing the buildings tactically, room by room. We did well on the assaults and room clearing. As an angry bunch, we were always aggressive and took the mentality of posturing hard and gaining fire superiority as the key. We cut through the village, took a knee for the after-action review, and moved back out to the company areas for a few weeks before gearing up for our JRTC rotation.

Joint Readiness Training Center, Fort Polk

After our ITC, it was on to JRTC down in Louisiana. Thomas must have wanted a break from me for a week, so I found myself on the advance party for the company.

It was Sergeant Trent Logan, myself, Specialist Chad Stewart, and two or so other guys. There was nothing for us to do when we got there, but there was also no official way to leave… legally. You see, we were on a military post, but because we were the poor grunts on the front lines, we were way the hell out in no man's land. Literally, the furthest outpost from main post in the swamps of Fort Polk is exactly where they stuck us. With the added burden of no civilian transportation, there was no way out of the AO without major recognition or being busted for leaving post without orders.

This is where some of our problem-solving abilities came in. I happened to have known someone who sold old police equipment after they stripped the cars down for decommissioning. I had asked him if he had any Panasonic Toughbooks around. If you have ever used one of these things on a worksite, it's a beast. It's a fully ruggedized laptop and even has a Faraday cage equipped internally. What does that mean? They can survive a damn EMP from a nuclear blast. They were the same piece of equipment as the issued computers the commanders were rolling around with at the height of battlefield technology at the time. So, when I pulled one out of my backpack, the guys kind of freaked out.

Once it was determined that it was, in fact, my personal computer and not stolen military equipment, Sgt Logan asked me if I could figure out how to hook it up to the commander's HMMWV that we were using as a ride that week. I quickly realized that the power and GPS antenna were a direct fit for my laptop. He then let the cat out of the bag and told us that he had family about an hour or so away and they wanted us to drop by while we were in town. Being the nerd I was, I rigged up some off-road Garmin software and navigated our little crew off post via an access road in the swamp. We headed down the back roads of Louisiana to the house of some of the nicest people I've met. We were complete strangers, but because we were with Trent, we were considered family. That's when we ditched the military vehicle in the back of Gram's house and went in a civilian vehicle to a local fish fry restaurant. I don't remember much other than our bill was paid by some nice locals, Sgt Logan had a really warm family, and it was the first time I tried some alligator bites. A little chewy for my taste, but not that far off from the taste of fried calamari.

Bravo Company gave Geronimo, the opposing unit in training, hell down there. I'm not sure if we "won" the war game, but I wasn't really paying much attention after being put through a month of the bayou in the heat and braving the mosquitos. We all just wanted to get back so we could knock back a few, get laid, and buy something stupid before we left for deployment. I wasn't as ridiculous as some of the guys, but I definitely have had a few of my own "joe moments" that involved indulging in an extravagant purchase or two.

JRTC was good for giving us the experience of being stuck in "the box" without a way of escape. For the most part, we just ended up sitting around a lot. There were a few classes, including some that went over types of IEDs and actions on when you hit one while on patrol. It was all basic overview training, but it was good for us to have that familiarization on the topics. Honestly, I wish I had paid more attention or that the classes were more in depth as it was information that proved to be a good foundation for what we were soon to face.

In a "react to contact" lane, it was Sgt Kornegay who proved to be the insane breacher that would pour a mixture of hatred and exhausted pent-up aggression. Kornegay was a mean son of a bitch. Laughing all the time, but bi-polar as fuck, he would transform into the big bad wolf on the turn of a dime. It was the kind of a "two face" villain character you would see in Batman. You never knew exactly what side you were going to get, but the two choices were mean and meaner. If there was anyone who was on the "violence of action" wrecking crew, he was one of them.

He was always there with his squad though. He was hard on them, but he also knew that as leadership in Bravo Company, you had to be. Sometimes, hard rode the fine line of insane as he would occasionally dip his toe into borderline abusive territory. He was still finding his own, but damn, you didn't want to be on his bad side. Kornegay had been in action before and felt right at home in the type of scenarios like a high-intensity fight. I have never seen anyone breach a door in the "live fire" lane than the way he did.

We were moving in on a village that was under question and it opened up on us as we approached. Same drill as any range lane that deals with shooting and maneuvering. There were near buildings and then a cluster that were further off and right next to the objective compound. Kornegay led the way for his team, crashing through the door and as he shoulder checked it open, the door flew off the hinges and he crashed into the dirt with his team flowing into the building without hesitation, stepping both over and on him. You could hear his laughing, like some maniacal cackling redneck as someone gave him a hand off the ground after it was over. God bless him because that's the type of crazy we needed in the coming shitstorm.

The final three days involved a base ops-type mission where OP4 (the team designated as the "bad guys") was supposed to breach our base defenses and test our ability to hold the line in a static position. I don't think anyone ever told command though because they split up between half supporting base defenses and SSG Hill taking half of us to create a maneuver element and take the fight to the enemy. The cadre and OP4 on Polk weren't expecting us to do that because it threw the script off in what was supposed to be happening within the "battle." We came out on top, but there were a large amount of casualties in the process. We hoped this wasn't a sign of how things were to proceed in the coming days.

The more experienced guys that were still in Bravo Company after the last deployment kept referring to something known as the "Mongolian Horde" during our time at Fort Polk. It gave the image of a small group of men being borne down on by a massive number of savages, and you know they are about to be slaughtered, but it's just a question of how many they get to take down with them. Think of a depiction of the Alamo where a small number of men face overwhelming odds until eventually, their gallant stand can no longer sustain against the onslaught of enemy bearing down on them. Little did I know, that was actually a thing.

It was a tactic that was used in Vietnam as well. The Viet Cong would just throw stacks of bodies at the US troops, and it was all about who could sustain fire superiority and for how long. I couldn't see how this would happen in the mountains or desert. How? There's standoff, but apparently, it had happened and was already experienced by someone in the unit. They just never talked about it.

CHAPTER 3

Out the Door

Green Ramp

Not too long after that, orders to increase the numbers of troops in Afghanistan had us rerouted on the direct word of the commander in chief, President Barack Obama. We had been originally headed for Iraq but I personally didn't want to be dealing with the Explosively Formed Penetrator (EFP) problems they were having in the urban areas, where the lines were blurred between civilian and enemy combatants. I wanted the expanse of the mountains and to see the country. I felt the chance for survival was better in a place where I was granted some standoff as opposed to a sprawling, urban environment with different dangers from block to block.

We had leave on the 4th of July and I was able to get to Pennsylvania to celebrate with my cousin Jeremy, the Marine, before we left for Afghanistan. We spent a good amount of time just throwing back a few beers, talking about past times, and lighting up a hookah that Jer had gotten while on shore leave. Somewhere in Bahrain, he bought this thing off a street vendor and would run various plants through its firepot.

Jer gave me a good look after everyone had bedded down for the night. "Listen man, I signed up in peacetime. I know that I almost hit the Persian Gulf War, but I missed it by a day in fleet rotation. You are headed on the express train straight to the front lines. Your crazy ass signed up for this in a time of war! I don't know if I would have signed up if we were in this mess. Keep your head down and don't do anything stupid unless you have to. Love you man." With that, we had a few more beers before hitting the hay and going to bed ourselves to contemplate everything that was said that night.

I had never even thought about it in those terms before. I would have signed up at my current point in life whether there was a war or not due to feeling the need to use the experience as a personal reset button. The way I had looked at it was there were good kids paying the price out there and I wasn't doing anything productive in society at the time. It was all about me up to that point. I felt that I had a decent head on my shoulders (I didn't) and why not step up to the challenge before the chance was no longer available.

The night before we were leaving, I went down to the Korean barbershops on Yadkin Road and got myself a three-finger high and tight. Fuck it, I was a SAW gunner with the 82nd Airborne. If I had to go do this shit with them, I might as well play the part. There were a few jaws that dropped about it, but the fact was, I was just within regs and there really wasn't anything they could say. I think the way my hairline was already receding helped me get away with it. SSG Hill pointed out that it was akin to the wild haircuts some of the guys that jumped into Normandy had worn. Not much was said about my hair after that and I think I was just given my "out" of the situation from having Sgt Thomas grab a set of clippers and take them to my head right then and there.

A final barracks-room inspection resulted in me being torn into for another few hours about the condiments and various nonperishables I had left for the next occupants. Wouldn't you appreciate a cupboard full of silverware, cups, and condiments stocked in your barracks common area when you reported in? (I told you these new barracks were awesome.) Apparently, Sgt Thomas didn't think so and I was left running back and forth to the dumpster for the next two or three hours for one last Fort Bragg smoke session. It wasn't the most pleasant night. Again… I wasn't wrong, but I still wasn't following things to the letter.

Government Cheese

What is the cheapest airline seat that you have ever flown? Now compress that room you had by about 40 percent and add weapons, assault packs, gear, and everything else on top of that. All that piled into a lowest-bidder-contracted Boeing 747 that has been modified to fit additional seating. This is the picture of what it is like to fly into a modern-day extended warfare engagement in the conventional Army. Fourteen or so hours to get to Ireland and then another 10 or so hours to Kyrgyzstan. Manas Air Base was a weird place with crumbling Soviet Cold War-era buildings surrounding the American compound that were showing their age and were pocketed with bullet holes. You knew that some of those buildings just off the flightline housed a few hundred troops at one time before the fall of the USSR.

Still, the surrounding area looked to be amazing. Surrounded by mountains, it was gorgeous. You would swear that it could have been the Pacific Northwest. Advertisement flyers were all over the MWR (Moral Welfare and Recreation Center) describing tours in town, hikes, and other available attractions for the airmen that were stationed there. There was even something about a pub crawl in town! None of that was for us. We were shuffled around the compound for about a week to get used to the altitude of where we were headed.

We weren't given much instruction except to stay close, stay out of trouble, and keep our mouths shut. This was to keep the joes from compounding too many issues as it was now "go-time" and sometimes, Army logistics works at a snail's pace.

We are the best in the world at what we do, but when you are moving this amount of equipment and manpower across the globe with what is essentially a bunch of young adults, you are still going to have issues.

When the word came around that there was a secret password for an unsanctioned "rub and tug" at the massage parlor/barbershop, ears perked up. No... I didn't partake, but I'm still a young male that is about to be hitting a combat zone. Don't think for a second that those needs take a back seat. Heck yeah, it had my attention at the mention of some last-minute possible physical release, even if it was bought and paid for. The mention of it would tickle the ears of any male in that age group within the same circumstance. Not my thing... but it's not outside of the morality of men. The same type of establishments were well known and accepted during the Vietnam War and really during every other conflict throughout history.

Something about asking for a blueberry muffin was the passcode to access the brothel service menu of the establishment. Probably some sick joke put out there by one of the guys that had been through here before, but it didn't stop the news from traveling down the PNN express story trail like wildfire.

There are philosophical discussions with the guys in between the action. You receive an honorary minor in philosophy when you serve on the battlefield, especially within the infantry. Some of life's situations are looked at in pure simplicity while others, that might seem trite to most, are picked apart and every possible angle is analyzed and gone over to length. It's usually the day-to-day mundane event that is scrutinized and becomes a satire, much like any *Seinfeld* episode you watch.

The other news was from the advance party that had headed to Helmand a month prior to us and had already been in some good firefights. This brought a round of excitement, as the one thing we didn't want was some boring dog-and-pony deployment where nothing happened and you sat around all day. I understand the value in wanting to keep the men out of harm's way, but at the same time, this is what you trained for. You're itching to get into it instead of being a non-combat infantry veteran your entire life. I can tell you with certainty that I would not survive a peacetime army where discipline falls to shiny boots and parade commands.

I don't wish war upon anyone, but there is an excitement and sense of adventure to it. My personal belief is that there is something to war or an incredibly difficult challenge that should be a part of the rite of passage into adulthood. It's the extreme instances and pressures that can either build a person or tear them apart. We were on the cusp of finding out who belonged where in the pecking order.

Kandahar Air Field (KAF)

Loaded up in a C-17 aircraft, we headed for Kandahar, Afghanistan. Flying into and out of Kandahar was a wild ride for sure. There is a mountain range on the far end of the airfield where Taliban would set up rockets to attack the current occupants of the base. The thing is, these bastards were really smart about it. They would set up a preset tube camouflaged on the far side of the mountain ridge with a time fuse. They could do this at night and get out of the area before the return volley came in to destroy the launch site. You never really knew when these devices were going to go off or if some crazy bastard was going to try to fire a Stinger missile at your plane while it came into the runway. Needless to say, the pilots have to come in hot and it's a bumpy ass ride. It would have felt more comfortable if I was in my parachute gear, rigged up in the plane like we would have been in the States, but I'm sure that wouldn't have made a bit of difference.

Kandahar was hot. Akin to the heat of the jetwash flowing off of the plane you just departed as you struggle down the runway carrying an overabundance of gear. It starts to hit you when you realize that you aren't near enough to the airplane anymore for it to be the turbines spooling down. At times, the ambient temperature in Kandahar is over 110 degrees with your sweat evaporating into the atmosphere as it exits your body. You aren't even aware you are sweating unless you keep an eye on the amount of salt that dries up on your uniform. When in a turret in Helmand, the temps are way higher. It's like the armor is a radiant slow cooker and we recorded temps of 140 degrees at times during our patrols on the highways.

We came off the flightline to a bombed-out and bullet-hole-infested building that served as the terminal. You could tell people had already died here during the Russian occupation, the initial American invasion, or throughout our tenure up until that point.

From there it was another week of mulling around Kandahar, doing hours of in-country briefings and trainings, while thinking of what last-minute stuff you would want to take forward with you. What you could snag that might be useful from this point, as you probably won't have the ability to buy much from here on out. What movies or games you could trade or put onto your hard drives to try to stay distracted from all the boredom that occupied any of the off time you might have.

The MWR on KAF is an interesting place with a special mention to the Green Beans coffee bar. I'm not sure if it's actually good coffee, but when you haven't had anything legitimate in so long, that particular cup of coffee tastes a lot better than any Starbucks you find stateside. It's an effect that I haven't really had since I've been out of the service. It makes one realize just how much you take for granted and just how good life within the USA really is. We have so much that we don't even realize just how much we have. Our problems within the world are trivial in comparison.

Kaibosh

There was a soul-crushing game the guys would play. It was covered and ended up under a different name in an *Army Times* article, but it was the same stupid and painful reminder of just how attached we are to things. A player had the ability to approach anyone within the game, at any time, and just smash whatever that person was enjoying into the dirt. They would have to yell "Kaibosh!" as they did it, so they didn't get their teeth knocked in. This was because whoever was just "Kaiboshed" was probably livid and in desperate need of an instant reminder that it was just part of the game. The target would get their chance later. I never joined in, but I saw my fair share of broken-hearted bastards moaning over something stupid, like a hostess cake.

It wasn't that the confectionary treat was all that delectable, but in the moment, a Twinkie represented an escape into the senses. When it was gone, the inevitable gravity of the situation in which we were involved would creep back into focus. The realization that, once again, there were X number of days left on the deployment. But for now, you could allow the dopamine to flood your brain. The sugar rush would hit and memories from back home would tickle the pleasure centers within your neurological circuitry. And then it would be ripped away from you in an instant, followed by heckling, laughter, and humiliation from the guys that were around you.

With no hope of any sort of resupply anytime soon, it could be the last opportunity to partake in such indulgences. Picture a grown man swearing up and down or driven to the verge of tears after having a Snickers bar almost touch his lips after a 48-hour patrol up a bomb-infested highway, only to have that source of escape forcibly knocked out of his hands and into the dirt of a country that most assuredly has an extremely high fecal content in the soil. You don't want to eat anything after it touches the ground out there… trust me.

There was a lot of sleep and guard duty in KAF. You weren't allowed out long enough to cause trouble (and rightly so… a bunch of idle paratroopers on the verge of ripping out to a combat arena is ripe for some real problems) but you still had to work out, do your daily duties, and try to keep from going a little stir crazy in the meantime. We were moved into a company plus-sized Alaskan tent that was insulated with spray foam to try to keep it cool enough to be able to sleep. AC units would be stolen by surrounding tents and God forbid you didn't have a roving guard on station inside your tent. Equipment, gear, and personal items would disappear and eyes on were needed at all times. People wouldn't steal from anyone within the company, but don't you dare trust anyone else… the same rules didn't apply there. The saying they have is true. There is only one thief in the Army, everyone else is just trying to get their shit back.

Not to say there weren't times later on in deployment when I was ordered to do a connex check with a wink. These internal "security patrols" were to peep around and see where units forgot to lock up their things. Cooks were notorious for forgetting to secure the food supply connex… so it's not a big surprise that there weren't many rip-its left for the people on the posting when we departed. Just saying that the backs of our trucks were sitting a little lower and were well stocked with caffeine and an attitude of hopped-up hatred.

CHAPTER 4

Helmand

Advon (Advanced Echelon)

When we arrived in Lashkar Gah, one of the main hotbeds within Helmand province, there was a flurry of meetings between the battlespace commanders and various agencies that were operating in and throughout the province. Between the political question of why we were there and the strategic benefit of how we could be used, we fell into the hole where no one knew why we were actually there. ISAF (International Security Assistance Force) met a whole lot of resistance among the international forces to going outside the wire and getting blown up. They all wanted to stay in place and maintain static positions within the country. The American troops joked about it and said that ISAF stood for "I Suck At Fighting" during the height of everything that was happening out there.

The British and the US Marine forces were focused on the various shaping operations at the time that led to the battle of Marjah in the February 2010 time period. With the various problems and issues that they had experienced with the mobile training team unit that had preceded our arrival, the British didn't want the American troops getting in the way of their current operations. It was Lieutenant Colonel Jasper De Quincey Adams that stated they couldn't afford "A bunch of American paras mucking around in the AO."

Quite frankly, their concerns were valid because all paratroopers lean a bit to the cowboy side of their mentality on the battlefield. You could very easily end up in a full-on Leroy Jenkins moment if you didn't have a unit that had any sense of discipline. The problem was that they had never come across a unit quite like Bravo Company before. You get someone that has the balls to jump into the middle of a fight and is comfortable with the idea of being utterly surrounded, you get someone who can be a mean son of a bitch when you bring them into the fight. Combine that with the battlefield discipline that Bravo Company brought to the table, you had a real asset in your back pocket if you knew how to use it.

Lash

We received word that the main body of Bravo Company would be moving forward to Helmand province to assist British paras and some Royal Marines that were getting hemmed up in the Lashkar Gah area. Finally… some action. We were all certain to get some gunfights and were itching to put our training to use. It was all over the news that Helmand was a hot area. Some of 2nd squad had been on the advance party and had excitedly reported news of firefights they had experienced while learning the battlespace along with the commanding officer of Bravo Company, Captain Adam Armstrong.

1st Platoon was a bunch of misfits led by SSG Matthew Hill. He was a rank below the other platoon sergeants but seemed to have more experience than they did. With five prior deployments already under his belt, Hill had a plethora of knowledge, but damn, did he have a temper. On top of it, he had one of the thickest Massachusetts accents I had ever heard… and I'm originally from Connecticut, so my exposure is higher than most. Anyone who has ever served with Hill could pick him out of a crowd of one hundred people with ease after hearing his voice bearing down on their position while in a fit.

2nd Platoon was led by Sergeant First Class Roy Frazier and stayed in a sectioned-off corner of the "swank" British-constructed FOB (forward operating base). It was complete with laundry service and a miniature PX that we loved to raid whenever we got the chance. They carried the standard lickies and chewies, but the candy was all British versions, which made it foreign and exciting. These were sitting right alongside an overstocked rack of Euro-smut magazines. Like locusts descending upon an unsuspecting farmer's field to demolish anything in their path, we would deplete both racks every time we happened by there.

The American area was in the back corner and had a large gate to it that opened up to a courtyard with a plaque wired to the Hesco walls that stated "Camp Dimond." One of the additional factors that made Camp Dimond the premier place to stay was the Aid Station on the British side of the base. The nurses were there were always super friendly to us "Yanks" and we would frequently drop by whenever we could to say hello. For some reason, the Brits took a notion that most of us Americans looked like Tom Cruise and judging from the teeth of some of the Limeys that were there, I understood why. Sorry for the cheap shot boys, but as an American, I couldn't help it.

There were instances where they had us easily beat though. First Sergeant Mcalister had the entire company assemble at Camp Dimond and be dressed in our best uniforms for a funeral ceremony one afternoon. It was intended as a show of partnership and a reminder how things could get bad at any second if we became complacent. We went out thinking that our freshly washed digital camo and brushed clean desert boots looked pretty good considering. It took about two seconds into the ceremony to realize that we looked like a bag of ass in comparison.

If you have ever attended a British military ceremony, you will know what I am referring to. The experience is one of precision and a crispness that I have only seen from units within the US Army that were ceremony based, such as the old guard that

Mcalister had come from originally. The starched uniforms and power that resonated within the voiced commands as the ceremony was flawlessly performed by the Brits were humbling. It drove the point home that the consequences out here were deadly.

The 1st Platoon housing situation proved to be different as we ended up remotely based in the middle of the city hosted in the ANCOP (Afghan National Civil Order Police) compound along with 3rd Platoon led by SFC Fox. Fox's distinct feature, like Hill, was his voice. Unlike Hill's though, it was laden with the loud heavy accent of a Minnesotan. You could hear it as a warning before he was in sight. His voice was mimicked just as much as Hill's because of how distinct and booming it was. There was no mistaking him for anyone else.

The ANCOP was staffed by the premier police of the district. They had multiple ceremonies and training exercises while we were there, but it always just seemed to be the same type of dog and pony that we would have back in the rear. The place was guarded by the Afghan police and there was no way we would have been able to supplement them with how large the compound was. We didn't have enough guys to supply staffing for that many towers and be able to complete the other duties we had to complete missions in the province. Even with the Afghan police providing security, we couldn't trust them.

There was an instance where two guards were talking at their gate posting and it ended up in an argument because one of them mentioned the other's sister during a heated spell that broke into a spat. The offended guard pulled out his pistol and shot his fellow sentry right in the face, splattering his brains all over the front entry gate. That was the premier force we were given to assist in training... great.

Hurry Up and Nope

We settled into a weird routine of having to drive through the city to link up with our counterparts for either side-by-side missions or for whatever other taskings we were headed out to accomplish. I wasn't aware of what the other platoons were doing because 1st Platoon was constantly patrolling/clearing the highway along with the partner training missions that involved the ANP (Afghan National Police). We hadn't been in Helmand long before we were getting radio chatter to stay away from the circle squares (due to our unit insignia patch) because we were what they considered a hard target and always poised in an aggressive posture. We had armored vehicles while the British troops would normally operate in Land Rovers and a few Jackals. I never saw much of anything that was armored besides the huge Mastiff troop carriers, but they never left the wire. Way easier to target the light-skin vehicles and a fairer fight for the insurgents, so who could blame them.

They knew... and you knew they knew. There was always someone watching. In combat operations, someone is always watching. The enemy looks for the days when the gunners aren't paying attention or maybe one of the vehicles or troops is falling back in the movement formation. They aren't stupid and they knew they had easier targets. The poor Gurkhas were rolling around the city in uncovered Land Rovers while we had a variety of HMMVWs, Cougars, and MaxxPros at our disposal. I think we were fielded some of the first MRAPs (Mine Resistant Ambush Protected vehicles) in Afghanistan when we headed to the second portion of deployment… not like we got to use them at that point though. The point is that the fight was stacked in our favor.

We maintained an aggressive posture and were pairing 240 machine guns with crew-served weapons systems such as the MK19 and .50 cal in every turret. Every culvert, dip in the road, and intersection needed to be cleared by dismounts or robots. It seemed like Lash was the IED training alley because we would find the damn things in the same spots every time we passed through. EOD (Explosive Ordnance Disposal) would just start to come with us because of the number of bombs we would find on a daily basis on the highway.

I was sent to this slick robot class to be able to operate a $250,000 remote controlled car that had tracks and a claw arm on it to "disarm" IEDs. Trying to keep the bomb robot charged and SSG Hill from playing with it was a challenge. He wanted to use it like any self-respecting guy in the military would do. Play with it until it breaks! It got to the point where I just wanted to pull on an initiator wire on a landmine with the claw so the damn thing would be blown up and I didn't have to lug it around anymore. It was slow going and painful, but we stayed alive. The second you let your guard down is the second you are in danger of being killed. The enemy would mix up the mine emplacement formula from time to time, but we did a pretty good job of finding the explosives. Mcalister's instilled discipline through his NCO corps paid off in droves here.

With all the pent-up advance news of action… nothing came. For weeks on weeks, nothing but hot desert, long roads, HMMVWs with AC that didn't work, and week-long mission sets with a refit at the end that lasted two to three days and then we would go do it all over again. The turret would get so hot, you would need to rotate the vehicle crew to keep everyone halfway coherent.

There was a lot of desert out there and the surrounding areas of Lash had large drug fields spread out around the area. You could smell the marijuana plants when you got within the radius and the poppy fields would contrast with the bleak environment. Of course, this had some of the guys chomping at the bit to get ahold of some of the buds, but we never got anywhere near close enough to be able to pull that particular type of mission off. There was talk of burn missions where troops would go and raze the crops of the local drug farmers, but we left them alone to their crops as we weren't out to do the DEA's job. Why smack a beehive when you are hunting for rabbits? They weren't our responsibility.

Some of those roads and routes in the deserts of Afghanistan get weird though. The area would look flat for as far as the eye could see, but there would be an offshoot access road so little used that you could barely see the previous travelers' tire tracks. About 10 minutes off the main road, you would dip into little valleys or fully irrigated desert crop fields with villages attached to them. It was interesting to see these little examples of desert living and what is required to get by in these environments.

Like a biblical city depicted in stories from Sunday School or a version of Tatooine from *Star Wars*, each little area would be self-sufficient in its own way. There would be a crude hierarchy and government rule of sorts. Here in the Wild West, you would find that your word was the most important thing, and you were expected to keep it no matter what. A promise out here could turn into a death sentence really quickly.

There wasn't much more from those drives through Helmand province for us to experience other than watching a local shepherd lose a sheep as we moved to Camp Leatherneck to assist the Marines in some capacity that I was never aware of. I've never seen a vehicle crush a human being before, but I can say with confidence that I made sure to steer clear of the tires of any heavy vehicle from that point forward. A local farmer was moving his flock parallel to us along the road when one of the lambs slipped and fell down a portion of the road right in front of a 17-ton vehicle whose driver and gunner couldn't see the immediate portion of road below. The animal let out a scream as it literally swelled and exploded from the overpressure inside of its internal organs, and the creature's bones gave way to the rolling armor of an American war machine. Not a way I would want to go at all.

Chi Boys

A disturbing practice in the country of Afghanistan is known as *bacha bazi*. Directly translated it means "boy play." Originally banned by the Taliban, who deemed that homosexuality was punishable by death, the long-practiced tradition involves young boys dressing as females to perform dances in front of men at parties or events because females are forbidden to do so. The boys used in the practice are essentially thrown away after they hit the age of 18 and by that time, have been raped, degraded, and psychologically damaged.

Traffickers prey upon the families in the poorest areas and essentially take young boys as apprentices to learn the practice of a "dancing boy." These kids are part of a human trafficking racket that purchases these boys and places them into personal servitude as sex slaves for their owners. It was a symbol of power and social status within certain circles of Afghanistan and began to regain its practice once the US forces removed the Taliban that were enforcing the prohibition on the activity.

During a training mission, SSG Hill came stomping out of the police outpost we were outside after a long day of side-by-side training with the Afghan police. He was in one of his moods and was anxious to get out of there that day. "I thought we were staying out here tonight?" one of the guys said. "Pack it up, we're getting the fuck out of here. Damn commander just offered me his chi boy for the night. This place is all fucked up."

Once I understood what he was talking about, it all clicked. In a land where we were supposed to be respecting the local culture and traditions, no one quite knew what to do when those traditions didn't equate to anything we had faced before. Were these kids willingly staying with their abusers? Did they need someone to step in? This was an accepted practice within a country we didn't understand, but there should be a universal moral code... right?

The answer from the DoD was to respect the practices of the local culture, but what did that mean exactly? We were living in an area of the world where they would kill a woman by stoning her to death if she was caught in a pre-marital sex act... even if that act was a rape. This is the dark side of Afghanistan that brought those familiar with the country to refer to the people as savages.

We were expected to be the model of an American soldier. Hell, even our patch reinforced the idea that we were composed of everything that America stood for as a proud member of the All American 82nd Airborne. Why was it that we had to turn and look the other way while children were being preyed upon by the very ones we were bolstering to "serve and protect" their fellow Afghans? But instead, we found ourselves packing up our outer security position to find a bed-down spot off the highway a few miles up the road.

Halloween Zombie Massacre

Partnering with a small crew of Afghan police that were huddled in the back of a Toyota HiLux, we drove up the highway in formation with a Cougar V-hull in front, myself driving the HMMVW behind with Lieutenant Sean Smith, another two vehicles, and SSG Hill bringing up the rear in a MaxxPro that was outfitted to be a medevac vehicle and was equipped with a CROWS. The CROWS is a remote-operated .50 caliber that is set up to be like playing a video game where the people on the other end of the targeting system really die. Think *Squid Game* turret of death during Red Light/ Green Light. You have a monitor, a joystick, and the ever-present bright glowing red fire button. The system can see in all environments or times of day due to the array of camera systems they had attached to it. Night vision, thermal, and a long zoom. Cool concept, but tough to learn on the fly if you haven't had a chance to use it in a combat situation. I don't even think that we had a chance to test fire or train on it yet.

The most dangerous time to be in a combat zone is when you have been in the areas where you know there is a threat, but you have been patrolling those areas with no results. You start to get complacent. We were a mix of guys who had been in combat situations before and a bunch of us "cherry" joes that had not had a taste of battle just yet. Fortunately for us, it was the ANP that were rolling with us that threw caution to the wind before any of us did. They showed us just how quickly Murphy can make the day can go sideways.

The trucks were about a mile or two away from an ANP outpost while doing our normal, painfully slow route and clearing the road in the process. The ANP figured that they were close enough to their buddies at this point and could wave goodbye, head out on their own, and watch us roll by in an hour or so as they sipped chai from the rooftop. We were also anxious to get back because it was October 31 and the Brits were promising a BBQ party when we got back that night. Real food was always a reason to be happy after five days of MREs and hot drinking water out of plastic water bottles from the back of the truck.

We continued to move slowly and clear as we approached a small roadside village in the middle of nowhere with a cluster of trees or some type of vegetation in the distance. The roads in this portion of Afghanistan were raised with ditches and wadis on either side. Some buildings were right up against the road on the right side with about a 10-foot drop down to the main village on the left. As we approached, you could see the ANP HiLux smashed into the side of a house on the right side of the road. As soon as the truck was in view, we started having the rounds zip by.

"OH SHIT, WE ARE TAKING INCOMING!" yelled Specialist Tyler Kohler up in the turret as rounds cracked around us. It was his second combat deployment, along with some of the other guys that were coming over from the 173rd Airborne out of Italy, so I was pretty sure he knew what he was talking about. The truck in front of us stopped and was blocking the view and we were stuck in place with their truck in the way of allowing us to maneuver and get the MK19 we had into the fight. Specialist Cannon was in the truck in front of us with a .50 caliber mounted alongside an M240 machine gun. The problem was that they were in a Cougar—this made the gun platforms about 15–20ft high along with a raised road of about another 5–10ft.

The ANP were popping out of a building on our right while launching HE (high explosive) rounds from grenade launchers into the village at random. Initially, they were more of a threat than the Taliban were at the moment. I realized we needed to get our gun into the fight and yelled at the lieutenant to ask permission to go around the truck in front of us. He gave the OK and as I rolled past the right side of the Cougar, I looked to my left and saw an enemy combatant pop around the side of a village building right in front of us.

The enemy maneuvering element must have had no idea we were in the fight yet, because as he popped out of cover, his eyes got to be the size of a saucers when he saw the large American vehicle fill his field of vision. The problem was the sheer height of the vehicle made the gun platform on the Cougar sit about 12ft in the air. It was so elevated, the gunner couldn't traverse the weapons system to engage the enemy at this range. SPC Cannon was instantaneously thrown a SAW from below by Sgt Rush and he jumped into the turret and drew down on the enemy combatant. BRrrrrrraaaaappppp… and down the enemy combatant went in a spray of red gore as every other truck in the convoy echoed the unspoken command to commence fire and unleash hell on the squad-sized element that was attacking us.

Our truck was finally out front and had a clear shot… but we are also majorly exposed on a raised road with rounds popping all around us. Dirt clouds were kicking up but I didn't hear anything pinging off the steel on the trucks armor yet. Kohler let loose with the MK19, right into the dirt about 75m away. "WTF KOHLER?" yelled Specialist Hammer from the back. Samuel Hammer was in the RTO position currently and was a real hard ass. I respected him as he was almost always squared away, but he was strung tighter than a pissed-off honey badger. "GET THAT SHIT ON TARGET."

Right at this time is when Murphy shows up for us. Lt Smith couldn't get anyone on the radio so he turned around and told Hammer to get the SATCOM (Satellite Communication) antenna up and running. We were too far out for the radios to let the guys in Lash know that we were in contact, so we needed to use SATCOM to reach HQ to let them know. Hammer started yelling that the manpack and SATCOM antenna were in the back of the truck. Lt Smith looked at him and told him, "That's an order Hammer!" "I get shot out there, I'm going to be fucking pissed, sir!" Hammer retorted as he now had to climb into the trunk of an HMMVW from the outside while rounds pop off all around us. Poor guy got screwed on that one but was magically not hit. Luck was on our side that day for sure.

I heard Sergeant Bobby Musil yelling over comms to "BRING THE HEAVY" as Kohler walked the next burst in onto the support by fire the enemy that had engaging us from the woodline. Once on target, Kohler just kept the trigger down. The whole first box was shot into the foliage in the distance. That's 48 rounds of 40mm grenades being rained down onto the enemy's head to make things especially shitty for them. "I NEED ANOTHER BOX," Kohler yelled as Lt Smith now exited the vehicle to assault the objective with the rest of the squad that was already on it. I reached back and threw an ammo box into the turret as Kohler was plugging away with the mounted M240.

The Assault

It was at this point that Kohler began screaming that something was wrong with the MK19: it was jammed and not firing. We just started yelling to use the 240 and forget the 19 as our element of dismounts was assaulting through at this point. I was scanning for weapon flashes and smoke trails as we continued to operate as a support-by-fire element in the trucks. Two RPGs (rocket-propelled grenades) were fired at the convoy, but missed and hit the buildings behind us. One of the rounds narrowly missed the rear vehicle as they lowered the rear ramp to dismount. One of the tactics the enemy will use is to shoot a round inside of a vehicle before the troops inside can get out. It's the money shot and will end up killing everyone inside as the shrapnel bounces around in what just became a metal coffin.

The firefight was over just as quickly as it started and was a textbook L-shaped ambush with the vehicles as the support element. I was a little sad I had been stuck in a truck at the time, but it was the job required in the moment. I was surprised after everything when Hill asked me if I took some shots out the window of my vehicle. I just looked at him weird and told him no. I wasn't sure what the value of having the driver unload a SAW through his window during a firefight would be. Especially if that open window was toward the contact and would leave the possibility of the vehicle being compromised. I get it though. Some of those guys think in pure aggression during a time like that. Which is needed, but not to the point of being reckless. I never said anything about it, but I think keeping my head, assisting the gunner in reloading rounds, and scanning for enemy threats in the area, tactical possibilities, places to maneuver that were constantly changing, and monitoring/ using the radio during contact was the right answer at the time. I found out later that he asked because someone else in the convoy had done so.

As everyone was being looked over and the intense battle stories were being swapped, some of the guys turned their attention to the dead, ashen bodies on the roadway now. I think we just grabbed three or four bodies before Hill said that was enough for the after-action drop-off. He was ready to get back to the house after a long week. There were more bodies out there, but none was seen as anything worth recovering. The Taliban combatants also had a weird habit of bringing their dead with them when they fled the battle scene. It was pretty eerie when you would find blood trails with no bodies after a shootout. Not sure if it was because of their particular religious views of needing to be buried before the next sundown. It made me think of the books on Vietnam where they talked about the Viet Cong being the "ghosts" of the jungle. I can see how someone could disappear quickly in a jungle environment, but in the desert... it was more than strange. Were did they go? Were they just swallowed up by the sand to be spit out after we had departed the region?

Miraculously, no one was hurt on our end during the engagement. Sergeant Tyler Anderson had a bullet hole through an armpit on his uniform top and Specialist John Culp had a rip in his helmet cover where a round skipped off it as they had assaulted. There was an enemy combatant that had survived the onslaught and Doc Ponce was told to save him. It was a teenager that was clinging to life after Private Harris had let out a burst from his machine gun to cut him down in his path. The kid had suffered from his battlefield injuries with both of his hands mangled, a bramble thorn stuck in his eyeball, and a testicle hanging outside of his scrotum. Doc begrudgingly patched him up as Tyler proceeded with a brief battlefield interrogation.

There is nothing quite like the feeling of surviving a combat incident, although this was mild in the terms of incidents to come or what could have happened if they had gotten an RPG into us during the engagement. The adrenaline high, the fact you survived, the antagonist lying dead at your feet, the sheer heightening of senses that was experienced along with a healthy dump of dopamine and adrenaline make for a nice little cocktail only to be known by those who have been there. This is where you start to recognize the hard chargers, the pipe hitters, the barrel-chested fighters, and the ones they compare to "woodpecker lips." After a moment like that, you get it. You understand what is at stake and why the discipline and urgency matter so much. You must give it your all or you won't be the one advancing. There are a lot of factors involved, but you can tell the men from the boys after an extreme experience like this... as I saw later.

After a brief AAR (after-action review) and dumping the bodies at the bottom of the driveway at the next ANP station, we headed back to Lashkar Gah where our cheeky brethren warriors (the Brits) had a Halloween cookout waiting for us with burgers just coming off the grill along with some other BBQ food. We had just been out for days, so being able to enjoy that delicious, grill-fired hunk of meat without someone yelling at me was the real prize at the end of the day. Everyone decompressed for the night after that. We had gotten a taste of action and the new guys had proven to be not incompetent. Everyone was unscathed which led to an even higher boost of morale for us. It was a good night. Two of the guys (Culp and Kornegay) even broke out some homemade Halloween costumes that they had fashioned from a mop, and other miscellaneous gear you find laying around in a foreign country police station. They were some kind of pirate mates with one of them sporting a full-on beard made from a floor mop's dangling threads and the other playing as a wench, complete with a coconut bra.

That night brutally exposed a few things for me. It made everything real. It's like that moment in Airborne School where it all leads to your first jump from an aircraft. You'll go through the motions for weeks before jump week happens. Even then, it wasn't real when jumping into the dirt on Fort Benning a few hundred times. It wasn't real when hopping out of the tower (although I think the 150ft tower is worse than the plane). Even after being released from that 300ft crane in the middle of the field of the airborne compound, I still can say that it wasn't quite real for me.

However, when the doors open on the plane and the cool air slaps you in the face... that's when it gets real. It can take anywhere from 15 minutes to six-plus hours to get ready for a jump depending on who you are jumping with, conditions, the aircraft size, crew, number of jumpers, and all of the other variables you have to deal with. So, after rigging up, being inspected, sitting in the pack shed, walking to the plane, sitting in the plane and taking off... all of this didn't have the feel. It was the motions. You could now experience the moment.

This is combat for a soldier. Everything up until this point was the motions. You had enlisted and had gotten to where you were now. You may have had years of training experience and shooting up until this point, but the sheer severity of you vs them isn't realized until after the fact. Yes, it's your job, but the fact is that there is still a very small percentage of soldiers in the Army that see combat. Once you've gotten through it though, it doesn't hit until later. You feel like Superman. The rush is unlike anything you'll ever get because you are operating at a level where most humans will never understand. It is you and them fighting to the death. One of you is leaving this world and one will move on to die another day. If you are in the thick of it, every fiber of your body is attuned to its surroundings (or at least it better damn be) and you have a hyper awareness.

I'll get into it later, but if you are exposed to these conditions for a long period of time, your body settles into this heightened state continually. It is exhausting but something amazing to have experienced. The body and brain are an incredible piece of hardware that can be honed to a razor's edge if you really have the fortitude to go down that road.

Mexican Standoff

After that firefight, things in Lashkar Gah got quiet for us. The enemy had lost all stomach to mess with our crew. We were already operationally stagnant and because of the recent experience, the Taliban in the area would see our up-armored vehicles and notice the patches and they would call anything off.

It was then we were brought onto an operation that included the British Royal Marines and some Afghan commandos. The 1st platoon element was stuck in a QRF/blocking position for something like 72 hours. It wasn't anything exciting, but there was an IED that tossed an Afghan HiLux through the air and over one of our vehicles. Other than that incident, the entire operation was a mess that included multiple vehicles getting stuck because they were just too heavy for the surrounding landscape. Anything larger than a HMMVW would break the smaller village bridges or get squeezed out of an alleyway due to its width.

In our position, it was just hot… really freaking hot. We would rotate in two-hour shifts between the three of us left in the truck. One would man the gun turret, one would monitor the radio and keep the turret gunner awake while checking the fuel levels and gauges, and one would sleep, or try to. You would try to dust off the weapons from time to time to make sure things weren't crusty in case things happened to escalate into a fight.

I was wearing a Sunnto watch that had a thermometer sensor along with all the other gadgetry packed into the thing. It read 142 degrees in the heat of the day. Just a miserable time where you just felt like you were baking in a convection oven, waiting for death by dehydration. If you were left up there for extended periods of time, it would have you delirious and you started to understand just how crucial water can be in a desert.

By the end of the mission, we had all been awake for a good amount of time and were exhausted. I was the driver, with Sergeant Malcolm Ackers as the truck commander, Sergeant Nesbit (a former Marine) as the gunner, and two others in the back. The particularly long convoy had a mixture of vehicles in it as the joint mission had all sorts of international warfighting machinery out for the hit. The truck in front of us was an Afghan pickup truck being driven by the commandos with about 10 guys piled into the truck bed.

Nighttime… roadway… everyone is exhausted. A combination for disaster if you don't have another person awake with you to keep you from dozing off. As we drove along, one by one they fell asleep. The backseat was knocked out before we were out of the town limits and I couldn't tell, but I bet Nesbit was racked out in that turret along with Ackers drifting in and out of consciousness between the drone of the tires and the monotony of everything. That's what you did. You slept where and when you could. You found places to do so, including ones that no one in their right mind would be able to sleep in.

My turn came last. I was kidding myself in thinking that it was all good. I never fell asleep in the car before. Would never happen. A few head bobs happened, so I cracked the window a little bit, pinched my leg, slapped my cheek, and the ever-present foot tapping. It still came as a blink and then my eyes jamming open hard, right before the initial impact. Full stomp onto the brakes doesn't mean much as there isn't much that's going to stop a vehicle at that weight very quickly.

I can only describe what happened as human bowling pins hurtling through the air. The truck bed of the Afghan commando truck was crushed up to the cabin and the soldiers went flying every which way one could imagine. Thankfully, something was watching out for us because no one involved was hurt except for one of the Afghans breaking his leg. We didn't know that initially though.

Remember everything I just told you about combat and heighted senses, emotions, and situations? These Afghan nationals just lost some soldiers and an American slams into their truck, destroys it, and fucks up their guys in the process. For whatever reason, we went into a full-on Mexican standoff. It was a dicey situation. Nesbit was up in the gunner turret and started asking if we were going to shoot them as the Afghans lined up and started pointing weapons at us. These are warrior people. These are also warrior people that demand justice swiftly and with severity when it comes to retribution. They don't mess around.

Nesbit is swiveling his .50 cal down to point into a lineup of AK-wielding commandos that were on our side up until a minute ago. The Afghan commander in charge comes up to my window, pulls a pistol out, and taps it on the side of the window while motioning me to get out. Afghans only use the pistol for one thing… executions. The Afghans wouldn't blink an eye towards an assault weapon, but you pull out a pistol… sheer terror! Goes to show you just how Wild West that place can get. Nesbit's adrenaline is so high at this point, his leg is shaking and he sounds nervous as he knows just how dangerous this hair-trigger moment has become.

It was the ugliest possibility of a CNN-type incident that could have happened and thankfully, someone came to our rescue outside of the truck on scene. I had to fill out sworn statements where the leadership determined that I was following too closely on advice from the TC. Sergeant Ackers saved my butt big time—I thought I was about to be thrown out of Bravo Company because I now had a second HMMWV crash under my belt. As luck would have it, they covered it up well enough and we continued on like nothing had really happened.

Afghan Gangsters: Lieutenant Demarest's Story

As the vehicle slowed, Lieutenant Vincent Demarest was jostled to coming awake. He was dog tired and doing part of his initial rotation into the command position as he was taking over from the 1st Platoon officer in charge. Lt Smith was showing him the ropes and pitfalls within the platoon. "Dude, what's going on?" Demarest exclaimed in his usual laidback speech pattern. Something about a truck crash that had just happened up ahead. Damn driver must have fallen asleep and had smashed into a HiLux full of Afghans.

The HiLux was the international version of the Toyota Tacoma and is the prime choice for just about any police operations in austere environments around the world. The Afghans had them everywhere with the 1980s blue lightbars and the forest ranger green paint color that stuck out against the tan backdrop. They would use them in every capacity and in the current mission role, they were troop carriers that had about 10 Afghan commandos that were armed to the teeth in the back of each of them. These weren't the standard-issue Afghan National Police, but the arm of the Afghan Army that was trained by the US Army Special Forces in counterinsurgency tactics and direct action against the hostile enemies within Afghanistan. They were a far cry better trained.

Demarest couldn't believe what he had seen earlier in the mission when one of the Afghan trucks that had been carrying guys in the back had hit an IED. The truck flipped up into the air, higher than the American forces' MaxxPro vehicle which stood at about 15ft high and was unrecognizable as the metal was twisted into a horrific deathtrap and the steel became a literal iron maiden, pulverizing its cabin occupants in an instant.

The Afghan troops that were in the truck bed suffered the opposite fate to that of the cabin occupants as the overpressure in the air from the blast completely ripped their bodies into pieces as they came apart at the joints. Arms and legs splayed out all over the ground, like someone had tossed a kid's toy box onto the ground full of broken-apart crash test dummies… but these weren't dummies. These were people.

Seconds ago, these had been living, breathing people with families at home and those that cared about them and what happened to them. Now, they were just meat on the ground that had been separated by the slaughtering butcher. The bodies were treated as such as another truck quickly pulled up to the scene and just began tossing the remains of the bodies into the back. They knew that this wasn't the time to mourn their comrades. These were hardened men.

These were the men that grew up watching their grandfathers and some their fathers fight in the various conflicts around the country. From a young age, they understood about loss and the brevity of life as well as the importance of taking the time to enjoy every minute of just how wonderful your time here could be. But it was a hard life in this country, and because they understood the importance of the freedom to experience a life without the imposed sharia law of the Taliban, these men took up arms to defend what they felt was something worth fighting for. Now someone in the convoy had just smashed into one of the trucks carrying these guys back. Hope no one was seriously hurt or even killed. Wonder who it was?

The report came back that it was one of ours that was involved in the incident. Oh shit! It was Ackers' truck! Ackers was 1st Platoon's 1st squad leader and one of the newer guys to the company had just smashed into one of the trucks after following a bit too closely. What was going on up there anyway?

"They say what's happening? Everything good?" Demarest said to Lt Smith.

"God damn it, the Afghans are lining up and getting ready to execute someone up there! We gotta go!" Lt Smith yelled. He jumped out of the vehicle and ripped open the interpreter's door and pulled him out. "Come on, Arman, it's time to really earn your pay today."

Arman was one of the interpreters that was assigned to the company, but he wasn't the good interpreter. It was like he was the B-team and was really new to all of this. As the three men ran at a breakneck pace towards the commotion about 200m ahead, Demarest could see that this was not good. There was a line of commandos with their weapons all pointed at Ackers' HMMWV and the yelling was intensified. DAMN IT!

He had just gotten here, and this is what he was getting into! Holy hell! Vince thought he was going to die right then and there as they had sighted the man in charge of the firing squad brandishing his pistol, out of the scabbard and motioning to the driver of the vehicle. "ARMAN... TELL THAT COMMANDER TO CALM DOWN. CALM THE FUCK DOWN!" Smith screamed at his interpreter.

But Arman was terrified! Shaken to his core as he knew that someone was probably getting a bullet in the head. Arman had seen the commandos do their job and knew the legends based around what they could do and would do to their enemies on the battlefield. That commander wouldn't think twice about turning Arman's head into an exploded watermelon if he said the wrong thing in the wrong way. His men were wounded, and this commander wanted justice and he wanted it swiftly.

"Uh... uh... uh, sir," Arman stuttered, making it worse. The commander turned a shade of purple as the men standing in a line with their guns drawn were nervously fidgeting. The turret gunner in the HMMVW was sitting low and the mounted. .50 cal was swiveled down at the line of men in front of the vehicle, its truck bed smashed right up to the cabin and no longer drivable, sitting behind them.

Damn it if it wasn't the most welcome sight in the world when "Gucci" showed up on the scene.

"Do not worry, sir. I will tell them what I need to do to calm this down," he stated in a curt, professional manner like it was something he was used to. He turned and instantly began spurting out a flurry of Pashto and Dari that had the other Afghans there reeling in confusion as they tried to keep up.

Gucci was a professional translator who had worked alongside Special Forces for years and had somehow ended up on this mission with Bravo Company 2/508 of the 82nd Airborne. It was OK work and Gucci liked doing something that helped out his country and working with the Americans. He wanted their way of life for his family and one day, his own kids. He spoke English fairly well, he was honest, the US Special Forces had vetted him, he knew his way around a weapon, and he wasn't a coward. There is a lot you can tell about a person and their loyalties when bullets start flying, but there was never any doubt of whose side Gucci was on or his beliefs in what he stood for. He was a good guy.

Whatever he said had the commander that had been brandishing the pistol a second ago turn his attention on Gucci, but at least he had his pistol down and wasn't screaming for retribution in the way of blood from the occupants of the vehicle that had hit them a moment ago. Gucci was catching hell though as the commander was still yelling.

Out of the corner of his eye, Lt Demarest saw the fast-moving figure of the Afghan battalion commander as he moved into the bubble of confusion and mayhem that was on a razor's edge from becoming a full-blown international incident like one they hadn't had happen in years. I think in the action taken to defuse the situation, the senior commander understood the full severity if this thing escalated.

WHACK, the battalion commander pulled his pistol out and in one swift motion smacked his subordinate in the face with the butt of the pistol. Vince could see the scorned commander's eyes and for a second, he swore they were about to see a full-on gunfight with pistols drawn while standing at the premier vantage point that one didn't want to be in while in a situation such as this. Those eyes were calculating the odds on shooting his own commander square in the face.

The senior commander barked out some stiff commands at the men lined up with their AK-47s drawn at the vehicle and they began to lower their weapons. Everyone was coming down off the adrenaline. He turned to Gucci who quickly promised that those responsible would be severely punished and sent back home to be tried for their crimes against the Afghan soldiers that had been hurt.

In a quick assessment, we found that no one was actually hurt except for one soldier with a broken leg but it wasn't a compound break; it would soon heal and he would head back to duty shortly. If anything, it was going to get this guy some much-needed rest as he healed up and he could take a break from the constant missions that were getting his friends killed on a regular basis.

So, this was what it was like to deploy to a combat operation with the infantry... great.

Thanksgiving

Our posting to the Afghan police station wasn't bad as far as places to stay in a warzone go, honestly. It was the full Third World experience though. There were hard buildings that we used as barracks. We were housed in a concrete building that was against one of the outer walls complete with a guard tower on the back wall and a small access road that surrounded the perimeter of the police station. As the hosts, the Afghans said they would supply security as was their custom and we were in their house. We could sleep as we needed, run missions out of the place, and use it to store whatever we needed.

We thanked the Afghans, but still parked our trucks in between the road and buildings, offering extra shielding against rockets or bullets that might come from the outer wall. SSG Hill posted a roving guard at the trucks with one truck fully locked and loaded and a sentry posted in the turret ready to blast anyone that tried to mess with our element at night. We had a single entryway and stairwell guards protecting against anyone accessing our building without being spotted and stopped.

Some might think it was overkill, especially when we would need to leave an element behind as guards for our building, run missions that went from three to five days on the road, try to get some sleep and maybe get a movie in before needing to go on a convoy to HQ for a briefing, pulling double guard duties, or just being berated and barraged by the NCOs with "hip pocket training." This phrase belongs to a lot of the stuff you would think a drill sergeant would be yelling at a recruit. Max velocity of a 5.56 round, questions about the cone of fire, running "down gun" drills with the SAW and 240. Weapons squad had some real studs on abilities to know the gun, be able to operate as a team in pitch darkness, and communicate effectively on the battlefield. This was all due to the work Staff Sergeant Scott Brunkhorst had put into his weapons squad.

Word circulated that Brunk had been in training to be a Special Forces 18 Charlie which was an engineer. He had made it all the way to graduation day and had gotten gigged with a DUI right before receiving his tab. So, it was off to the 82nd as the SF regiment didn't want to take a guy with such a stain on his record before he had officially obtained his tab. This was the beginning of the big joke that DoD imposed on their soldiers, even though it had fostered a system of alcoholics that glorified drinking for decades prior. I don't agree with a DUI ending your career and I don't think guys should have their tab taken for certain actions that could have been a teaching experience. The teams were full of guys with alcohol-related incidents and it was an inside joke that you would never make it past E7 without getting one. I'm not saying I agree with the drinking culture either. I do think that we are getting better as an entire society that is informed and educated to the very real risks of alcohol. However, it shouldn't be a decider on your career when the very organization that fostered the risky behavior is the one doling out punishment with a heavy hand. Either way… Staff Sergeant Scott Brunkhorst was a good dude and they were lucky to have that amount of knowledge in the squad.

Days in Helmand back at the ANCOP would be long and drawn-out with intermittent electricity fueling the brief time you could charge whatever equipment you had or go and take a shower. Sometimes, things would calm down enough and you might be able to get a chance to rotate into playing a round or two of video games on an X-Box one of the guys had stolen from the National Guard compound at Camp Diamond. Someone had brought the newest modern warfare saga that included a mini game where you needed to survive the zombie onslaught as the progressing levels brought more of the horde to bear on your position.

The separation between platoons was very real and they always fostered this sense of being in "the best platoon," but there was even some trickledown to the squads. You knew that Sgt Musil's squad in our platoon was the best without question. Second squad was known as "anger squad" for good reason. Weapons was tuned for what they did, but Musil's squad were the guys that were generally outperforming everyone else. They were aggressive and they were suited for how they were used throughout the deployment. Someone had mentioned that Bobby was the "angel of death" in reference to a firefight they got into in a prior deployment when he was a PV2.

The story was told to me after having had to help Bobby out of a screaming fit during a nightmare one night while on guard. He had been on a particular mission and in the turret of the lead vehicle. They entered a village that they were headed to attend a Key Leader Engagement (KLE) that day and the entire village had been infiltrated by Taliban. The enemy opened fire on the vehicle and the driver "stalled in the doorway." He literally freaked out and hit the brakes when the ambush hit. No one could get around the truck and they were being hit with everything the enemy had to throw at it. Bobby was a maniac up in the turret: just started to gun them down. I couldn't believe it, but they told me to look at his dress blues when I got a chance and see that he had a Silver Star for it. That's what was told to me anyway. I never asked him about the story personally because that's not the type of thing you ever want to ask a guy. If he wants to let you into that world, then you can listen to what he has to say. That's about the best you can do for guys in that position.

I was in Sgt Ackers' 1st squad. I had left Sgt Thomas from 3rd squad and was placed under Ackers at some point during the Helmand mission on this portion of deployment. I remember liking the move because Sgt Thomas got in my butt about a lot of things. I was also with his squad when I first arrived at Bravo Company, so a lot of screwups along the way were probably burned into his memory. He had a lot of attention to detail and could always find something wrong with what you were doing at the time. It wasn't a bad thing and I understand now just how important knowing your trade is. There was a lot of the discipline that I needed, but it was being taught in a language I didn't understand. We did not mesh very well... so, he was probably grateful when I was moved out of third squad.

Ackers was a good leader. He was strict, but he gave you a chance and taught the lessons in a way where I think things started to click. I didn't enjoy my new roommate, Norton, but at least he came off as more mature and didn't really bother anyone for anything. He just did what he was told, would rarely bitch about anything (although he would mutter curses under his breath), and was generally knowledgeable about everything in the unit handbook. He didn't like attention, so he just kept in his lane. He was a good gray man. SSG Hill was also convinced that Norton had a switch and was going to snap one day. He used him as his driver because he stated that the kid was going to go mental one of these days and he wanted to be there to see it.

I was the polar opposite of him. I was always looking to do a task more efficiently, with less effort, or improve upon how it was being done currently. Either that... or looking for a way to get out of it all. It must have driven Ackers batshit crazy. However, Ackers was patient and a good teacher who took the time to understand his guys and the way they operated, and figure out how could he put them to their best use. I liked Ackers because he was another leader that had discipline but was fair. Once you started to gain trust by proving it, you started to be able to relax a bit. I'm sure it's also why I was sent to the bomb robot school. They knew I wouldn't screw up too bad while away from the flagpole and I would be enough of a geek to operate the gear that it came with.

Those skills came in handy more as the deployment went along, but we were a ragtag bunch that were getting tasked out for any possible duty imaginable. I am sure that somewhere in the 82nd bible (DIV PAM for those who know) there is a reference to something to the effect that "an idle private is a problem one never wishes to have... especially when a paratrooper."

I probably don't remember much from Helmand because I probably don't want to remember much about Helmand. I do remember the latrine duty on the initial move into the ANCOP building. The place was disgusting... when I was told by Sgt Musil back in the states that the country was inhabited by "savages," I immediately thought that I had signed onto Colonel Custer's long-lost relative's paratrooper brigade. I wasn't looking forward to the last stand somewhere in Afghanistan with a bunch of goons. After living alongside them for a little while, you start to think that maybe they are, in fact, savages. I realize that it is an entirely different culture and world, and at this point, I know the place is even worse off now that we are gone. Most, if not all, of the country is going to be forced back to Old Testament times due to the enforcement of sharia law.

I honestly thought about that at times. It was the weirdest thing. I would be watching a guy lead a donkey through a mud hut village, caked with mud and his little flop hat on with a shawl placed around his shoulders. You would think for a minute that this picture is exactly like it was back in 250 BC. No electricity, have to get fresh water from a well that was in the village center, and that donkey was probably his most expensive possession, and then you would catch that his sandals were Adidas and he was sporting a digital watch. It's about the weirdest thing, but it gets weirder when Apache gunships show up and start doing gun runs and dropping ordnance.

We opened the door to the latrine compound and were greeted by the foulest smell that you could ever imagine. This is due to the Afghan diet and the fact that they never seemed to be able to hit the target of a giant hole in the ground while dropping their feces. You learn to appreciate the invention of the seated toilet when you take a look at this porcelain slab in the ground that resembles a farmhouse sink but with no depth and a much larger hole in the middle. The method of use is to stand, straddling the fixture, and let your bathroom business drop into the hole. Not only were they complete amateurs at bomb runs but then they would either kick the feces when they were done or throw it around the damn room like a pack of monkeys had gotten into the latrine.

It took what seemed like forever to clear out a good portion of the bathroom "fit for use" alongside having to work around the intermittent power schedules and dodging the camel spiders that lurked in the moist environment and would shoot up the walls if you entered the stall. After a while, we had the place looking pretty good. By Thanksgiving it was good enough that HQ and 2nd Platoon left the luxuries of the British compound for the day to come over to our posting because it was the only place with enough room for our little celebration to be held all together.

The Army has a tradition of the officer corps serving a hot dinner as close as possible to a traditional dinner back home in America. It did not disappoint and was a holiday that ended up seared into our memory. Not only for the good-natured jokes tossed around ribbing one platoon against another, but for the shotgun incident as well.

Some of the guys had gotten new PSP games and were trading their old cartridges or illegally downloaded ones that were loaded via ROMS or jailbreaking. Dinner was fantastic! The turkey was probably left over from a chow hall somewhere on Bagram, but everything just had a sense of what one could consider "normalcy." It was a good day. Captain Adam Armstrong was carving up the turkey and portioning out the slices. I didn't really think about it at the time, but now every time Thanksgiving comes around, I hope those same guys are enjoying a hot meal somewhere with people that give a shit about them. If there is any time during the year that brings up memories like this for the guys, it's the holidays.

Sgt Tyler Anderson was giving SPC Nesbit a class on the shotgun because he was supposed to be moving into a team leader position soon. We carried shotguns for breaching and Nesbit would need to have one with him from time to time. Nesbit had come over from the Marines. I can't hold it against him, but damn if he hadn't already eaten his fair share of crayons already. Tyler was showing him how to clear the weapon, and for some damn reason, Nesbit only dropped one round from the chamber before deciding that was all the tactical shotgun he was clearing held. He proceeded to manipulate the safety and fired the damn thing into the wall.

We were lucky as hell that no one was hurt or killed as all it did was take a good chunk out of the wall. A bunch of the guys lost some hearing frequencies that day and ears were ringing. Unfortunately for us, Anderson was moved within the company after the incident. He was a really good team leader and I was sad to see him go when he did. He ended up traded to 2nd Platoon and Nesbit went to 3rd.

Not long after that, we received word that we were leaving. It was good to get out of there because it was a boring assignment that wasn't using us for what we could offer on the battlefield. There was the necessary task of training the Afghan Army and police forces, but fruitless results regardless of the blood spilled, limbs lost, and lives changes forever. We weren't told where we were headed, but we were told it was going to be a hot area. We had been proven in combat, but only touched lightly up until now. I was to realize soon just how many ways you can wage warfare and just how ugly it could get.

FOB Walton

The flight into Helmand on a Chinook had been like a scene like out of a movie with the rear tail of the bird cracked open and door gunners on miniguns ready to rock. You have a ton of gear piled on top of you but you don't really care as it's one of the coolest rides in your life. The desert is rolling under the bird and we see a herd of wild horses get swallowed up in a swirling ground sandstorm as we fly by overhead. The gunners dust things off by running a "test fire" over an uninhabited area about midflight. This is what a gun bunny lives for as a Dillon Aero manufactured weapon pours 7.62 rounds onto a target at a rate of 6,000 rounds per minute.

Leaving Helmand wasn't as glorious. We drove out with everything we had strapped to the vehicles with our bags inside of a connex that was being shipped via jingle truck to where we were headed in the next two weeks. I know how that goes, so I was one of the guys that strapped my stuff to the exterior trunk of one of the vehicles. There are so many shipping containers loaded to the gills with DoD equipment that end up being found on the Pakistani border or elsewhere, completely gutted with only a shell of steel remaining.

What do you do with a combat unit when in between mission sets in a country? Bringing everyone back to Kandahar for refit and "redeployment" would not be a great idea. You have a bunch of guys in an infantry company that have been cooped up doing operations for the last three or so months. Bringing them to a place like Kandahar would only bring things like pregnancies and soldiers maxing out their credit cards on dumb stuff at the boardwalk. So, you bring them to somewhere like FOB Walton.

FOB Walton stands for forward operating base Walton. They would name various combat outposts (COPs) or FOBs after those killed in the unit that was over that AO at the time of death. Maybe it was done as a sort of memorial, but it also served as a constant reminder of the severity of the situation you were in. You would usually see the history on whatever plaque was tacked somewhere near the entrance. Something bigger like Kandahar or Bagram always had its threats, but nothing like these areas. The damn towers in Bagram were given paintball guns and pen flares at one point as a deterrent because they didn't want a jumpy joe to go killing locals if they thought they were trying to breach the wire. The threat just wasn't there. Somewhere like Bagram was big enough for the Taliban to know that it was a futile endeavor to attack those points.

I can understand those fears because one of our own guys, who we had received from the 173rd, had killed a local elder while he was trying to free a goat from the surrounding concertina wire. It was an accident because it had appeared that he was attempting to breach the wire, but if an extra second had been taken to positively identify the situation, someone's life may have been spared. That's a tough call. I think it was the fact that it was an elder of the village that upset the locals so much and put a black stain on the soldier's record. It's one of many choices that are made during war.

Sometimes, you get the enemy, and the day is saved, but sometimes, it's just someone in the wrong place and wrong time with the "fog of war" introduced to the situation. You must make a call, and it doesn't always result in the desired outcome. While in the role of an Infantryman, your job is to stay alive and to keep your guys alive around you. That is not to say go full cyclic on every situation but be aggressive and with an aggressive posture. That is your mission. If it falls under the umbrella of different ROE (Rules of Engagement), that will be dictated by the current commander's directive. You are the one to live with your actions for the rest of your life. I don't feel there was ever an instance when it was a gray area for me, but I do know that the sentiment among some of the men was to kill them all and let God sort them out later.

Walton was one of those areas that was a good choice for the unit to refit. We had a gym, a small chow hall, tents, and a few hard buildings. More importantly, we had electricity on tap all the time! Someone had seen my jailbroken PSP with all of the emulated original NES games on it while we were having a little down time, so I was circulated into the frenzy of guys wanting their video game fix. With the mass sharing of hard drives from the guys came a torrent of virus-ridden computers, so I would usually end up with both electronic devices in my lap.

I had been around a little bit now, so I could start to talk to the other guys. Up to this point, I had been running around with a damn machine gun and 1,200 rounds of ammo strapped to me. What I really wanted was the job of the RTO. It had nothing to do with being able to get rid of a little weight. Honestly, the radio and batteries weighed about as much as what was in my assault pack prior anyway. It was because I wanted to be an 18E (Special Forces communications sergeant) and I wanted the experience of the job. I knew that I was going to go back to selection and was going to make it this time around, so this would be the best form of experience for the job I wanted to be doing. A lot of people don't understand just how much goes into a soldier's position, knowing his craft, and making adjustments while gaining practical experience along the way.

Take my job as a SAW gunner. I had a separate machine gunner rig where I would carry 600 rounds with a 100-round "nutsack" loaded into the weapon at all times. A "nutsack" was a cloth ammo carrier that is riveted to a plastic carrier mount that attaches to the underside of the SAW. I largely preferred it to the normal plastic 200-round box that the 5.56 link comes in and you get told that's all you get. The problem is that the boxes are clumsy, noisy, and break off with any sort of hard impact. If you were using a "nutsack", the rounds didn't bang around and make noise as you were stalking other humans during a mission. It was also lighter, which assisted in the heavy frontal weight bias the SAW had that the M60 didn't share as an attribute. Sometimes, your squad would have a box with better equipment in it from guys who had left it behind. The most assured way to keep your gear and not have it constantly lent out was to just buy your own. This way, you own it, you maintain it, you know every little nuance and factor about that particular piece of equipment. This is the level of attention to detail that you needed to have. Maybe it was my OCD but it worked well with that situation and I've put it to use ever since.

It was also kind of weird that you could use this stuff while on deployment, but if you ever dared to use it while training stateside, you would have 1SG and the SGM chewing your ass for the duration of training because you were thinking outside of the box. Adapt, overcome, and win the day, I guess. It was all part of knowing where your range limits were for each situation.

The logistics nonsense was amplified in situations like when we had the SAW swap out prior to deployment. The unit had a bunch of busted and beaten-down weapons in our arms room that they would strip down, swap parts with, and were useless otherwise, but had serial numbers we had to retain. I understand the concept of being supplied with equipment in-country, but when you start to see the experienced guys talking about the state of equipment that we were heading to combat with, you get nervous. I had trained with one particular SAW myself for a while. I had that thing down to a science. There were a few deficiencies when I was first handed it, but after bargaining with the arms room for certain parts, swapping out the worn-down springs, and practicing at constant ranges, I had that weapon running better than anyone else's in our platoon. I mainly thought the 249 was a piece of garbage, but this one was all right.

Well, about two weeks prior our deployment, I was told to pass my machine gun off to Specialist Joshua Simas while being handed a deadlined one. I couldn't believe it! It wasn't just that we were heading out and I now had a useless weapon; the guy they handed it to was someone I had zero respect for. Some of the guys called him Slimas behind his back because he showed favor to those that could get him what he wanted, but anyone else was pretty much useless to him, so he treated you like shit. On top of it, he had been on deployment with the guys prior, so he had a combat patch. This was an internal type of ranking where guys with combat patches would get more credibility than those without. Two E4s side by side, but one of them had a "slick sleeve," so guess who was the boss?

I had no problem with respecting rank or time in grade, but this guy wore it as a badge of ability to sham harder than anyone else. He wasn't a bad guy, per se, but he wasn't one of those guys that had leadership qualities. He wanted his guys to fall in line, do the work, not make his life hard, and get by with having to do the least possible. Even that would be OK, but he didn't do it from the front. It was always him screaming to get something done and we would go make it happen... then we would have to find him again. Usually at the PX or hiding out in someone's room playing video games. So, seeing I had my own axe to grind with him, it was a struggle to give my death-dealing machine that I had cared for so well up until now to someone that I had considered to be a turd.

RTO

All of that didn't matter at this point because I wanted that RTO slot... and you know what an RTO didn't have to carry? THE SAW! I was a joe at that point and didn't know that they were looking for the next RTO. I also didn't know that it was recommended an RTO only carry the radio for up to six months due to the amount of frequency power that the radio puts out. What I did know is that the current RTO, Hammer, was leaving for mid-tour R&R leave during refit at Walton. This could be my only opportunity.

I talked around and weaseled my way into at least putting the word out there that I wanted the job and I wanted it bad. A lot of the guys looked at the job unfavorably. Hammer put it best when he stated, "I'm out here shooting off radio signals when I should be shooting off bullets. I didn't sign up for this shit!" I had a different view. I saw that the radio position would give me access to the battle picture happening around me.

In a modern-day conflict, the ability to call for air support, medevac, situation reports, or whatever else is key. Even more so when you add some of the other capabilities that we have these days. SATCOM was the pinnacle of communications where you could send a small team in anywhere in the world and have them communicate securely via satellite using a handheld radio unit and a specialty antenna that was the size of a Folders coffee can. If you give me the right azimuth and altitude, I can show you how to set one up. It's incredibly easy and must have been space-age tech during the 80s. These days battlefield capabilities are insane. If you lose communication on the battlefield in the modern day, you stand a very good chance at losing the battle.

The threat of EMP and other various jamming methods out there is very real and there is a reason for that. We are very reliant on technology in the current day and age because it has done us well. It's interesting to note that even with all of these amazing advantages over an enemy, we still have trouble fighting an adversary like the Taliban or ISIS. When you learn to fight "off grid," you can immensely disrupt a modern-day adversary. It's scary to see the disappearance of things like fieldcraft when you are leaving the service because you know just how important it is to be able to live off the land or in extreme austere environments. You appreciate the edge technology can give you, but you also need to understand the element of the land as well.

I was the only guy I knew who actually wanted the job and that probably made the leadership suspicious. Being RTO also gave you a few perks the other guys didn't get. You were under the Weapons squad leader who was usually the most experienced—but also busy enough with the gun teams to not worry too much about the RTO. The platoon RTO will also be an assistant to the platoon sergeant and the lieutenant. Between being farmed out to do their business or attend meetings with them, you got a lot of autonomy. That was exactly where I excelled but exactly where I think that most of them were worried that I would screw up.

SSG Hill called me into the platoon hut to talk to me about it and pretty much gave me the shit end of the stick on the situation. He knew we were going to lose Hammer for the initial push into our new AO and I wanted the job to fill in for him while he was gone. I could have the job but it was temporary and I wasn't losing the damn SAW either. Looking back on it, I know he was just messing with me, but damn if that didn't piss me off. Not only was I going to be carrying a crap ton of ammo into a hot objective with a machine gun, but now a radio too? How was this even going to work? What the hell?! Good on them for making me sweat it out until about two days prior to our push.

Determined at this point to not screw up the opportunity, I had to set a better standard than Hammer had done in the job. The platoon loved that guy. The deck was stacked against me on this one, but I was going to do my best. Hammer was a good at what he did, but he was very high strung and an asshole that would be on your case the second you screwed up. It was like he lived for that moment. There were a few guys in Bravo Company like that. The thing was that he was never wrong any time that I can remember. I'm sure he had his moments, but it never showed. He was one of the few guys that could get into me about something, but I could respect him about it, even if I hated him for it.

I grabbed inventory of everything, wiped all the data sets that were on the radios, and set all of them to a standard with the same preloaded frequencies across the network. There were batteries cross loaded through the squads. I inventoried all of our equipment along with our new Lt and then ended up signing for everything in our platoon. I very quickly learned to sub-receipt everything out to the respective squads as I didn't want to end up responsible for a few million dollars in damages.

It was a bit of an ass pain in the beginning, but I quickly figured out the role and had a working knowledge of the particular equipment before long. They gave us a new version of radio known as the 117G. Command had even brought us to a class on the equipment that involved waivers and paperwork. Probably because the capabilities included digital spectrum cryptology, full-on internet, and the capability to stream live drone footage while on the battlefield. No shit, you throw a laptop into your assault bag and you can watch a live feed from a 1,000ft view above the battlefield playing out in front of you. Crazy type stuff that was never utilized. I tried to bring it up on a few occasions, but I don't think they factored in its usefulness or wanted to rely on the tech. Murphy does tend to show his head at the most inopportune times.

The Last Meal

Constant awareness of areas that were left unsecured or unlocked connex containers were a thing at FOB Walton. There wasn't too much to do at Walton and we didn't want to do anything that was going to get us in trouble, so we would keep it mild. A case of rip-it drinks here or a package of steaks from the mess hall freezer. It was a small outpost and hot, so you could move about without too much attention, but you also had to be careful about who you let into the fold. Who were going to let into your little underworld?

The downtime also allowed me to order my first AR15 from a computer at the FOB MWR. There was a little makeshift wooden shack on one corner of the FOB with 10 or so computers with dial-up speed capabilities. It was better than nothing. The rifle was a Stag Arms 8L with piston impingement and a left-hand ejection port. For some weird reason, I shoot rifle lefty but pistol right-handed, and all without an issue. It has always felt natural for me and worked out really nicely when I moved to transition ranges down the road in my service. It also brought me undue attention from Kornegay one day as he told me, "Who do you think you are, Ranger Rick?" Again... my mentality didn't conform to how Big Army wanted me to do things.

The night before we rolled out for the Arghandab River Valley, it was around 11pm after all of the briefings finished. We had received mail a few days prior and I had gotten a box from my parents with some things I had asked for. I remember running across Specialist John Meier as I was headed to the chow hall because you couldn't eat anywhere else on the FOB. The rats would get into everything if they smelled a hint of food in the living areas. I think John had been waiting for midnight chow they occasionally held for the guys getting off mission or on tower guard rotations.

Meier and I sat down and demolished an entire package of salmon, cheese, and crackers. It was the best damn thing that we had tasted in a very long time. Between MREs, UGRs (unitized group rations, the even worse version of an MRE that requires an army cook to pull a tab to activate the warming chemical reactions… cooks are useless in a combat zone except for a select few), or eating someone's version of roadkill, we hadn't had much real food up until that point. I haven't the slightest idea of what we talked about, but I remember the feel of everything that night. It was the calm before the storm, and everyone knew it was coming. It was a true turning point in how events had unfolded for the men of Bravo Company up until now.

CHAPTER 5

Entering the Arghandab

Area Recon

We took a Chinook ride into the valley to get onto a joint patrol with the currently embedded unit and perform what was supposed to be an area recon. The current battlespace owners were rendered combat ineffective due to the heavy number of losses they had sustained up until that point. It was a Stryker unit out of Fort Lewis, Washington that was dubbed in a news article as "Harry Tunnell's ill-fated Stryker brigade." If I were to go into depth about the situation we were about to take over, it would require another book.

They had come into the valley under orders to conduct counter guerilla operations and had the motto "Search & Destroy" emblazoned on the sides of their vehicles. Colonel Harry Tunnell was in staunch opposition to the COIN (counter insurgency) doctrine currently being adopted and had his own ideas of how insurgencies were to be dealt with. Unfortunately, his personal doctrine and tactics were hard pressed to be effective in this area and the hard-charging infantry within his command had spiraled into a campaign of hatred towards the populace.

Word from one of the guys I talked to when we first arrived was that the unit hadn't even been patrolling into the town within the last month because the area was so bad. During the joint side-by-side patrol that we performed, it took ages for them to reach anywhere we could observe the area they were trying to show us. The men on patrol with us were scared and extremely jumpy while we made our way down the hill and over a series of walls that stood in our way. Two civilians were gunned down by the patrol leader as he called in a gun run from Kiowas above and we watched the two "insurgents" brought to a quick end. Two younger males had been digging with shovels in broad daylight at the edge of the riverbed about 800m away. We looked at each other and one of the guys asked what the threat was. "They were emplacing charges," was the answer we got. Bombs don't go boom when they're wet, so I'm not exactly sure that was a viable answer.

That area of the country was ripe with a history of invaders losing men to the Afghans that would resist the occupying invaders. One thing about the Afghan people, they are a warrior race of people who operate primarily as tribal nomads. However, when there is a common enemy, they will put aside their differences and collectively fight that invader until that enemy is dead or gone… then, they will disband and resume fighting one another. Col Tunnell created a nightmare situation in a valley that was saturated with insurgents while producing a terrified populace who were trapped and along for the ride.

The Russians had lost with a brigade-plus-sized operation in the Battle of the Arghandab within the Arghandab River Valley during 1987. The responsible party was an insurgent force that battled an element of 6,000-plus men with tanks and air support alongside ground troops. There were still signs of the conflict that included a massive rocket complete with hammer and sickle buried into the side of some old man's house in the countryside. It was wild to see and even crazier when you would catch one of the older residents of the area donning a Soviet officer's belt.

When I talked about Helmand being the IED training site, I wasn't exaggerating. The insurgents in the Arghandab were the masters at IED emplacement and didn't waste any time in figuring out a way to disrupt the American forces. They would double stack anti-tank mines to compromise the hull integrity of the Stryker the troops were riding in. The most recent charge they had emplaced blew a Stryker in half and sent pieces all over the countryside while instantly turning everyone that was inside the vehicle at the time into a goo. When the Americans stopped moving around with vehicles, the Taliban pulled out the ordnance and repurposed the explosives into smaller anti-personnel mines that would either pink mist you or forcibly remove your legs from your body. It was a shit show.

We inherited the battlespace after Lieutenant Colonel Jenio had asked General McCrystal where our battalion of paratroopers could be used best. The plan of attack brought Two Fury into the Arghandab as the replacements to the battlespace. We weren't being effectively utilized in Helmand and the British or US Marine forces weren't letting us participate in the shaping operations for Marjah that were taking place at the moment. The next best thing was to take a battlespace that was to become part of the main effort to clear out Kandahar in 2010.

The plan for Bravo Company was to infill the area via an Afghan National Police outpost just off the main road and outside of one of the many local villages. This one was a traditional Afghan village made of mud, clay, and whatever else the landscape had provided them. Half of the town had electricity and half didn't. It was weird because there were hard buildings that were five stories high just about 500m away from there. We saw the main roadway I referred to about three times the entire time we were there.

From the police outpost, we were to stage the vehicles and leave 2nd Platoon behind as QRF (Quick Reaction Force) and guards for the equipment while we pushed forward with HQ and 3rd Platoon to the objective. They were looking for somewhere that was fairly central to the valley and could reach the surrounding inhabitants via foot patrols. After looking over maps, seeing overlays, planning, and calculating what the best place would be to embed the company, Captain Armstrong determined the spot Bravo Company would operate from for the next nine months.

Infill

About two days prior the move to the Arghandab, I was handed an M4 rifle and told not to fuck this shit up or it would be the last thing I ever did with the company. Got it… fair warning and quite honestly, they were taking a chance on me. Up until this point, I had been real joe material. SSG Hill told me later that I wasn't a bad soldier when I was given some leeway and responsibility, but I was a downright terrible joe if left to my own boredom for any amount of time. I can't argue with him there. I'm someone that needs a constant pile of stuff to do because boredom leads to me making a mess of things.

Nothing could have prepared me for the arrival. I was warned about working for SSG Hill before and I had seen how he could get during what they called "situation black." I wasn't sure if that is because he just got "black" on patience or everything went blackout for him… I'm still not sure, but I did know that you didn't want to be on the receiving end of it. I had the misfortune to be on the receiving end of it on this one.

The vehicles were being parked at the outpost when I heard screaming coming from SSG Hill's vehicle. "YESKE!!!" Oh shit! What now… what the hell am I missing or what did I forget? Thoughts are racing through my mind as I yell out "Moving sergeant" and I run towards the red-faced, screaming figure of SSG Hill. Just as I start to lift my head, I catch an image of something flying at me. Thank God I still have my helmet on as SSG Hill's MBITR radio catches me square in the forehead, giving me a good smack to the cranium. Weighing in at about 2lbs, it was like getting hit in the head with a brick at full force.

Once I snatched the radio up along with my pride, I ran up to SSG Hill to square away whatever issue he was having. I didn't even mention anything about what had just happened. "What's going on SSG Hill?" Between his twisted face, heavy Boston Irish accent, and lack of understanding when it came to technology, he screamed that his radio wasn't working and if I wanted my job, I better unfuck it right the fuck now. Looking calmly at the radio (which was still on) revealed that it was on the wrong channel. I flicked the switch one channel over, did a radio check, and hooked it into his kit like nothing had happened. I asked him if he needed anything else for now.

I'm not sure if he even realized his actions at the time, but that incident was what made me want to be the best damn RTO the company ever had. It also revealed to me exactly how much I needed to make sure I dumbed down the system when dealing with these guys. It's all about perspective and how you look at the situation you are in at the moment. Sure, I took a hit to my pride right there, but I learned that if I created a foolproof system, then I wouldn't get hit in the head anymore.

We waited until nightfall in the staging area that became an outpost later and around zero hour, began our movement into the gates of hell. Everyone was in expectation of heavy resistance coming into the valley. There were Canadian troops attached to us that had been working alongside special operations in the area, an ODA (Operational Detachment Alpha) was on standby with 400 troops of militia at the ready in the event it went terribly wrong, and there were more resources on station if it came to that. The element ended up staying in a compound on the outskirts of the radish field that ultimately became our primary outpost site in the valley. We had been given a packing list that was short and meant for an assault, but it didn't include plans for any situation that was sustained.

Even having a poncho liner draped over us, sleeping while curled up with others to retain body heat, and lighting cow manure on a fire to stay warm, didn't help fight how cold it got that night. Probably one of the coldest times I've experienced in my life. Not sure if it was the adrenaline from the movement in, the massive temperature drop, or the particular climate, but it was frigid. I was on guard duty with Specialist Will Ross, sitting on a rooftop while manning an M240 machine gun at one point and just quietly talking in an attempt to stay awake while your teeth were chattering and your muscles were racking against you. It's a bitter type of cold and we hadn't been allowed to stash any extra snivel gear. Whatever would have helped us those first few days was back in the trucks where we came from or still on the way in a shipping container.

After about three days of running patrols from that compound command decided to park our new home right there, smack in the middle of a radish field in the valley. We had a little standoff from the village and there was a clear view on most sides. We were waiting on resupply and Specialist Adam Voelker sauntered up to me while eating a radish. I was in disbelief! You mean, I could just pull these things right out of the ground we were standing on and eat instead of starving while waiting on rations?! The radishes weren't bad. Honestly, some of the best vegetables I've ever had, but after a while, it gets to be a curse. You begin to hate the radishes along with the fact that your new home is living out of a mud field in the middle of nowhere because someone, somewhere said it would be a good mission for us.

The conditions the company lived in were austere at best and the workload was immense. One day, a truck full of Hesco barriers showed up and unloaded what were to become our "walls." A Hesco is like a modern-day sandbag that is comprised of fencing with a strong nylon/burlap cloth material inside of it that can be laid flat for transport, but when unloaded and stood up and creates a cube which you can fill with whatever dirt you have available from the surrounding area. This creates a bulletproof and mostly bombproof wall with minimal effort or needed material. However, we couldn't get any dirt into them. We stood guard behind a façade of a fort in what would become one of the deadliest places on the Earth during 2010.

The problem was there was no equipment supplied to fill the barriers with dirt! First Sergeant Mcalister started a continually tasked element of soldiers to erect Hesco barriers and create a wall system, complete with a flight landing area and serpentine along the entry control point. Expedient guard positions in the form of HMMVWs were posted at all corners and manned while one lucky squad would get picked to attempt to fill the Hesco barriers with hand shovels during shifts that ran 24 hours a day. Three days passed before just one barrier was full and there had to be close to 700 more that surrounded the perimeter.

It Begins

Deployment got real. There were constant patrols rotating through the area while trying to accomplish the necessary base improvements and maintaining base security. It was insanity. There should have been engineers attached to our element because we were worn thin and it was starting to show in the attitudes towards one another. Around this time is when Thomas and I got into a shouting match due to how thin we were spread on sleep.

The patrol needed to clear the LOC (line of communication), which was the bottom portion of the main road that came close to our field and provided access into the nearby mountain village. There was an area the Taliban would emplace IEDs in the upper portions of roadway that were past the mountainside village. I would usually enjoy going on those patrols as the route often had some good views from above. The serene nights offered a slice of solitude and broke up the rest of the madness that was threaded throughout the day-to-day taskings. It would have been great, but I had just gotten back from an all-day patrol with another squad an hour prior. I snapped on Thomas when he delegated to me the duty of accompanying the patrol.

It was because I was being treated akin to when I was a member of his squad. There was an expectation that the team was going to do what he said, no matter the objection, and outside factors didn't matter. We had an additional forward observer (13F) by the name of Paul Martinek that could have done it, but Thomas was convinced I was the guy for the job. It was Martinek's exact job to assist in helping out the platoon RTO due to the op tempo, but that fact didn't matter. We got into a shouting match about his lack of common sense and my inability to follow direction.

Fuming, a reluctant PFC Yeske tossed on his equipment, still sweaty from just an hour prior, and headed out of the ECP (entry control point) and up the hill with the rest of 3rd squad. I was pretty pissed off for the first half of the patrol, but then all anger was lost at some point as we were looking over the moonlit village and the little lights that dotted the landscape as a blanket of night covered everything.

Maybe it was coming to terms with the fact that Thomas was still the sergeant in command of the patrol and ultimately, in the right for grabbing up someone he trusted to get the job done.

In all the stillness, Thomas came up alongside me and I apologized for being an ass earlier. He said back to me, "I know you try really hard; I see that you do. I just don't see 'it.'" I think the "it" he referred to was the fact that I was still determined to go the Special Forces route after we got back to the States. He wasn't wrong, honestly. It was a mixed statement that was put out to me. It meant I needed to be better if I was going to make it through the challenges that were headed our way. It was just the type of motivation that I needed. The kind that makes you want to prove the doubter wrong and push harder than what was expected.

Nights in Afghanistan can be incredible and some of the best examples of how serene the landscape was at one point in time. In a lot of ways, I prefer it. The stillness and lack of outside influence on the world, such as streetlights and sirens. As we moved back to our outpost, you could see the glow of civilization in the distance, but it was far enough removed that we didn't have to deal with any of it in our slice of Third World mud huts that dotted the landscape.

The area also carried nighttime predators that would skulk about after us as we passed through pomegranate orchards, across mountain areas, and over farm fields. We couldn't walk the roads because they were laden with IEDs. We had to constantly change our tactics because the enemy wasn't going to make it easy on us. At some point, we found a daisy-chained complex IED set up in a staggered road march pattern about 500m from where our COP (command outpost) was located. COP Ware was established in honor of Sergeant Albert Ware who was killed in an IED attack on December 18 as they were bringing a HMMVW through. These were the first of the finds as we moved throughout the valley and quickly learned that this was nothing like Helmand province had been.

Johnston—December 26, 2009

Time became a blur as it was constant patrol after patrol while manning guard towers and trying to keep up with what command wanted to see accomplished as base improvements. We quickly became jealous of 2nd Platoon, who had gotten to stay behind where we had staged the trucks.

Christmas had come, and as it was in a combat zone, it was just another day. I was excited because I had my mid-tour leave coming up any day now and I had already planned a snowboarding trip with my little brother in Vermont. The plan was to stay in a lodge by the Killington resort and I had already treated myself to a new Burton snowboard along with equipment to go with it. I was totally stoked to be able to take a few days and just enjoy myself outside of the hell of constant work. Maybe fate would have me return to a finished outpost!

The day after Christmas, 1st Platoon had a mission based on intelligence about a bomb maker's house in the area. Seeing the saturation of IEDs there, this could be a nice turn for us if it proved to be good information. We had scouted the area and had found multiple bombs during our patrols already, always in roadway areas. The locals had a fairly good idea of where bombs were, so it showed us that the Taliban were living among the villagers, even if they thought we couldn't tell.

We were skirting along a lower portion of road when we followed a shepherd as he drove the flock down the road. The interpreter talked with the shepherd as we walked along. We came to what would be considered a choke point and mutton chops were made as a sacrificial lamb took the brunt of an anti-personnel mine that was meant for a US soldier.

The tactics we took in order to survive and adapt in an ever-changing environment would constantly change as we charged into the thick of things. That day, we weren't farther than 800m from the walls of COP Ware as I sent up our position. I had made it a point to send up an updated grid position any time we entered a new compound or as we moved over different walled-off terrain features. It was drilled into me to be annoying with the number of times I would call up our position, but the precaution was for a reason. The dangers lurking weren't always apparent, but the type that lie in wait.

This particular compound was set up in a typical Afghan fashion with an outer wall surrounding an inner walled-off living area. A gated villa would be a way to try to describe it but not the luxurious type that you would find when someone says "villa." Think of it as a mud house 10 years after people abandoned the area and the vegetation and local wildlife had moved in. SPC Culp was on the mine detector up front to clear a path into the house and make sure there wasn't anything to worry about. We had found quite a few mines already, including some that were inside of our walls at COP Ware because they had already been in the ground when we dropped our walls into the field a week or so prior.

Everyone was on edge because we had just been walking a route through the surrounding area earlier in the day, so this was going to be a nice change of pace for a bit. The plan was to set into a patrol base with overwatch on our objective compound for a few hours. Pretty soon, everyone would be setting in security, grabbing a bite to eat, and creating a rest plan. I was walking mid formation with Lt Demarest and following in the previous man's footprints ahead of us. It just made sense as we tried to minimize any risk of stepping on anything in an area that was cleared but not completely cleared. In the valley, your next step could be the largest risk you took during the day.

There was a concrete slab in front of the house that would constitute what an American would think of as an outdoor sitting area or porch. I walked to the far end of the compound and hung a hard right. I couldn't set up communications inside the building because we were already having radio issues due to a high iron and mineral content in the soil. It would be best to stay out of the way of the patrol as the building was cleared and security set in. Lt Demarest would need to send up a situation report and it turned out that the only radio capable of reaching out over a distance past two compound walls was the larger manpack radio I carried. This fact made it essential to keep the manpack radio operational at all times as it was the only piece of equipment that would reach out any distance.

After crossing the length of the slab, I put down my assault pack and as I was raising the long whip antenna, I glanced back at the rest of the squad coming into the compound. Sgt Thomas was giving orders and pointing out security positions to his team leaders as everyone filed into the compound. Lt Demarest and SPC Culp were clearing the living areas along with some of the others. Doc brought up the rear along with Weapons squad and SPC Voelker carrying the 240 that was brought as a heavy defense to beef up our SAWS. Ross and Specialist Jason Johnston were scaling the wall to get onto the roof and provide support a machine-gun emplacement for the overwatch position.

Johnston wasn't really someone I knew personally as he was one of the guys that had been in the unit for the prior deployment. He was friendly to anyone and everybody, but there weren't many opportunities for mixed conversation internally within the company as they tried to keep squad integrity. I happened to have a whiskey shot with him at the Fayetteville Texas Roadhouse a week or so before we shipped out for the 'Stan. Jason was out with some of the other guys and they were all headed out to the Cadillac Ranch after getting their dinner. I hadn't seen much of Jason because 1SG Mac had told him to make himself scarce because he had a shaving profile. He didn't want that type of undisciplined behavior on the front lines with us. Jason had developed these nasty bumps from shaving, and he was trying to figure out why. Womack Army Hospital had taken skin samples and there was word that they ended up at the CDC as something to be aware of in the previous area he had traveled to in Afghanistan. He stood out like a sore thumb as we were to be always clean shaven, even while operating within a combat zone. We laughed because the Afghans thought he was Special Forces due to the additional facial hair.

As he was straddling the top edge of the wall, Private Stephen Towery stepped on an area almost adjacent to where Johnston was seated. EOD had cleared the pathway and everyone had just walked over the same spot when our element had come into the compound. I had stepped over the same area myself just less than a minute prior. For whatever reason, the step that Towery made was a costly one. In what was a flash, but what seemed like an eternity, the entire side of the compound I was watching the men cross over disappeared in a massive cloud of dust with a resounding boom.

If you have ever experienced an IED close up, you know it's a real "end of days" type moment. You can see the shock wave fly over the vegetation as it thumps out in front of the path of destruction that follows the invisible force. Your brain goes into an instantaneous survival moment and provides a level of hyper awareness that few ever get to experience in their life. I had experienced this a few times prior, but nothing like to this magnitude. These are the moments when you know it's all on the line. This is when it matters.

As the dust washed over me, I picked up my hand mic and simply stated, "Bravo 6, this is 1–6a, we just hit an IED, our location is my last front line trace, we have urgent surgical, but I'm not sure how many yet. We need dust-off and maybe an extractor. I'll have to get back to you, how copy, over."

Johnston: Specialist Ross' Story

SPC Ross hadn't even wanted to be on this patrol. With the frequency of everything that was going on at COP Ware, there was no time to get anything done, much less sleep. He was always exhausted because if there was a detail to be done, he would be the one that always seemed to be snatched up. Having been there longer than the rest of the lower enlisted in 1st Platoon, it seemed to be a curse because there were some NCOs that would depend on him if they needed anything done. They knew he would get it done and it would be done right.

As they approached the compound, he felt a chill. Like those that you get when you enter a haunted house, and the temperature drops 10 degrees unexpectedly in the matter of an instant. Ross shrugged the feeling off and followed in everyone's footsteps as the area we were coming in on had been cleared already. Lt Demarest called to get a team on the roof of the building because he was worried about spotters calling out our position to the insurgents in the area.

Ross had been bored on this day and Johnston was already headed up onto the wall to get eyes onto the surrounding area. "I'll go!" he exclaimed, as he could use that moment of solace to just get away from the bullshit going on within the compound. A breath of fresh air would be nice and Johnston was just the guy that would understand. They could enjoy the silence and the scenery together on the rooftop as they shared a smoke. It had been a rough week and with his fellow weapons team members on leave, Ross would fill the gaps in the patrol needs as well. It was utterly draining.

Thomas was pissed as he had been heading for the wall when Ross had just jumped out there and started immediately scaling the wall. He edged up only a few feet behind Johnston. It was a weird wall that had some breaks in the structure and sloped a bit up to the roof of the building that was within the inner areas of the walls. It wasn't unlike a lot of the other tricky mud-built architecture you would find everywhere in the valley.

Towery had a walking stick or something and held it up for Ross to steady himself as he made his way up. Just helping a guy out, as we all had to while crossing some of the terrain and manmade features that peppered the landscape and made going any amount of distance miserable.

All of a sudden, he felt like someone had cracked him in the back of the head with a bat or something. What the hell? It was right underneath where the protection of the helmet ended and one of the vital areas in the neck that hurt like a son of a bitch if you were hit there in any capacity. I've seen guys go down from a proper cuff to the back of the neck in that spot before. BLACK…

What in the hell just happened… his brain was catching up. Where in the… what the fuck? Everything was tilted and his neck hurt something fierce. It took a moment to realize, but he figured out that he was outside of the wall and on top of his head. There was dust everywhere and his mouth tasted terrible. Oh, shit. With a sinking feeling in the pit of his stomach, Ross figured out that they had hit an IED.

There was a grunting coming from the orchard in front of him. The orchard… He was the only one outside the wall! His brain started to panic as he knew that the enemy would probably be coming soon. He was outside of any sort of security perimeter and completely alone. He started to come out of the fog and quickly scanned the area for his rifle and his assault bag. He had everything he needed right there. Let the bastards come. Could there be any better way to go for an infantryman? His family had history in the Vietnam War with an uncle who was killed in combat after having been up and down the conflict areas and even into areas of Cambodia. Let them talk about how Ross took his chances on a last-ditch effort to take as many down as he could before they cut him down. There was no other option for someone like Ross. This was it.

There was that grunting noise again. What the hell had happened? Was something hit out here? As he had finally gotten his rifle in hand and was trying to make sense of the entire scene, he turned his attention to the pile of material that was making the noises. As his eyes came into focus and his brain started registering what he was seeing, his curiosity turned into horror as he realized that the shape had a uniform pattern to it. It was Johnston.

It was as if Satan had come to the Arghandab to play a sick and twisted marionette puppet show with a patrol squad of soldiers. As the puppet master, he had tossed the figure of Johnston into the air and had just dropped the figure onto the stage in a discarded pile. Johnston was folded over and in half with his face in the dirt and was trembling as his body was starting to move and go into shock. The noises were changing now and getting louder.

"OH JESUS! OH MY GOD! OH GOD!" Ross could hear Thomas screaming in the compound as the realization of what had just happened was washing over him. Ross needed to get to Johnston, but there could be mines everywhere out here. He was flying blind here. Ross decided to crawl as low as he could to the ground and do a series of checks for IEDs as he made his way to see what he could do.

He couldn't believe there was any way that Johnston was alive. It looked like every bone in his body had been broken. Ross got to him and got what was left of

Johnston onto his back in the field. "Dude, it fucking hurts, man," he said to Ross. Ross couldn't believe Johnston was alive and actually talking to him. There was no way this guy was going to live through this. Fuck it, he had to try.

Ross pulled his own tourniquet out of the medical pouch on his rig and got it around what was left of Johnston's left leg. It was pulverized, but his right leg was already gone. There was his femur sticking out of his left and what appeared to be enough structure to press down on and seal off the bleeding from any arterial wound. Although who knew how would that even work as it looked like Johnston's entire pelvis had been smashed. Ross could literally see into his organ cavity.

Ross started to crank the tourniquet down to hopefully stop some of the blood loss. That's when Johnston started screaming. "I need someone out here!" Ross screamed for help as this wasn't something he could handle alone. He needed the doc out with him and he needed him right now.

Doc Ponce finally made it over to the scene and Ross could see that he had gotten fucked up from the explosion as well. Doc was half blind but operating at a level of focus that can only be explained as a properly trained combat medic doing his job. Ponce ripped his medic bag open and threw Ross a package as he started ripping into another and packing Johnston's wounds with curlex to stop the bleeding. There was so much going on and with the both of them working at a breakneck speed to save him, the pair synced in a pattern of efficiency that allowed them the feeling that there could be a chance.

Johnston was still talking to them and asking if he was going to die and how bad the damage really was. Ross didn't even know how bad it was. He just told him that he was going to be alright and to stay with him. Just keep talking to him. Johnston started to say that he was having trouble breathing along with everything else he was talking about.

Bobby Musil and the rest of the QRF were the most welcome sight Ross had ever seen when Bobby crested that wall. The pararescue helicopter had just gotten there when Johnston's eyes went cloudy.

Johnston: A Man Who'll Fight

Bobby Musil had been carrying a toughbox across COP Ware when the boom occurred. He dropped the box and sprinted off for the TOC (tactical operations center) to see what the initial word was. He said everyone questioned the call over the radio because of how calm I seemed over the net. I can only attribute this to the multiple exposures I had of high-adrenaline moments up until this point in life, including those while jumping out of an airplane. I believe the ability to adapt and stay calm in high-stress environments is something that comes with repeated exposure. I also think this is the reason for the heavily instituted airborne skill badge within the special operations community. There is something to be said for General Gavin's statement, "Show me a man that will jump out of an airplane, and I'll show you a man who'll fight."

After sending the original transmission and immediately going to find Lt Demarest, I crossed the compound through the dust to see Demarest running from the building towards me and SPC Culp running towards Towery, who was on the ground near the blast. The upper half of the wall behind Towery was gone, as were the men that had been on top of it. I heard screaming on the other side of the wall as SPC Will Ross was yelling out that he needed someone over there, fast. This was a mass casualty situation.

Thomas, Doc Ponce, and Voelker were all heavily peppered in the face with dust, dirt, rocks, wall, bomb fragments, bone, shrapnel, and any other ungodly piece of garbage that was in the atmosphere within that particular town. Voelker is screaming that he can't see and Thomas is yelling to get up security while half blindly leading Doc over to where Towery lay. Thomas was experiencing a flurry of emotions and trying to hold it together as he had just realized that he was no longer in control of the situation and one of his guys was most likely dead. Demarest got the word over the net that the company was sending up the casevac even though I hadn't sent up numbers or injuries yet. He told me to try to assist Doc at this point and he would take over the radio for now because my EMT training was needed more currently.

After handing off my assault pack, I ran over to Doc Ponce to ask what I could assist with. Doc was already in action and throwing a tourniquet on what was left of Towery's leg. As he is actively talking to Towery, doing a blood sweep, and treating other wounds, he tells me that Towery is going to be OK and we need to get over the wall to check who is hit out there. The screaming hasn't stopped but only gotten more urgent at this point. I turn to head out of the compound when Thomas grabs me by the collar and yells that we need to clear the path first. He's not wrong, I get it.

I turn back to Doc to assist as he is finishing up with what he can for Towery. "What do you need Doc?" I ask and he tells me to double check Towery and make sure he is alright as he needs to check on the other guys. As I'm talking to him, I see that not only is Towery's leg gone from around the knee, but he has some fingers missing and a few other things going on. Doc had thrown some gauze on the fingers, but with any wound in that country, one of the biggest issues is infection. About all I did was make sure his leg stump wasn't still bleeding and give him a quick blood sweep of my own while talking to him. His fingers that were left were held together with gauze in an attempt to save some of them when he was moved to surgery.

I made light of the situation as he was looking a bit dazed but sloping into the side of despair. "Welcome to the club, motherfucker!" I held up my own right hand that was missing a pinky due to an injury that I had sustained during childhood.

Towery cracked a smile and it was right then I knew that the kid was going to be OK. "You're an asshole, dude, but I fucking love you man." Maybe Towery was starting to feel a little loopy due to the effects of the drugs Doc had just injected into his system. I found out later that Doc never gave him anything for the pain.

I hear Doc move past Thomas and run into the orchard towards the screams. "You going to be alright until the bird gets here?" I ask Towery as chaos surrounds us and is blasting us from every side. These situations are always so weird. With the sheer amount of yelling, orders being tossed around, screaming, and pain, there are these bubbles of calm that exist. Even with all the commotion along with being wounded, Towery was actively hearing and responding to everything going on. We had a quick joke about it was bullshit that he was getting out of here ahead of us and what a way to sham out of the rest of deployment. Meanwhile, the screaming over the wall intensified.

"I need someone out here," comes the call from over the wall again. I hit the wall of Thomas once again as he yells in my face that they need to clear for mines. I yell back that "Doc went though and was fine. I get blown the fuck up, then it's on me." It's a definite moment of full-on bullshit that neither of us wanted but there it is, front and center in the middle of a shitstorm. "Go get yourself killed, whatever, Yeske," and he moved back into setting up security and checking his other men over.

I moved out of the compound towards the clump of uniforms on the ground. What I came upon was one of the worst instances of what a human body has the ability to survive. What was left of Johnston's pants were rags hanging off of him with one side noticeably longer than the other, but the entire crotch area was totally gone. There was just enough of a flap to cover the business end of everything down there. One of his legs was missing almost entirely with a fragment of yellow bone sticking out and the meat that surrounded it just hanging off. The other leg was still attached but mangled beyond recognition of anything but a twisted mess of flesh and bones. I could see the thigh bone snapped along with every other bone in that leg being pulverized beyond anything the body was able to withstand.

Doc was looking frantically back and forth and going from his bag to grab one thing or another while he did everything he could do to save Johnston. Doc was good. He was on full autopilot at the moment. He had attended one of the special operations medical classes that dealt with bleeding out goats and having to save them in real time. It was a controversial subject during its operation, but it was a training that is vital to medics having the ability to save lives on the battlefield.

Johnston was calling out that it hurt and was fully conscious as Doc furiously worked on him. There wasn't really much I could do. Ross was alongside Doc and seemed to have been helping already with what he could. Ross looked pretty concussed as he had been right next to Johnston when he was hit. Damn, what a fucking trooper Ross was. Right in the middle of the damn blast and still keeping it together. Johnston asked me what everyone that is hit by an IED on the battlefield asks those looking over them at that point: "Do I still have my nuts?" I had to do what any self-respecting soldier would do in this combat situation and check but I could already see that the bomb blast had taken more than just his legs.

Johnston was in a position that when that main charge bomb went off, he received the full force of the explosion to his pelvis and legs. Towery had stepped on a toe popper that was daisy-chained to a larger charge placed within the wall and was meant to kill or maim the entire squad. Those tricky bastards had used something known as a hockey puck initiator that had no more metal in it than the size of a sewing needle. This fact, combined with the high iron content in the soil, it made it damn near impossible to tell that there was a huge squad-killing charge in the wall adjacent to the initial charge. Det cord doesn't have metal in it either.

The blast had basically gutted Jason. His pelvis was shattered in multiple places and anything that was left within that cavity of the body was just spilling out as Doc was holding things in, packing the wounds, and attempting to bandage the area to make sure he could stop the bleeding. I was struck with amazement that Jason was conscious and talking to us. There was nothing left inside of him and I had no clue how he was still able to communicate.

I gave him the thumbs up and assured him that everything was all good down there. I looked over at Doc for some sign of reassurance that maybe he thought we could make it through this one with Johnston surviving. I could tell in Ponce's eyes that he was doing everything he possibly could to keep him alive, but it wasn't looking good. I scrambled for anything that I could think of that might keep Jason going. I dumbly said something about having a smoke for him once I got my pack back from Demarest. We all had our fair share of smokes that we would bum off each other from time to time, but Johnston was one of those guys that seemed to dip into the community pool a little bit often. It was the stupidest thing I could have said, but it was the only thing my brain came up with at the time.

Doc told Johnston that he was going to give him something to help him with the pain and shot him up with some more morphine. Doc didn't have much left that he could do and he was tapped to the point of just trying to keep him somewhat comfortable without crashing his vitals. Between Johnston crying out about the pain here and there, Doc trying to triage someone who shouldn't still be alive, Ross holding down the fort while talking to us as he assisted Doc, and myself trying to say whatever dumb thing that came to my mind to keep his head going, it was all about as real as death could get for a soldier.

I saw Jason Johnston as he passed from this world and his body went gray and slack. I remember the look of defeat on Doc's face. I remember sitting there and feeling utterly useless. Right about then is when something rained down from the sky.

Johnston: Specialist Martinek's View

SPC Martinek and Lt Demarest were coming out of the rooms within the compound because something didn't feel right. Things were too clean and there was leftover MRE trash in one of the corners. This had meant that someone had been there before. It probably also meant that someone was tracking the Americans who had been there prior and would have left a little surprise in case they returned. You hear about this kind of thing which is why normally battle space owners will hand off information such as patrol routes, observation points, points of interest, and enemy tactics as they hand off the battlespace.

As they headed back out, Martinek saw Towery's step as a loud crack hit the air. A black tendril of smoke wrapped around Towery's leg as the slow-motion event unfurled before him, powerless to do anything about it. Following the crack was a much larger boom and the entire squad disappeared in a cloud of dust, smoke, and debris.

It was as if the entire space-time continuum slowed to a crawl to imprint the details and danger into everyone's brains. The shock wave was visible as it swept across the compound and flattened anything in its path. The large, imposing figure of Sgt Thomas was thrown through the air backwards, with his arms out, like in a superhero movie as our hero is hit with a fatal punch to the gut and flies backwards about 20 feet before coming to a stop in the far corner with a wall providing the assist to bring his body to a screeching halt.

In that moment, Thomas flattened Doc Ponce, who had been directly behind him, but also inadvertently ended up shielding Doc from a large amount of the blast as well. Something else had flown over the wall that Martinek couldn't comprehend, but his mind had placed the dark figure as a plastic bag being tossed into the air as a rag-tag flopping mess with all of the turbulence that had been created from the blast. As time started to come back to what we consider "normal speed," his brain caught up with the fact that it wasn't a bag that he had seen. It had been a person. Some poor soul had been right on top of this thing and had been blasted high into the air during detonation. Judging from the screams coming from across the wall, it wasn't good.

It was when Martinek was headed over to Johnston's position, outside of the wall, that he saw Bobby Musil and John Meier fly over the far wall that was across from where we were. About the same time, there were medical birds coming on station. The Air Force had a casevac team of pararescue soldiers by the call sign Pedro that was on station for dust-off. The huge HH-60 Pave Hawk helicopter that came burning in towards our position was like a gigantic bus being hurtled through the air.

"God damn, they are coming in fast," thought Martinek as he watched in amazement and wondered if they would overshoot our position or if this was a flyover and return situation to make sure there was nothing else in the area that could shoot the bird out of the sky. It was as if a little kid was playing with his toy as the chopper came to a last-minute 45-degree angle to allow the prop wash to slow the bird to an almost instantaneous stop in the air.

Unbelievably, a head popped out quickly, disappeared, and then a rope, followed by a body, was chucked out of the now hovering chopper. Two Air Force pararescue soldiers fast roped down to our position and one headed towards the compound where Towery still lay. Johnson was a grayish white at this point and his pupils were dilated different sizes. It didn't look good... not good at all. If he lived through it, he would likely have sustained a head injury that would affect his life heavily for the rest of his time on earth.

Dust-off

The crew by the callsign Pedro was a group of Air Force pararescue soldiers on standby off the flightline of Kandahar Air Field for instances such as these. Sgt Musil was on the scene and told the pararescue soldier this guy was down, there was one back in the compound missing his lower leg, and there were various other injuries. As Demarest came up, he handed me my bag and I grabbed it as I knew my usefulness here had just rotated back to my primary job as an RTO. Just as I was about to check myself and equipment over, the rest of 2nd squad comes barreling in over the compound walls like a bunch of crazed warriors ready to fuck shit up.

PFC Chris Wiesner, SPC John Meier, and Sgt Musil were the first I remember seeing arrive to the scene. Meier was immediately sent to see what he could do for Towery as he was the other EMT-trained guy from our platoon. I had attended the school along with him prior our deployment and knew he was good at the job. Musil was angry at the situation and let out a flurry or swears as he punched the tree next to where Johnston lay. But Wiesner's reaction is the one that is etched in my mind.

There are scenes in war movies when the hatred towards the enemy is spewed out of soldiers on the battlefield. I had read about it in multiple books on war that I had pored over as a child. He looked down and saw the mangled and broken body of SPC Johnston lying there ashen gray, and he went white. A blank look instantly fell over his face and he began to shake. First his foot and quickly following, his leg.

The blank look on his face transformed into a snarl and quickly became a look of hatred. His M4 was equipped with a loaded 203 that now swiveled up to the low ready as he turned toward the Afghan police that were attached with us on this mission. "You see this, you pieces of shit, this is what you've done!" he screamed at the Afghans. "This is on you!" As he said that, I knew something wasn't right. This wasn't the Wiesner I knew. He was a downright angry little bastard, but he wasn't like this. This was pure hatred and battlefield fury. This is what was dangerous in the guys if it spilled over into something outside of what was needed in combat.

His barrel began to come to the high ready in the direction of the Afghans hen I grabbed him and his barrel and started telling him not to do this. This wasn't them. Don't do it.

Musil realized what was going on at that point and told me to lead him over to somewhere where he could supplement security and not be near where Johnston lay. I was able to corral Wiesner into the compound area facing away from the blast area and then turned him over to Culp to help establish security within the compound walls. It was back to the RTO job as I was trying to put my long whip antenna into a position we could maneuver in while moving through the orchards without snagging branches. I had to duck down to do it and as I was looking up, I ran smack dab into 1SG Mcalister.

When I say, ran into him, I mean I ran into him. I stumbled back and knew instantly I was fucked. Mcalister was rough and I had seen guys hemmed up for days for offenses in front of 1SG. Maybe not by his direct order, but the NCOs made sure that we knew to never interact with Mac unless he came to us first... even then it was a tense situation every time. He looked at me with that instant piercing gaze at first, but then it quickly changed. Something in his eyes showed me that he was hurting right now. That he cared about what had just happened and knocking into him at the present moment wasn't important at all. He moved on and went on about the after-action assessment and planning of how they were going to secure the AO for further assessment later.

As I circled back around to where Towery was being treated, they were getting him into a hoist to lift him out of the building and into the hovering chopper. Towery's last words to SSG Hill as his platoon sergeant were, "Sergeant Hill, you are the best platoon sergeant ever... but you're a real asshole" and as if on cue, the hoist lifted Towery, much like a guardian angel, away from the amazed but swearing platoon sergeant who was just so openly blasted by the casualty. Towery never meant it in a crude way at all; if anything, it was a paratrooper's way of letting his superior know that he had the upmost respect for him, even in the moment where he could have gotten away with much worse. It's humor like this that sets apart the guys on the battlefield and would become a stress relief in times to come as we pondered our own fates in the valley.

Jason's body was so broken, they couldn't put him into a hoist to get him out of there, but they needed to get him out of there along with some others. They were bagging him up and putting the other pieces of his body they had found in the surrounding areas into the body bag. At this point, I had linked back up with Lt Demarest and was awaiting further instructions. Since the other squads were on scene along with the headquarters element, there wasn't much to do other than process everything going on and what had happened. I watched as one of the EOD guys placed a charge onto a wall adjacent to the orchard we were in that had enough space to land a helicopter.

"BOOOOOOOOM." You know that saying, "if you can't tie a knot, tie a lot"? The same isn't recommended with explosives. EOD had overcompensated and ended up concussing himself and a few of the others nearby. He got the worst of it as he was throwing up and dizzy after the incident. "Jesus Christ, you idiot, what're you trying to do, blow us all the fuck up. The damn Taliban didn't get the job done, so you tried it out yourself. Fucking hell!" Hill was teetering on situation black again as we loaded up the lost EOD captain, Johnston's body, and Voelker to be transported back to the Kandahar flightline and to the various trauma stations that waited to triage their wounds.

Later

Our original patrol element was relieved by one of the other squads and we headed back to COP Ware to refit, get some food, and process what had just happened. I remember the tent that night and the tears that were shed. Guys hugged one another and offered each other support as some sobbed over one another's backs and let everything out that they felt like they needed to. I felt like an asshole because I knew that I had to go back out the next day because they were going to need the RTO again for tomorrow. Tuck down your feelings and deal with it all later. It's just something that happens. I cleaned my weapon, gave it a good coating of oil, reset my magazines after dusting off all my ammo, checked all my batteries, and made sure my commo stuff was ready to go for the next day. I felt like even more of an asshole as I remember wishing everyone would just be quiet as I just wanted to drift off to sleep… and at some point, I finally did.

Ashes

That next morning, the mosque continued to play music. It was different even. What were they playing? Ross went and got Gucci and gave him a look of dead seriousness. "What are they playing on the speakers? What is that music? What are they saying?" He had a feeling and the look on Gucci's face confirmed it. Gucci didn't want to tell Ross. "What is it, Gucci? What the fuck are they saying?"

"I'm very sorry, sir. They are celebrating." Ross' anger was rising. "What the fuck are they celebrating Gucci? What the fuck is there to celebrate?" Ross demanded between clenched teeth because he already knew what the answer was going to be. "They are celebrating the death of your friend. I'm sorry, sir." Gucci hung his head, ashamed to even be associated with a culture that would do something like this.

It was then that Ross understood the reasons why the stories existed of villages being burned to the ground during the Vietnam War. The rage built up within his system and he now knew why soldiers had gone and slaughtered everyone, burning it all to the ground afterward. There is no saving anyone that would do this… they all needed to die.

Back at the blast site, the guys that had responded the day before were shivering as the sun came up over the horizon. It had been a miserable night in the silence and cold. Bravo Company had just lost a soldier and everyone had different memories running through their heads as they did everything they could to process what had just happened.

The security circle was tight and the guys were huddled up to share any sort of warmth because they were missing any of the "snivel gear" that you would have in the bottom of your assault pack. Not thinking, they had all just grabbed ammo and water as they hurried to get to the blast site as quickly as possible.

Hill was sitting next to Doc Chris Bridge when Morton, one of the SAW gunners, started to break out into a yell, muffled at first while growing in intensity. His face was white as a ghost and his body was backpedaling from his machine-gun position while his mind reeled from what he had just experienced. "GOD DAMN IT! FUCK! OH, MY GOD! FUCK!" rang out in the quiet orchard as the steam was lifting off of the ground, creating an eerie low fog hanging over everything.

As Morton's screams echoed over the valley, everyone out there realized Morton had been laying on top of what was a portion of Johnston's missing leg throughout the night. It had been dark by the time everything settled down for the overnight stay and no one could see the ground as they set guard positions in. Morton had been laying over what he had thought was a tree root or something all night long, but it was Johnston's leg that we couldn't find.

They pulled Morton aside, the company medic, Doc Bridge, put the leg in a body bag he had. As Cpt Armstrong moved to their position with an EOD team to do an assessment on the explosion site, his RTO, Kyle McFarland, saw a boot on the ground in the neighboring orchard. "What the fuck?" he thought to himself as he moved over to check it out. It looked like a desert tan Oakley combat boot… why was it out here? He quickly realized that there was still a portion of foot in the boot as he picked it up. As they moved into the security bubble, he linked up with Doc to join the leg with its foot to be sent back to Kandahar.

The Hardest Job

Sergeant James Lee had just gotten back from his midtour leave when they got the word that someone from Two Fury was hit. In a little more discovery, their small group of guys returning from their respective leave quickly learned that it was Bravo Company. "Shit." James muttered. "Already?"

SSG Scott Brunkhorst was returning along with Lee and Specialist Leeson and they headed for the hospital triage area to see if they could learn more or find out what had happened to the element on patrol. They were on edge as the news hit them when they came through the door that it was Private Towery held within the ward and was missing a foot and some digits on his fingers. He was going to be ok and was babbling off to them and the command team that was already in the room about what had happened.

He was extremely loopy as CSM Puckett and LTC Jenio were at his bedside trying to ascertain the situation unfolding on the ground in the Arghandab. Puckett made a crack to bring the kid up and he started to tell the sergeant major he wanted Walter Reed to fit him with a peg leg during his recovery.

Someone came to the door and motioned for the commander to meet him in the hall so they could talk discreetly. Towery turned to the guys that he knew from Bravo and smiled. "What's up guys! This sucks, but at least now I don't have to go back to that shithole!" The guys, who were soon returning, nervously chuckled as they hadn't caught what had happened. All Towery could tell them was that the patrol hit a landmine when coming into a compound during the patrol and Johnston was hit really bad too.

On cue, CSM Puckett came through the door and asked, "I know you guys don't want to do this, but we need someone from Bravo to come with us to identify the body." Puckett was on edge. He had been through this before, but this one was weird because he had personally allowed this kid into the fight on this one.

Specialist Jason Johnston had come to CSM Bert Puckett during all the work-up the battalion was doing in preparation for their deployment to Afghanistan. First Sergeant Donald Mcalister had given him severe grief about his shaving profile and the condition of his face, that he had told Johnston he would be staying in the rear echelon because of his skin condition and Mac didn't want to see his unshaven face. It was a stain within his ranks and formation.

Johnston had thought about it and like anyone in the same situation and thought of the pros and cons. Sure, he could sit this one out and get into any trouble that he wanted to on rear detachment. They never really kept a good watch on those that stayed back due to one reason or another.

He couldn't do it though. He couldn't watch the guys leave and get stuck twiddling his thumbs in the barracks until he went searching for some mischief to liven his environment up. Johnston knew better and he also knew that it would gnaw at his conscience if he didn't join the fray on the journey to combat the horde of jihadists that awaited them in the deserts of Afghanistan.

Johnston went directly to Puckett, which went against any previous behavior. Jason was a low-key sort of guy and the type that would never be seen within eyesight of the command group if he could help it. After their interaction, Puckett had gone to Mcalister and asked his thoughts on the matter. Mac gave him the grooming standards reasoning that he had justified his previous commands to Specialist Johnston.

"Mac, you can't hold a guy back from that. He's got a damn skin condition from the last deployment that they don't know what the hell it is. Just tell him to keep it clean. It'll be fine. The kid wants to fight, let him fight." CSM Puckett replied. Just like that, Johnston had been brought over to fight alongside us and die in the valley that cold day in December.

Now, Command Sergeant Major Bert Puckett found himself asking his men if they could come identify the man for him. He knew very damn well who the kid was and what seeing him in a body bag would do to one of these guys, but procedure was procedure and he needed to have one of them verify.

"I'll do it. I'm the ranking one here anyway." SSG Brunkhorst said. Sgt Lee stepped forward. "If you don't mind, I was his team leader and I knew him pretty well. I'd like to go if that's ok." Brunk was relieved but didn't show it. He had enough to deal with back home during his mid-tour. He wasn't even supposed to be on this rotation, but Specialist William Ross had traded leave slots with him after hearing that Brunk was having serious relationship issues back home. Ross said that it was more important that he try and use the time to sort that out as Ross didn't have anyone back home waiting for him.

Sgt Lee followed CSM Puckett and LTC Jenio down the maze of hallways and to the designated room where Johnstons body was held. As they came in, Lee saw that the bag was unzipped and was open down to Jason's chest level. The thing he can never forget though is his face. Lee wished he never saw the contorted scream of pain that was held frozen on Jason's face that night. "Yeah, that's Johnston." Lee said without really believing what it was that he was saying. The gravity of the situation and the burden was already hitting him as he numbly turned to walk out of that room.

The second that Puckett had seen the shadow of the beard on his face, the situation hit him like a ton of bricks and he felt the full burden of responsibility that lay with the soldier on the table in front of him. It became very personal, very quickly and he felt tears well in his eyes and other reactions he hadn't had before throughout his long time in service. Perhaps it was the gravity of all the previous years that finally broke the hard shell of an exterior, but Puckett started to crack.

LTC Jenio came alongside him and whispered in his ear. "Not now. You know that. You can't do this here and now, it's not the place." Puckett straightened out and regained his stoic bearing during the rest of the procedures that day as they were headed over to talk to General Scaparrotti soon after everything was cleared up here.

When Lee arrived back at COP Ware, Specialist Culp nearly jumped on him to get the details of everything. He knew Jason had passed away, but they had been friendly in the unit as well. "How did he look, Lee? I heard you saw him in KAF. Was he alright looking? He wasn't too messed up, was he? Did he at least look like it wasn't a painful death?"

Lee faced the immediate dilemma of what he was about to tell Culp. They had just gotten to the Arghandab and this wasn't a healthy place to be at the time. He had done his homework over leave and seen some of the articles that had come out about the previous unit that had been in the area.

"He looked good, man. His face didn't look touched at all and he looked like he was at peace when he died." Lee lied. He couldn't tell him. Shit, he couldn't tell anyone about this. Not if he wanted the men to keep their heads about them as they moved in the valley, because James was sure of one thing. There were probably going to be more casualties to follow.

CHAPTER 6

The Lashings Continue

Mid-tour

My mid-tour leave happened just a few days after our first casualty had been experienced in Bravo Company. I never thought about just how much of a culture shock it was to be in an area of combat like the one we were operating in and heading back to the States for some time around the holidays. Especially around this time of year with family buzzing about with Christmas and the New Year. I spent New Year's Eve in Kuwait as I made the trek towards my snowboarding plans. Maybe it was because I had just counted mid-tour as another "mission" that I never really processed the moments that had occurred not even two weeks prior.

The week or so it takes to head home might be frustrating at the time, but it's a good buffer in place that ensures not getting back into civilization too quickly. Even with that time in place, I was still a bit uptight and high strung with family members. It went with my personality, so I'm not surprised if no one raised any red flags. After a few days, I headed up to Vermont to try to catch some good times on the mountain before heading back into hell. I had determined not to let anyone know just how bad of an area we were in, but I am sure eyebrows were raised because of the recent stories on the news.

There was an argument that left me flying solo and partying with a group of investors from New York City vacationing in Vermont for a last-minute winter vacation fling. They were all college friends that had gone into buying investment properties along the east coast, so they owned the cabin that they were crashing in that usually served as one of their short-term rentals. They loved the war stories and they brought me into the fold while I was there. The ride home was spent in mostly silence and I was saying goodbye once again to rejoin the unit.

The layover in Atlanta was conveniently missed as the schedule required me to switch flights from Connecticut to the international terminal. If I had rushed, I could have probably made it, but I wasn't going to rush the proverbial door when what lay beyond it wasn't particularly friendly. The plan worked and I was able to stay an extra night in Atlanta before continuing the long trek back. The night wasn't memorable, but it was just one additional night I didn't have to be in Afghanistan.

My rescheduled flight didn't leave until later in the day and it was lunchtime at this point. So, I found the best restaurant in the Atlanta International Airport… and it was housed in the international terminal as well! If you are ever in the Atlanta airport, I recommend One Flew South. Best food you'll find in the airport. Don't kill me when you get the bill though. What can I say? I am a bit of a foodie and I like to eat well. I was traveling to a place that wasn't guaranteed your next meal so can you blame me?

The waitress approached after I had ordered a few hundred dollars' worth of food and told me the gentleman across the restaurant would like to pay for my drinks. I let her know that I was in uniform and there was no way I could accept him supplying me with drinks, but thanks for the sentiment. She came back a while later to tell me that the gentleman was going to cover my meal… damn it! I mean… not exactly, but holy crap. I don't think this poor soul knew what he just got himself into. I thanked her and had to go say something to him. I went over and thanked him but told him it wasn't necessary. He told me that it wasn't a big deal and that he was in the military at one point and now he gets paid to do his research by government and he doesn't mind giving back to the guys from time to time. I was then told his name was none other than Dr Grossman.

I must have come off like the dumbest joe on the planet as I had never heard of him. I was new to all this and had never heard of the books *On Killing* and *On Combat;* I further didn't know that Dr Grossman had come out to personally speak to my unit before the previous deployment. How funny is that? Either way, I fumbled through a thank you and got to enjoy what I thought could very well be my last great meal… and what the hell, it was on someone else!

Back to the Suck

Coming back is weird. You don't really want to be going back into a hell hole, but at the same time, you don't want to miss out on everything going on. You don't want to let the guys down. You completely tune everything out when you leave, but coming back, you are anxious to get back into the fight. The thought of not heading back to Afghanistan never even crossed my mind, but I know that there were a few of the guys that had gone missing after their mid-tour flights had left. I guess things just hadn't gotten bad enough yet.

The route back into the Arghandab went from Atlanta to Germany, Germany to Kuwait, Kuwait to Kandahar, and then someone would arrive from battalion to snatch you up and bring you back into the fold. During one leg of the trip, I ended up across from Command Sergeant Major Sturdevant who was new in brigade and the group that was around him were talking about the leadership changes at battalion. I started to wonder why leadership was being switched up mid-deployment.

We had two powerhouses as our battalion command when I arrived at 2/508. LTC Frank Jenio and CSM Bert Puckett seemed to be able to provide infinite resources and had three-letter agencies popping up during our tenure in the battlespace. Maybe it was the extent of their networking or maybe they just had a bit better of a hustle than the rest in the Brigade. They were a good team and had been out there during the times we were being pushed to perform. There was even a tradition where the two would meet up with the battalion and perform a godawful number of pushups and flutter kicks with the men. They had a good dynamic and the men had no issue following these two through the very gates of hell itself. The men might have done it with a little griping here and there, but that is just the mumblings of an infantry company. It's considered a job requirement for some of the soldiers.

The switch-up seemed to have stemmed from a toxic relationship among the brigade commander's wife and the FRG (Family Readiness Group). There was pushback from Jenio along with others and she made good on a threat to get him fired. This was even brought up by his commanders to the division commander himself. Colonel Brian Drinkwine dismissed his peers and even said that his wife spoke for him as she held the same rank. Yup...we had one of those wives that thought they needed to be addressed as his rank as well. It escalated to the point of multiple battalion commanders lodging complaints about the conduct that was occurring at Brigade.

Someone slipped what was supposed to be a humorous "demotivational" slide into a PowerPoint presentation that depicted a Black man in chains taking about being liberated from the chains of oppression. I had never known those two to be anything but professional, but they took responsibility for not reviewing the deck beforehand and were thrown into the trash compactor faster than I'd ever seen happen before. I would assume it was because we were on the eve of a large push for the Army to have more EO officers, focus on sensitivity training, and jam so many "death by PowerPoint" slides down our throat that it overshadowed our actual training time. No, the slide was not appropriate, nor was it anything that should have been even joked about in this manner. People do weird shit on deployment and sometimes others pay for it. Unfortunately for us, it cost us the two warfighters that may have gotten us through the meat grinder in better shape than we made it through had they been allowed to stay and do their job. All conjecture, but a lot of the men had the same sentiments.

The replacements shuffled into place were Lieutenant Colonel Guy Jones and Command Sergeant Major Timothy Guden. CSM Guden was brought over from 4th Infantry Division where he already had experience as a CSM. I didn't know much about LTC Jones, other than he had been on the alternate list and wasn't really supposed to be in country anymore. This was not a good scene to come back to. Our company had just pushed into a new area of operations that was extremely dangerous with the full extent of the situation being unknown. Now we had a replacement commander who was rumored to be a puppet for a man who removes commanders on the recommendation of his wife. Tell me this isn't shaping up to be the recipe for the coming disasters in the near future. I know one thing was certain... morale wasn't so hot about the situation at that point.

COP Ware

I came back to the tents at Ware ready to get back into the swing of things. As I opened the flap of the tent, I saw my cot with all of the contents of my bags strewn about the floor around and under my cot. For someone with OCD, I hit full stupid mode pretty damn fast. "What the fuck is this shit?!" I yelled as I came into the tent. SPC Hammer looked at me and said that 1SG Mac was missing a set of night vision goggles, so they had to toss the place looking for them. They just cut the locks and dumped everything out. Common sense would dictate that they were not in my possession at the time of the loss seeing I was over 1,000 miles away in the USA on mid-tour leave.

He just shrugged his shoulders and looked right at me and said, "Why, you have a problem about it?" Yeah, I had a fucking problem with it, but I also knew I didn't want to have a problem with Hammer. He was a former tree-climbing lumberjack who was heavily muscled and from the backwoods of Tennessee. The guy was a fighter and had no qualms or fear about jumping into a fistfight any time of day. I wasn't a fist fighter and was way out of my league if I was going to try to tackle Hammer. I was mad, but technically, 1SG probably would have had them cut my damn locks even if they had tried to save my area from the mass layout they had to endure while I was gone. "Fuck this shit," I spat as I turned and started re-organizing my area. Yeah... I guess I'm right back in the suck at this point.

COP Ware had become something of a reality by the time I had returned. The Hescos had been filled by local contractors with earth movers; there were ANA (Afghan National Army) stationed on one end of the outpost; we had a gym now that comprised a few bars, some plates, and a few free weights; and there was a makeshift chow tent. They had also put in a landing area that was walled off and had made some wonky-looking guard positions. The biggest improvement was internet! There was a 25-series and some minions that arrived to provide satellite communications along with some extremely limited internet capabilities. It wasn't fast, but anything was better than nothing out there. This was akin to the speeds of dial up, so trying to view anything like a modern-day website would time out before loading the full page.

It's hard to imagine just how far the internet and our capabilities have come in only 10 or so years, but there we were happy as hell to be getting a 120k/sec connection in our tents from time to time. There were cell towers with a data connection, but also nothing like we have today. The Taliban had control over the cell towers and would turn off towers at night. They also seemed to have hacked into the control portal and were watching for American phone numbers on the net. They aren't stupid and you can just do a simple location-based tracking when USA recipients start to show up. So… don't use phones in a combat AO unless you've got the battery out and it's a foreign throwaway.

The problem with these base improvements is that you need to guard them while still maintaining a presence in the area and keeping the additional reaction platoon within the patrol loop. The rotation of patrols and duties out of COP Ware was brutal. We had a mountain cave observation point (OP) we needed to keep manned at all times so that we could keep an eye on the valley with night vision, along with a Javelin on standby in case it was needed. It was nice to know that we had guys above us looking over our movements. However, it just added to the list of duties that needed to be filled while having that area of responsibility within the valley.

The idea of being up on OP165 was great but I was never allowed to stay up there as they needed me below for patrols with the platoon. The platoon would have the squads on rotation to man the OP location for a week at a time. It was mainly a week to go and freeze your ass off in an outcropping over a mountain but that meant a week of not having to risk your legs on patrol or pull guard duty over a burn pit. I did get to go on an escort patrol up to the OP during our stay at COP Ware and was able to experience just how incredible the view could be. You don't really realize how high you are on some of the mountains as you are attempting to pay attention to everything around you at once while trekking to the summit. When a helicopter passes below you that you realize is at its maximum altitude and there isn't enough air to maintain that altitude, you start to appreciate the different aspects that make your job as the boots on the ground worth every experience.

Kit

There are significant challenges as a machine gunner, especially when it comes to the Squad Automatic Weapon or SAW (M249). One of the crucial details while serving as a SAW gunner is maintaining your balance with a crap ton of rounds on your body while retaining the ability to maneuver effectively. It's your job to send rounds downrange to suppress the enemy as quickly as possible. Your rounds might not even actually hit anyone in some instances, but anyone on earth will drop to the ground fast as hell when hearing automatic gunfire from the opposing side. It's about the "mad minute" principle of gaining initial fire superiority due to the amount of lead flying towards the enemy.

Eagle Industries produced pouches that were better than anything I had used that was issued to us and the material would not 'sag' while webbed to the Molle system due to the weight of the rounds you carried. I would personally adjust the loadout and carry two of the 200-round drums up front and high on the belt position so that the bottom of everything sat flush with the top of the equipment belt when loaded up. I would then put another two 100-round drums in smaller sized pouches adjacent but flush with the top of the 200-round pouches. This created a shelf and the height of the smaller pouches allowed for full squat movement as your hips had extra space. You would then include your IFAK (med kit) off to the side and rear so that whoever was providing aid could get to it. The bottom of the rig would usually sit at about my belly button and would allow freedom of movement because I had full range of motion with my lower body and legs.

Throw in the fact that the pouches create a functional shelf, you minimize the risk of running your arms to exhaustion from carrying the machine gun. You wouldn't use it all the time, but the ability to give your arms a break here and there goes a long way. The M249 is an outstanding piece of equipment while doubling as a giant piece of garbage. Weighing in at roughly 20lbs and having poor balance, it's still an improvement over the M60 it replaced. The M60 weighs in at 22lbs without ammo but adds 35lbs to your loadout for just 500 rounds of the 7.62 ammunition. You would feel it after walking around while carrying one at the ready, whether you were deployed or back in garrison during training.

Everything on your equipment kit is rather front-heavy now, which is where your assault pack comes in. I would always have a three-day bag on me with additional rounds and equipment to balance the load out. There would be another 500–600 rounds in my pack depending on what the mission called for and how I had the rounds broken down into ammunition combinations using 100- or 200-round drums. I would usually carry a 100-round "nutsack" loaded on the SAW because it cut down on the weight and the bulk of everything on the weapon. Go ahead and hold one sometime with both versions of drums attached and see the difference for yourself. The other problem was the 200-round drums that were issued were bulky and made of a plastic that was sturdy but would snap if you were moving at speed towards an enemy objective on an assault. The 200-round cases were better for situations when you were in a support by fire roll or providing suppressing fire for any amount of time.

When I had been carrying the machine gun, I would carry around 1,200 rounds at all times when we were on a mission. After switching to the RTO position, I had sold the SAW rig to SPC Morton and changed my gear to a lightweight rifleman hybrid rig that I had bought from a small company known as Mayflower Tactical that had been founded by a disabled SF veteran. That lightweight rig increased my ability to maneuver and climb over the walls in the region far better than anything that was provided by the gear that was issued to us. There is something to be said for being properly outfitted. The military is getting much better about what they provide due to the lessons learned during the steep curve that war provided us. The same can be said for the private sector that continues to innovate in incredible ways.

That rig was also worn high and over a plate carrier which allowed for better freedom of movement than the IOTVs variation of body armor we had been wearing during our stint in Helmand. After switching out to the plate carriers, the IOTVs were reduced to flak jackets that we hung at the head of our beds in case someone tossed a mortar into the compound while we were sleeping. The chest rig had room for six 30-round magazines built into it, a grenade pouch down low, a general-purpose pouch, the radio pouch, my IFAK, and two small pouches in which I would keep a compass and a can of Copenhagen.

I also used an Escape and Evade (E&E) pouch with breakaway clips that was attached to my plate carrier. I had the system broken into stages in case it came to certain points of desperation while on mission. I wanted to keep the weapons and ammo portion separate from the plate carrier in case I needed to drop the carrier for weight purposes or freedom of movement. There are times when speed and mobility are going to be the primary function needed. If you must resort to only keeping your small E&E pouch on your person along with your weapon, with a magazine or two stuffed into your pants pocket, that's going to be a really bad day. The E&E pouch contained things such as a Gerber multitool, a civilian space-saving compass, a 9v battery, an infrared chem light with a cricket flasher, a LifeStraw to provide a clean water source, some para cord, a few hundred dollars, and a prepaid cell with an Afghan sim in it. I removed the battery because the Taliban would take over the telecom towers in the area every so often and I didn't want them triangulating our position. I really hoped that it would never come to that, but if it did, I wanted to be prepared for it.

Mayfield

Out of COP Ware, we found ourselves at the ECP and responding as a QRF element with 1st squad after Lieutenant Eric Mayfield was hit by an IED during patrol. When your drill sergeant yells at you in basic training for needing enough drive to get to the fight and then actually be able to fight on the objective, he means it. I would have never thought that running a distance into a firefight would be a thing, but it was that day as we hauled ass over a mile to where we assisted the platoon that was under attack. I remember looking back and seeing SPC Cannon huffing as he lumbered over the plowed fields with the 240 over his shoulders as we ran.

The company commander, Armstrong, had grabbed Sgt Ackers and been out of the gates in minutes. Looking back on it, the urgency in which we left the ECP was matched in intensity on the run across the fields. It's a wonder we didn't hit another landmine as the group did a rag-tag sprint over the terrain. When we got there, there were two Kiowa helicopters performing gun runs and directing fire from above. They had to break off due to being low on ammo and fuel, but one of the helicopters landed and attempted to load Mayfield into the cockpit because his head was bleeding so profusely. Mayfield started fighting the guys that were tossing him in the chopper and the crew realized that it was a bad idea to stuff a wounded animal into a two-person flying machine.

Armstrong was frustrated because it had been a decent solution to the problem but now they had lost another 10 minutes trying to get the casualty on board instead of just calling for a casevac. Thankfully, Pedro was on station that day and arrived on scene quickly. We lost yet another to the halls of Walter Reed that day, but at least he was still alive and breathing.

Muddin'

Rainy season on COP Ware was not fun. The ground was carved out of an existing farmer's radish field and we had essentially plunked a large bulletproof barrier (after they were filled with dirt) of Hescos around the outskirts of the field footprint and set up camp. Two or three Alaskan tents to start and a bunch of the green GP Medium tents were put up in short order with the dirt as a floor. It worked out OK in the winter, when the ground was bitter cold and frozen, but as things thawed out, the trouble began.

Mice, bugs, rats, snakes, and everything else would be found infiltrating our living areas and you had to make sure to shake anything out before wearing it because God knows what was hiding out inside, claiming the "shoe cave" for its own selfish purposes. On top of the local infestations, we had to deal with the soft soil that had done great for the farmer and his previously well-tended crops. Now, it was a constant fall mitigation to go outside to use the bathroom. Guys would pee in bottles and toss them in the burn pit in the morning because of it. Sometimes, some of the dirty bird types would forget to throw the bottles out periodically and would face the wrath of their team or squad leader if it was noticed.

We started grabbing any piece of wood that wasn't bolted down in order to create some kind of flooring, so we didn't have to be slipping around all the time. Maybe it would dry out the tents just enough to be livable. Those times would mostly just be spent in your rack anyway because life never stopped at COP Ware.

It was one of those dark and wet nights that Sergeant James Lee stepped outside to use the bathroom in between his sergeant on guard duty rounds when he saw a figure writhing on the ground through his night vision. "Hey, who is that?" Lee said as he approached. The figure stopped moving and turned his head towards him. "Uh... I don't want to say," the figure replied. It looked like it was one of the guys, fully kitted up with their assault pack on and everything, fresh back from a patrol.

He had fallen over backwards in his trek from one end of the compound to the other and was essentially on his back, futilely trying to flip forward or roll to the side in order to get back up. It was so slippery and he was so laden down, he was like a turtle on his back, writhing around in the mud in the night. Lee couldn't help but chuckle to himself as he approached the guy to help him up. "Come on, let's get you up."

As he lifted the figure off the ground and he came into view, it was instantly clear why the reason for the embarrassment... it was our company commander, Captain Adam Armstrong.

Ichabod and the Horse

It was one of those dark nights Afghanistan was known for... really dark. One where the moon wasn't existent and there was no real amount of lumen available for our night vision to work. There were quite a few times where my night vision was turned on, but it was useless. I would have the eye cups against the brow of my forehead so as to not illuminate my face for some asshole to target a green pumpkin floating through the night. You would be surprised what the smallest pinprick of light looks like in the dark.

Fortunately for Ross and Cannon, they weren't having to deal with the technicalities that come with moving through the surrounding terrain during the witching hour. Instead, they were squared up on an intersection near the village of Bibihowa to monitor patterns of movement and who was moving around during the night. Because of the climate and the work being done, most of the farmers would be working in their fields at night to irrigate or do the field work maintenance. You would start to recognize people and they would start to come up with ways to show they weren't a hostile combatant.

At one point, it was standard to just grab the fabric of their long tunic and hoist it over their head to make it clear and certain that they weren't loaded up with a suicide vest. They were just as worried as we were that they would face the reality of certain death alongside the combatants within the valley. Just a matter of what side the reaper was on that day.

Ross was a good soldier who was always thinking... sometimes a little too much. He would get in his own head about just how crappy it was living in the area, or how pointless that particular patrol was, or why did it always seem that he was the one to be lugging around the most amount of ammo. He was sitting at the apex of a point with the 240 gunner, Cannon, when their whispers of conversation were interrupted by a noise.

"What the fuck was that? You hear that?!" Ross struggled to continue whispering. Cannon strained to listen because he had heard it too. It was like a strange psychotic heartbeat in the night. It was distant but closing rapidly. This was something out of the ordinary and unusual and in a job like this, it was the unusual that could kill you. Like the scene in *Jurassic Park* when the T-rex's ominous footprints stomp closer and closer until the inevitable burst of the ultimate predator coming onto the scene, the audible thumps closed in on their position.

In a climactic scene, a huge black horse came thundering out into the intersection and slice of road they were covering. Clearly unnerved and sensing that he wasn't the only one there, the horse gave a loud snort, turned on its heels, and bucked back the way that it had come. No rider, no saddle, no explanation. In a part of the world where a horse was more valuable than a car and more akin to getting around in a Rolls-Royce, you didn't just see one roaming around like that.

Ross and Cannon both looked at each other and shrugged their shoulders. Chalking up what was just another one of the weird experiences that made up our time in the valley.

The OP

Morton was scanning the valley from high above COP Ware on the mountainside with the Javelin computer system one night on OP165. Ackers was pulling night shift along with him by his side but curled up in a sleeping bag. You would have four or so people on the observation point at a time and would be in buddy group shifts. If one of you on guard was feeling tired or if you needed to verify something, you would wake your buddy up and go into action on whatever the incident was.

They would usually serve as an overwatch of sorts for patrols that would be moving throughout the valley at night or would watch the local patterns of life and report them back to the COIST team (Company Intelligence Support Team) at the TOC in COP Ware. The COIST team was a group of soldiers that would develop reports and enter data observed into spreadsheets to analyze and share with other agencies within the area. It was what you could consider to be a small intel team composed of some of the HQ elements.

The TOC is your radio and communications area where you would also host any of your briefings with the NCOs and pertinent people that would need to know the operation. As an RTO, you can get in on most of this stuff where a lot of the other guys wouldn't hear this info and would only be focused on the job at hand. Better off for focus purposes out there as it was. The job of looking for threats while watching your step is no easy task and would leave you drained by the end of a patrol if you were doing it correctly.

The advantage of the Javelin system was that it had multiple vision capabilities that would allow for verification of the target. If you see two guys digging in the field, you can tell if they have left a land mine due to the temperature of the metal versus the ground temperature. You could verify with the thermal vision, switch to standard green night vision, snap some pictures, and if they let you, warm up the weapons system and have a missile headed their way within two minutes' time.

There would usually be an SDM (squad designated marksman) up there with a sniper rifle ready to pop anyone if they wanted to save the ordnance and only cost the taxpayers around $2 as opposed to the $80,000 it costs to buy a replacement missile from Raytheon. We pay taxes too, you know. I guess it comes down to the discretion of the ground force commander at the time as there was an instance when we were told to hold the Javelin shot while the headquarters scout unit on the opposing mountain completely missed the shot and lit up the valley with a 240 machine gun from 1,000m away. This led to the quick escape of a three-man bomb emplacement team in the area and frustrated us to no end. Why they didn't have sniper rifles up on OP160 that day and decided using an unsilenced 240 was a good idea, I'll never know.

But there Morton was, scanning as usual when there was a huge shape on the thermals just below the ridgeline and to the left of his position. "HOLY SHIT!" thought Morton. "What the hell is that?" It was about the worst position to be in right then. It was cold and damp, and as such, the guns that were on the ridge with him were bundled in tarps to keep them dry. You could see forever up here, so the possibility of needing a long gun was minimal and there was enough standoff where you would have time to get to anything you needed.

"Ackers," he whispered. Nothing. "Ackers!" he said a little louder as he kicked his foot in his direction. Ackers slept on as the creature turned and revealed the shape of a cat. A big ass mountain cat that was about the scariest thing outside of a bear that you could find up there. In some instances, this was worse. The distance that this animal could cover in an extremely short amount of time was huge. It could be on Morton within a second and it was pure muscle and sinew as the cat had a hard life surviving in this part of the world.

Morton was a hunter in his past and sized this feline up to weigh about 120lbs. From the look of the massive head on it, it could have been more panther than anything else. Whatever it was, he knew that if this thing got any closer, it would be detrimental to everyone there. A big cat like this would defend its territory and would mutilate anything that reared up on it in the night.

With what he considered to be a light yell, but in reality, was probably just a whisper that roared in the night, Morton tried to get Ackers up again. He couldn't blow their cover on something like this. There was no way he wanted to take the shot without confirming first but if he couldn't get the word in the next second, he would have to make that choice on his own. He had been locked onto looking at this massive creature the entire time as he was frantically trying to get ahold of Ackers. The animal came right up directly in front of their position, stopped as if it knew they were there, and continued on its way like it understood that the threat of mutual destruction was very real, and it had overstayed its welcome.

His heart pounding and the cold sweat starting to leave chills on the back of his neck as he came off the adrenaline rush, Morton could finally relax again, but that didn't happen. He still had a job to do and now he had to fight the aftereffects of an adrenaline dump. You start to get sleepy and just want to curl up and have a little nap to allow for the body to replenish its stores for the next encounter. So, fighting the urge to fall asleep, he stayed up and continued to scan in the stillness of the night, all the time waiting for that cat to pop up and eat him during their stay in the mountainside chalet known as OP165.

Morton never saw that cat again, but damn if there were more run-ins with nature out there in a region of Afghanistan that held a bit of everything for us to experience. It wasn't just insurgents that had it in for us, but mother nature as well.

Nature wasn't the only threat in operating as a small team within the mountains out there. You had to make sure that your assets knew you were a friendly force out there. It complicated things further when you took into account that some of the air support was from other NATO forces that weren't on our radio channels or comsec. Comsec is a cryptological code that would be encrypted and sent out among the radios across the battlespace and changed on a weekly basis during a zero time. One of the jobs as an RTO was to ensure that all the equipment was changed over to the correct comsec profile during that particular time. So, you would wake up during zero hour, no matter what, and load the new cryptological security key into everyone's radios. Sometimes they would be sleeping, but you would slide the radio out of its owner's pouch and do radio tests afterwards to make sure everything transferred correctly.

There would be times when you would have to run a patrol to meet a patrol position and load their radios with the current comsec keys so you could talk to one another. The other tactic was to leave a spare radio on the old security key so that you could talk to the patrol that was operational and change it after they got back to the base. Both methods offered their own merits and were used from time to time depending on the situation. You wouldn't want to blow an observation point by having someone roll up mid-mission to essentially update your firmware. I would imagine they developed an over-the-air solution to upload crypto keys these days with how advanced everything has gotten in the military.

Whatever the case, when the team at OP165 noted an aircraft that had gone by and then begun to circle back around, there was no real way to talk to the pilot. Chances were that the surface radar had picked up the Javelin system heat signature and locked onto the small force of human targets on a mountainside in Afghanistan. Sergeant Jason Spottedhorse was out there that day along with Sgt Ackers' squad in an attempt to offer his FIST (Fires Support Team) services to the onlookers at the mountain observation point.

In reality, it was probably to just get away from COP Ware. The tempo of duties would crush your soul and an occasional trip up the mountain to freeze your ass off was a welcome change of pace from time to time. Morton described it as being the one place in that hellhole that offered a bit of peace in all of the noise. Spottedhorse was a tree of a man from the Kiowa tribe in Oklahoma. The job of the FIST as a 13F was to offer fire and support service to the ground force.

This means that they can facilitate gun runs, drop bombs, call for artillery, help drop mortars, and use a whole bunch of other really cool ways to destroy the enemy that require a position on the map to eradicate. Look up the Army HiMars system. You can vaporize everything on an entire grid square and essentially clear the area with just one missile. The FIST guys will have all the listings of alternate channels where they can dial in the correct frequency to talk to the guys in the air. What they don't show in movies is that the time you have to get a message to an aircraft on station is about 10 seconds if they are just cruising. Another reason why they get referred to as "fast movers"… because they are.

So, when you see an aircraft with those capabilities circle around… you start to wonder. The French Mirage was starting to go into a pattern above their heads and Sgt Ackers grabbed Spot to start talking on any channels he could to get in contact with the pilot of the craft. "Get your damn helmets on!" Ackers yelled to the other men on the ridge as they were scrambling to do anything they could to ensure they looked like US soldiers out there. "OH, SHIT!!! GET THE FUCK DOWN!" he screamed as the plane did a 1,000ft flyover combined with a salvo of flares shooting off which left a crack in the ears of anything on the ground to experience it.

As the plane began to climb and circle back around, Ackers yells at one of the guys, "Get the fucking Javelin up and armed and see if we can't either get him to veer off on a radar lock or if we have to, fire it at him! I'm not going out like this! Fuck this shit!!! Anything on getting that pilot or HQ about it?" he yelled at Spot. "Nothing man, shit!" Things were getting frantic. This plane was about to go into a kill run to blast anything that moved on that mountaintop that day and it was just the flick of a switch for the pilot.

Somewhere between the scramble to relay the issue, the jet lost interest in the guys on the OP and veered off elsewhere. They never confirmed what actually happened, but it's not outside of the realm of possibility that a Sidewinder could have been locked on to eradicate the perceived threat in what were ultimately friendly forces. Just another day and another bump in the road in the Arghandab River Valley.

Patrols out of Ware

Pir-e-Paymal was a town that was past the LOC route we would occasionally patrol. There was always a suspected enemy influence in the area, but we couldn't pinpoint it. We had intel along with our own suspicions that one of the insurgents in town was using a system of birds as a signal when we would come through. I had never thought to look for a method so old in practice before, but why would I when I lived in a world where cell phones took the place of ancient methods long ago?

We were performing a nighttime outer cordon for the current task force in the adjacent town of Chahar Dahaneh that particular night. It wasn't the typical operation and as we set in position, an AC-130 started to circle overhead and comms crackled with their callsigns. They initiated comms checks with everyone and lit up the whole countryside with what is dubbed the "God light." A floodlight on the bottom on the plane streamed down from above and illuminated the entire AO for the operators that were coming in via chopper. This is not a normal floodlight from a plane, but some crazy directional IR spectrum light that only helps if you have night vision goggles on. The entire thing was over within five minutes as they came in hard and fast onto the roofs straight from the rails of the helicopter. Off the bird went to circle around and provide cover fire if necessary.

Two flashes followed by bangs and the teams breached quickly, hit hard, and were already on the exfil before anyone in the village realized what had happened. These are the night raids you hear about and were normally performed in snatch-and-grab missions by Special Forces or task force soldiers. These guys were definitely the latter of the two for this mission. I don't think I had ever seen an operation go as smoothly as I did when those guys hit the kill zone. It exemplified the "slow is smooth, and smooth is fast" mantra you would hear echoed around the gun ranges on Bragg.

It wasn't a regular occurrence, but we would receive the after-effect that brought various villagers to our door asking for money to repair damages to their residence that were incurred during the nighttime. It was part of having to live amongst the locals. The Special Forces guys would stage out of the large FOBs and perform the surgical missions based on intel while we were in the danger zone every day as we plodded along in the muck of the fields and orchards that surrounded us. This picture is very backwards with how the system is supposed to operate according to doctrine. Special operations will place the Special Forces ODAs, whose primary mission is FID (Foreign Internal Defense), embedded with the local populace to essentially work themselves out of a job as they train and assist the host nation counterparts. Maybe that's part of the reason why we never got anywhere in the overall picture of this war? Higher command was swayed by the sweet sexy sounds of the CIF (Commanders Interdiction Force) teams and the focus turned towards direct action as opposed to the core function of what Special Forces is supposed to be performing as a mission directive.

We never paid the villagers that would show up, but I know that the policy was to hear them out and generate a report. I'm sure it included pictures of the one asking for handouts and maybe even a biometric scan on the HIIDE (Handheld Interagency Identity Detections Equipment) unit. Someone somewhere had been compiling people from all the battle theaters and we would get townspeople who were in the military fighting age range showing up as being seen in Iraq and other non-friendly countries within the entire Middle Eastern portion of the world. The concept wasn't strange, but it makes you think about the fact that these fighters were pouring in from other areas of the world so they could essentially wage a crusade against you because you were the representation of the United States of America and you needed to die for your beliefs.

There was more traffic within COP Ware as supporting units and analysts started trickling in and setting up camp in various portions of the outpost. People would get shuffled around and tents would change hands on a weekly basis. There was no relaxing or place to call home here. We received some cooks on the outpost, but with no real cooking to be done due to the lack of freezer assemblies, they just doled out MREs from their pallets. The worst occasion was when they would pull out the UGR cafeteria-style warming tray meals. Imagine just how bad the taste of MREs had gotten by this point. The government has gotten better over the years but has consistently screwed up when it comes to creating shelf-stable meals for extended portions of time in a lethal area. Go eat an MRE for fun and see what I am talking about. They are disgusting; however, the UGR is taking the fun out of guessing which terrible meal you are going to end up with and getting to share it en masse with the platoon. So now, you don't get the other portions of an MRE which make it semi-OK even if the main meal is horrid. On top of that, the meal tray never heats evenly so your chance of getting an evenly heated (or heated at all) spoonful of slop is pretty much nil.

Soldiers within the infantry have cursed me out about the various comforts I would splurge on with my earned pay. I never wore issued boots except for in basic training and I was always analyzing a situation or my gear to make minor improvements or learn something in order to improve my situation. There are two distinct trains of thought on this. One: these improvements can help a warfighter hone his skill and take the focus that would be spotlighting possible equipment failure or bad design and redirect it towards the present moment in the fight. This is what my line of thinking was. Two: what was issued you was good enough. The job and fight will be miserable no matter what. Embrace it and improve from your time within the misery. It will make you a harder and a better soldier. It doesn't matter anyway when you are in the thick of it. It's going to be a miserable time anyway. Enjoy it. Honestly, after the experience I've gained, they are both the right answer. If anything, the best-case scenario is getting to experience the hard times before being allowed to make the improvements once you fully understand what you are getting into. There is a lot of "snake oil" out there.

Even with the base improvements we had, it was still a rather spartan situation on COP Ware. I can remember the day they ended up bringing in the shower stalls. This was after three months of going without what was considered a normal shower. It was too cold to hang up a solar bag and quite frankly, we couldn't spare the clean water as it was. Not only did we have a shortage, but the water source provided was packaged in those cheap, super thin-walled plastic water bottles that developed issues if left in the sun or heat for too long. Everyone there will probably develop cancer on using those bottles alone, much less the rest of the particles that were still floating around the atmosphere in our area. There was talk of leftover chemical warfare residue from the Russians. Not every military entity in the world thinks long term. The USA does a pretty damn good job when it comes to clean up. However, it's almost assured that there are traces of toxic elements within the soil of the Arghandab and you could see it in some of the birth defects of the people that lived there.

The Russians still harbor some nasty feelings against the USA because they will unofficially place bounties on American heads operating in areas of interest or commission some Chechen kill teams or snipers to raise some havoc. It goes both ways when we have truckloads of supplies heading into Ukraine on a daily basis these days. We assist people to be subversive in areas around the globe and our enemies do the same thing to us.

You could surmise that our body odor was horrible after the initial shock of the first week not showering has worn off and then we return after a period of about two to three weeks of constant patrolling and guard. At first, you think that the baby wipes are doing their job, but this is a lie. Your clothes become stiff and then start to rot due to the threads being eaten by the copious amount of bacteria soup that is living on them while being created by your movements along with the current environment. Patrols would be routed through riverbeds and creeks just to be able to get a quick rinse as we waded through sections of rivers and irrigation within the valley. Later in the deployment, we were sent buckets to be able to do laundry, which mainly just saw our t-shirts, underwear (if you wore any) and socks anyway. You were better off just letting the uniform take the elements and allowing the added grime from the environment to aid in camouflaging your forms as you patrolled.

Being out on patrol was better than being back at the COP anyway. You were out of every other duty and could focus on the present moment. There was a beauty among chaos or even the constant threat of death that loomed over our heads. I found myself snapping a picture in an orchard with trees that were beginning the blooming process. There were cherry blossom trees in full bloom with a compound off to the right in the distance and a road that led up past the nearby village. You can see the soldiers fully kitted up on a combat patrol but otherwise, this scene could have been in a magazine spread for *Better Homes and Gardens*, Third World edition.

This was a world where both extreme ends of the spectrum of life existed. The possibility of a peaceful and serene moment could flip to full-fledged chaos in an instant. The adrenaline spikes experienced could give you the shakes as if you spent the day becoming hopped up on caffeinated drinks, but then you get cold and sleepy after the action calms down. The crash ensues. However, the local animals didn't share the same sentiment towards the danger around them. The realization came to me while out on a patrol when the EOD team blew up a mine that we had uncovered. We were huddled down on the opposite side of the berm while the team leader snapped the det cord. I was watching a cow that was grazing in the field adjacent to us. The damn animal didn't even flinch when the boom hit. I don't think we had a clue what we had gotten ourselves into.

Welcome to Boomtown

The few times that any supplies ever came in, they would follow the main route clearance patrol (RCP) that consisted of engineers who were equipped with vehicles that had massive IED defeat systems on them. They would travel in a convoy that had attachments of EOD to take care of any large charges that needed to be disposed of and had additional assets to patch roads, fill the infrastructure, and provide support and logistics while traveling through the region. Akin to a massive Mad Max nomadic convoy with a constant roving mission that brought cheer to remote territories, they provided a brief window to the outside bubble we were in.

Some of the units would have female truck drivers or medics that would use the quick opportunity to create a brief love interest with one (or more sometimes) of the guys on the outpost as it was a convenient "no-strings" arrangement for them that didn't require any commitment from either party. Most of the time, life doesn't afford enough time for any serious relationships in the military, so we just make do with what we have. To hell with what traditional society thinks anyway.

Times where this can prove to be dangerous is when you enter into a combat scenario or one that calls upon you being able to separate and discern between emotions and facts. The urge to protect the female sex in the event of a crisis is massive and ingrained at a biological and societal level. They are the genetic pathway to another generation and the survival of the human race. If a female cries out or is hurt on the battlefield, our attention is drawn to that particular area. Our brain can't help it… it's biology. Even within the special operations community, where the lines between roles of the sexes on the battlefield are blurred further, you will have problems stem from within a group of extreme alpha males with the presence of a female. We didn't have this issue as we were about 100 males from an infantry company existing in a radish field. Just a pissed-off, testosterone-fueled, all-male unit.

Every mission for us was dismounted patrols with the very rare opportunity to drive to Kandahar to pick someone up or for some officer to drop off paperwork that was needed. This means we walked everywhere. The human body can adapt to any situation, given some time and motivation to continue moving, but the terrain within the Arghandab River Valley was highly varied. High mountains peppered the region with a river dividing the immediate area of operations and feeding an entire irrigation network of farms and villages living around us. You would go from rocky and dry all day to humid and plodding through the mud, all within one mission. Some of the areas that we stalked had my mind running through the pages of those books I had read about the Vietnam War. There would be farmers flooding their fields and small canals that we would have to travel down or cross at times. Mostly, it made for some really slow moving. The bright side was that while you were in the muck, you had to appreciate that your legs were probably safe for the time being because it was impossible for the IED teams to lay explosives in a mud field or a river.

Helmand had been the testing ground if you compared the tactics and quality of work when it came to laying in IEDs and their tactical effectiveness. The enemy would have tactics such as using multiple people to stage a mine emplacement using an assembly lineup. One guy would come through just scouting and drop a marker, the next would wander by and dig a small hole but leave it open. He may even just drop the shovel and shuffle off. Someone else would meander by with the charge and just plunk it in the hole and get outta Dodge before ISR sent an alert that would have a Hellfire missile tracking him shortly. The initiation wire and detonators would follow and it would be an artistic masterpiece by the time the sun crested the horizon. Sometimes, the Taliban were brazen enough to perform the mine emplacement during broad daylight following a patrol that was passing through the field. You could never come back the way you went in. The enemy's tactics helped them minimize the chances of someone being caught with solid evidence of explosives on the scene. We couldn't kill them if we didn't have positive ID of weapons or explosives. Even if you knew someone was up to no good, you couldn't do anything about it without solid proof to justify your actions. It's what separated us from them, I suppose.

Another brilliant tactic they would use was laying the mines in place and covering before sunrise while wetting the area, so the top layer of soil looked uniform with the rest of the area with no signs that anyone had just disturbed the earth. They were tricky. Daisy-chained mines with varying depths under the ground were found along with different possible ways the charges were used. Landmine equipment from China and Russia was found along with a handful of other homemade devices that would make life a living hell while we continued to survive in the valley.

We faced our own challenges of adaptation as well. A lot of the time we fell back on tactics that recon had used in the Vietnam War era. A single file line is a terribly ineffective way to move in a battlefield situation, but when you had to minimize the amount of space the guys walked on the ground, it was one of our few choices. The machine gunner would be the second order of movement to maximize the initial return fire as guys maneuvered on line to get an assault in place or would begin to peel off in a retreat. There would be times when we combined tactics and fanned out over open spaces and would collapse back into a file while traveling in high-risk or low-visibility areas.

If you stuck to any tactic for any amount of time, the enemy would be sure to exploit it. Battalion had a tracker that estimated a window of 27 to 32 days before the enemy would adapt to the current tactics we were using. It was a defined area of time that we had to figure out how we were going to start operating next. We found landmines in the shape of our patrol formations on more than one occasion, so the element of needing to constantly adapt was vital for survival. Taliban would take notes with details such as the distances that we were spaced apart and then adjust the explosive charges to have maximum effectiveness within the desired attack. Everyone was always watching, villager or not. The indigenous people weren't "dummies" or "savages," and between the enemy being integrated into the region and the village inhabitants willing to sell us out for some quick cash, it was a nightmare.

Fortunately, the tide began to turn once the villagers realized that we weren't killing people at random and something was different in the way we operated. It's sad to say, but it probably took our troops taking losses and bleeding alongside their countrymen for them to realize we wanted to make a change in that valley. Kids within a village are always curious about any activity to escape the harshness of their reality. Life in that area of the world is hard… really hard. I remember watching those kids on more than one occasion and wondering how many were going to make it. How many would go on to be fighters and on what side would they fall? What do you have to look forward to in a country where your biggest request from a foreigner is a pen or pencil?

As a youth growing up in America, your problems could have a wide spectrum, but nothing akin to what these kids face on a daily basis. When an adult male would show up, the children would usually scatter because one of the kids was about to get cracked in the head for a behavioral infraction. Maybe it was just because they were out during our presence? There was a hierarchy even amongst the packs of children that would roam the areas. You couldn't just give stuff out to them because they would get into fights over anything you gave out. One little girl was seen taking a large rock to the face from one of the neighborhood boys after one of the guys had thrown her an MRE bar.

That was another problem of humanity the inhabitants would face out there. By the luck of the draw, where you were born and what gender you were determined a good amount of how terrible your existence would be. Females were treated almost as being subhuman. If you were born a girl in Afghanistan, chances would be extremely high that you would be married or sold off by the age of 14. With no education or hopes of being able to attend a school, you were guaranteed an existence of servitude to the husband and family for the rest of your life.

The soldiers would joke about the laws imposed upon the women of the country and would call the burka-clad shapes that would move about the villages "Ms Pac Man." Sometimes, you could hear one of them making sounds like the noises from the classic arcade game. The mystery and allure was what was under there anyway? Sometimes, a male terrorist would get caught sneaking around urban areas in a burka to avoid being caught. There were also stories of suicide bombers using the same garb to cover up their motives and close the gap to improve the effectiveness of their explosive's payload.

We didn't have an FST (Female Support Team) with us to be able to interact with any of the females within towns that we came across. It was forbidden for a woman to talk to men so they would quickly disappear from any area where we would cross paths with them. If they were caught talking to us, it would ensure a merciless beating from their husband at a minimum.

Night Letters

Because we were living in such close proximity to the villages, we started to notice particular people and normal patterns that you could recognize in the town. You started to become attuned to things that didn't fit in. People that would show up on our biometric systems who had been seen in Iraq and other war zones. There were a good number of foreign fighters that we would encounter within the region, and there would be a different dialect, clothing, or mannerisms. The interactions between people that had grown up in the region and those that were "visiting" were decidedly different.

It wasn't long before we started to become aware of the balance of power operating in the area and who held the power within the villages. There are two people you need to know when getting anything accomplished in a village within Afghanistan. One is the village elder, which a lot of times is also the mayor. They are sought after in their wisdom and understanding because of their age. The other is the mullah, or the religious leader of the village. They run the mosque, prayers, and the community within the village. Between the two, they make the town come together. The ratio of power that they hold will vary depending on the village you are in; that's why it's so important to understand the particulars in the situations housed within the area of operation.

Once the villagers decided we were different than the other Americans who had been there, they started to warm up to the idea of talking with us. The kids were never scared unless an adult male from the village came around. I never worried when the children were around because the chance of an attack was fairly low. No one wanted to be at fault for any kids being a battlefield casualty. Situations with kids will almost always sway the populace in the favor of the ones opposite of those at fault.

The mayor of Mian Juy, a small village between COP Ware and the outpost that became COP Johnston, started talking with us because the people of his village had started receiving "night letters." These were threats to the village occupants that included dismemberment and death if you cooperated with the Americans. Maybe because we would go through the area daily to show face and try to show enough presence to convince the people that we were trying to help and not just make things more complicated in the valley.

We became stuck in town for an extended period that was way over the allotted mission time and our guys ran out of water. Food wasn't a large deal, but water was a detrimental factor out there. A little hunger will just make your senses sharper and reactions quicker if you get into a fight. But lack of water will bring a patrol to a grinding halt as you need to ration what amount that you have and limit movement during the heat of the day. I had been slowly working on being able to adapt to the local parasites so I wouldn't get threateningly sick in an instance like this. No, I don't recommend this method, but it seemed to have worked out for me.

From the moment we got into Afghanistan, I had started to brush my teeth with the local water. Then I progressed to a swig of it to rinse my mouth out daily every morning. Soon after, I would take sips of the water here and there until it was a small glass every so often. I never experienced any large issues and figured I wouldn't go down from dysentery if it came to resorting to the local well as a main water supply.

The patrol ended up going "black on water" with no idea of when we were going to be able to get re-supply or back to the COP. Something had happened involving EOD and we became a QRF or blocking position of sorts until it was sorted. We redistributed water and rationed what we had left among us. The villagers gave us permission to use the well and we pooled together some money for food to be brought out to us by one of the kids. We weren't too worried about anything such as poisoning, but it was always a risk. The gyros the local kids would bring us beat anything you've experienced at a restaurant or street vendor in the USA. The most authentic source might manage to pull off 65 percent of the full experience. Between the freshness of the ingredients that were wrapped in the flatbread and the way they would flatten the bread with their feet before baking it in a brick oven by the side of the road, they had a mouthwatering product. There is nothing in this world like fresh, hot Afghan foot bread that just came from the oven. Cringe if you might, but I would bet Anthony Bourdain would have given a thumbs up.

One after another, the guys started having stomach cramps and episodes of dysentery not too long after they had started drinking the well water. The climate left little choice as they also risked overheating from getting nothing in their system to hydrate. I never experienced the slightest bit of gastrointestinal distress. Maybe the water trick worked. I should probably ask a travel expert or Bear Grylls what happened at some point.

It became our job to fend off a bunch of bullies that were armed and liked to slap around those that weren't trained to deal with this type of situation—nor should they have to. A lesson that the current generation should take note of. If you have a troubled neighborhood, send in a bunch of guys that have a moral compass and are armed to the teeth with gear and training. Guaranteed, the troublemakers in that area of the world will get really quiet really quick, as was the case with us. It seemed to work out and the people of the village seemed happy enough that they were able to get a night's rest without the worry of being dragged out of their beds at night to be strung up or hacked up like others that hadn't been so lucky. If any freedom was won for anyone during that mission, it was providing sleep and security to those who may have never really had that experience before. You have to experience hell to be aware of just how strong of a presence a squad of US military personnel can provide.

My advice to the new guy about to face the situations you'll come across in a combat zone is to not overthink it and stick to your lane. If you overcomplicate your tasking, you will be overwhelmed and either freeze up or make some really bad decisions that could get yourself or one of your friends killed. Learn from those around you and the mistakes that you will see, and make, along the way. Most importantly, keep your head about you in all the chaos. You'll be OK, but when you stop actively processing things and adapting accordingly, you go into a react mode. That is not where you want to be at any point. Be proactive.

We ended up leaving the village a few days later after the majority of the squad couldn't hold anything down. Water was going through them at a rate that was dangerous to continue and the short rest that was allotted after the mission was nowhere near the time needed to recover from a health problem like that. But that was life was in the valley. It was a constant pressure cooker of Murphy showing up anywhere you turned.

CHAPTER 7

Away from the Flagpole

Adaptation/"Hajinuity"

With the challenges this area of Afghanistan offered, it was no wonder we faced issues. Mountains surrounding the valley rose past helicopter altitude allowances, irrigated farming orchards and grape fields would suck your boots off if you didn't have them laced tight, rivers and canals flowed through the place and cut off various avenues of approach, and finally, the dry, arid desert towns and villages that speckled the landscape provided safe harbor to insurgents living among the locals.

The Russians had lost an entire battalion in the Arghandab River Valley at one point with an emphasis on the battle of the Arghandab in 1987. There had been a huge push into the area involving artillery strikes that were followed by rolling in with tanks and heavy support from a motorized rifle brigade (mounted infantry). Funny thing about the whole ordeal was that they wrote a lot about the inability to move throughout the valley in any sort of mechanical capacity. The Russians suffered heavy losses due to a lot of the same things that the Stryker brigade had faced prior to our occupation. Our unit was able to circumvent these because we were light infantry and walked everywhere. After spending time in the valley, one can see how a minimal force could cause havoc to reign supreme on a large conventional unit trying to saturate the battlespace. The terrain and elements just don't allow it and they heavily favor an insurgency.

A lot of experimental gear and tactical equipment would be brought out to us, but we always found that the best way forward in the valley was usually something that was self-built from the environment that was surrounding us. There were a lot of situations that forced you to think outside of the box. This is a country where they would stack piles of luggage on city buses that were twice the original height of the bus and then pack it with people to transport to a neighboring district. It made me think of *Star Wars* elements combined with Bible stories alongside a healthy dose of modern explosives, technology, and terrorists all thrown into the mix. George Lucas would have been all over it. There were times when you would see the most bizarre things, like men shoveling concrete mixture three stories in height using a vertical assembly line that involved shovels and precision tossing. We coined what could be considered a bit of a racist term for the quirky but intelligent methods known as "Hajinuity."

When the Army would send us things like a "magic box" that could see through walls, we would use it once or twice, understand that it wasn't practical for what we needed, and figure out a way to render it "non-operational" so the powers that be couldn't force us to continually test it. A lot of the equipment was heavy as hell and then you have to consider that we had to carry it with us everywhere we walked. Special operators get to use some insane gear, but they literally fly in, make the hit, and fly out. Sure, give me a specific role on the hit squad of goon boys that has me running up the breach wall with a scanner for the first mad minute and then flow into the objective, but carry that bad boy across the Arghandab while crossing 10-foot-high walls, checking every wall along the way, and all while struggling with the standard 55+lbs of gear we already had on? No thank you.

The mine detector wands were mainly a false sense of confidence due to the metal content within the soil. Someone was flown out to calibrate the units in an attempt to tune out some of the noise from the metallic soil, but it was never perfect, and you were better off staying observant of the environment around you. Distance flags hung in a tree or soil differences in the pathway could tip you off there was a landmine up ahead. Constant scanning of the terrain in addition to your plethora of jobs on the battlefield is exhausting if you are doing it right. The more complex the terrain/area, the harder it can be on your senses.

We received another robot to use as we were searching for alternatives to waiting on EOD to arrive every other patrol because of the number of landmines we were finding. This one was smaller and supposed to be able to be tossed into a backpack. It proved to be a terrible use of resources because the tracks it was equipped with couldn't deal with the mud and soft soil of the area. The vehicle needed mud tires, not tracks, for this particular portion of the world. I could have quickly saved the developers a million dollars if they wanted an all-purpose IED finder that could work. Most of the youth that race RC cars could have come up with a design better than what the TALON robots provided. Just up the road, the track version would have worked great in the dry and desert-type areas that make up the majority of Afghanistan. We carried one of these robots out to an IED site and then it got stuck halfway to the suspected charge. One of the EOD team ended up jumping the wall to get the machine unstuck, just to have it become entangled just shy of the necessary point. Like I said… useless.

We were also given these electronic radio jamming devices that needed to be used in a sequence to create a bubble that would jam incoming RF. They technically worked, as one of the HQ patrols found out when they passed by a hay bale with an IED set up inside. The patrol had made it past when the damn thing exploded about 20m behind them. The charge must have been meant for the midpoint of the patrol which usually held the lieutenant, captain, or other leadership. We taught them well when the CIA trained the Mujahideen to fight a modern conventional force.

The large problem with these radio jamming manpack units was that they slowed us down, were a detriment if we took contact, and caused a lot of the guys to start having health issues. They weighed about 25lbs each, adding to the total weight of our current loadout, and were cumbersome. Guys kept getting headaches from wearing the damn packs and I was just happy that I had the radio with me, which kept me from having to wear one of them. I knew I was still being exposed, but not as badly as some of the guys. We saw the value in having something that could save our butts if it was a mine that utilized RF, but most everything used against us used a command wire to set off the charges, so the packs were useless.

Sgt Thomas decided to get rid of the "manpacks" when after we were leaving the wire, one of the guys' noses started bleeding accompanied by a splitting migraine. We immediately rerouted the patrol through one of the surrounding rivers and submerged the packs in the process. When I say submerged, I laugh because I want you to picture the large 250lb intimidating figure of Sgt Thomas leading the guys across a shallow river and halting midway through. This was waist-deep water and we set up security on either side because the nature of the canal would render a crossing squad useless. They were mid-river with the manpacks slightly submerged and the cooling fans sputtering as the units were taking in water and continued to attempt to cool off whatever secret squirrel equipment that was housed inside.

Half of the squad had no idea what was going on as they grumbled about being waist deep in Afghan river water that we have seen used for everything you could imagine. Irrigation source, clothes washing, water the flock as you pass through, get drinking water for the house, discard your bodily waste in the river, and drink directly from the river as you watch animals pee into it upstream from your location. You never knew what possible bacteria infected the waters, but you learned to ignore it. The team leaders knew what the end goal was and told the guys wearing the packs to take a knee in the water. Still not understanding, one of the guys protested and was jumped on by SPC Simas to get his ass down in that water or his day would be miserable when we got back in later.

As the manpacks overheated or succumbed to the onslaught of water they were exposed to, the mission was considered a success as the units would no longer power on or charge. We shuffled them off into a corner for repair in case a repair unit dared to come through and either repair or replace them. We were given a new set when we hit COP Johnston, but they never saw the light of day and were kept in a corner behind the RAID (Rapid Aerostat Initial Deployment) tower controls room in the TOC. The destruction of unnecessary gear was a task that had to be accomplished because if we didn't render the equipment inoperable and some sergeant major somewhere said they needed to be on, then they would need to be on our backs with no questions asked.

Some of the most effective methods for finding mines and exposing tripwires were found via ingenuity from our own guys. They thought up of IED defeat devices such as securing a baseball to a length of 550 parachute cord and having the point man throw the ball ahead of the patrol and drag it over the pathway we were about to walk. It was used to find any tripwire obstacles we couldn't see in our path. This tactic could be especially helpful in finding fishing wire that was used in fields at night and was designed set off a shallow-dug antipersonnel mine or grenade. One team member even used an adjustable wrench to throw out ahead of them as a drag weight at one point, but that would prove to catch on a lot of things. The most ingenious was when someone was sent a kid's fishing rod complete with lure weights to supply the ballast to reach out over the distance. Simple solutions would prove to be just as effective as a million-dollar product that was funded by the DoD. It further proved the disconnect between higher support echelons and the troops on the ground.

An addition to our growing pot of resources was a dog team that was sent to assist us by sniffing out explosive devices. A former Marine showed up and was now working as a contractor handling the bomb squad dogs. You would see a lot of this in Afghanistan as the funds that were doled out in a year's time easily amounted to what you would earn as a service member over a five-year period. Nice fellow, but most of the dogs they sent us were useless. One of the dogs found det cord on a mission that chained an explosives array together; however, it was one of the local dogs that joined us that proved to be more useful than his trained canine counterparts. It's like he learned the behaviors from the working dog crew but knew how to do the job better than they ever could.

There was a running order to shoot any local cats or dogs on the outpost as they carried diseases and were a risk, but no one had the heart to kill animals that were perfectly healthy and didn't pose any sort of problem or threat. Having one or two cats around the FOB can help out with any rodent issues that you may have, but if you don't watch it, you'll have two dozen of those little guys around spreading fleas, pissing everywhere, and creating a real mess of things if it's not controlled. Cat pee can be toxic and release a bacterium that causes Leptospirosis and other ear, nose, and throat issues. Not something you want to be dealing with in the middle of nowhere if a simple order can prevent it. Thankfully, it was never much of a problem and the base "pets" found refuge with us during our stay.

The locals in Afghanistan would keep dogs for another reason. They would use them as a guard source and that was the extent of their duties. A compound would just have a wild dog they had caught chained up in their compound courtyard or just outside and it would bark at any human or threat it might hear. They were barking mostly because they hated anything and everything that disturbed the bubble radius that was around them. The Afghans would beat the animals and leave them in the searing sun to serve as a proximity warning. They were thrown a hunk of whatever scraps of the meal might have been left over and were left malnourished and dying in the harsh elements of the countryside. At night, you would catch a glimpse of a pack of wild dogs that were roaming throughout the region and hunting whatever easy target they could exploit.

There was a lone Afghan mountain dog that showed up out of the blue one day. He seemed reasonable enough and didn't behave like the other dogs we had come across. It seemed that he may have encountered Americans before because he was friendly towards us, but if any Afghan got anywhere near him, he would growl and snap at them in a warning to not come any closer. I can't even remember how he came to live with us. I think he came back with us on one of the patrols and would spend most of his time at the entry to the COP or following our patrols into the town areas. He would halt with us, never made any noise, would bed down in a patrol base, and was a fantastic alert system. It was like he knew what we were doing and could have been a soul of a soldier reincarnated onto the battlefield in canine form.

Someone nicknamed the dog "Bowser" and the name stuck. That's how we ended up with one of the coolest local dogs in the country. He chased off the other dogs in the area, served as an early warning for the ECP and an additional deterrent for locals, and never took anything off anyone's plate unless it was given to him. He would just sit there and would never beg for anything. Scraps were always offered to him when we were finished and it's like he knew they were coming anyway, so he was patient. If there wasn't enough for him to be satiated, he would head out into town and would come back later to spend the night.

One night, we were out and headed into the town of Morgan when it seemed like every dog in the neighborhood wanted to announce our presence. There was barking and yapping from all over the town when Bowser reared up and let out a bark three times the size of himself (and he was a damn big dog already). Dead silence followed and nothing else barked at us that night. It was eerie, and only one of the strange occurrences we encountered while in the valley.

In contrast to the friendly local wildlife, we had instances of being stalked by other animals during the nights within the orchards of the Arghandab. The observation outpost that was overlooking the valley provided overwatch as we patrolled the valley below them. They were a helpful pair of eyes and could provide support by fire if needed. One of their capabilities was possessing some thermal vision goggles on the site. Yes, predator vision! They could see the overview more effectively that we could during the dark and cold nights and would observe the other creatures moving about the orchards during the night alongside us.

Something was tracking us one night as we moved through the pomegranate trees and towards the group of suspected compounds that we were to watch that night. Word was that they were a sort of guest room for Taliban migrant fighters. Halfway into the second walled-off orchard, the OP called us to report they had seen movement near us. We halted movement and the creature was spooked when we moved into a defensive position. The OP continued to watch and said they saw an Afghan bear moving away from our position. I didn't like the idea of being torn apart by a seven-foot-tall fur-covered killing machine that called the dangerous region his front doorstep.

Other instances were stranger still as some of the men whispered of paranormal instances and seeing things (that could have just been actual hallucinations due to sleep deprivation) such as Russian patrol units and Mujahideen fighters moving about during the night. I never experienced anything like that, but I did observe a few instances of a strange temperature drop that was local to a specific area. It was different than the goosebumps you feel during the "hair on the back of your neck" effect. The only other time I felt that way was in legitimate haunted areas. The sixth sense is a real thing. You have an ingrained sensor that tells you when something is not right... learn to listen to it.

There were times when you could see the fog of moisture as it was held under the green canopy and the scene felt like it belonged in the original *Predator* movie. Instead of the muscle-bound crew of the silver screen, you found yourself fumbling around the valley as an ill-equipped bastard on the front line. We tried moving in a wedge throughout the orchards, because a single file line is a terrible way to move tactically. It either increased our chances of hitting a land mine or would lose a guy during the night within a pitch-black orchard. Even night vision needs a little bit of lumen from the stars to work, but there were some nights that didn't provide that and consisted of an inky blackness that would suck you into the void. You could almost lose sight of your hand if you held it out at length in front of your own face.

There was no taking the roads as they were already packed with land mines. The enemy had adapted to putting ordnance into the ground so efficiently, they would place them behind your patrol as you traveled so if you retraced your patrol route, you would hit a landmine. Never retrace your patrol route while on a mission. Always find a different way back and constantly change your patterns of movement. It's tougher on your mind than one would think as your brain will follow the path of least resistance due to its programming. The habit is engrained into your psyche from birth and it takes a lot of work and effort to break it. If you ever found yourself passing an area a previous patrol had walked within a week prior, it was probably going to be a bad day.

This is a great example of the catchphrase known as "hard right over the easy wrong." When dumbed down it just means to always choose the harder path because the enemy is an expert in human psychology. They know that the human mind intends to follow comfort. The entire American culture has been built around comfort and convenience. What better way to undermine the very teachings that the empire, known as the United States of America, had engrained into their people for years? Seek comfort and convenience. It's the American way.

The other difficult task while adapting to the constantly changing environment was fighting the urge to settle for complacency. Don't ever go into a day-in and day-out routine when in the fight. That thinking kills faster than any other deficiency you might have. You had to stay sharp because the Afghans were always watching, and you needed to learn the rules of the game. We started to notice "farmers," contractors, or even the Afghan police counterparts on their cell phones when we would leave on patrol. They were obviously calling in our step-off time and the direction we were headed, so we started to plan the patrols to fool that discouraging element as well.

ECP guard was notified to watch the ANP that were stationed on our COP and to take note of who got on the phone and when. The patrol would then get out of sight and reroute over an area that would flank anyone trying to get the jump on us or laying anything in to blow us up. War is more complicated than people realize. Sometimes, you had suspicions about some of the other men there, but there was nothing that could be done... even though you wanted to drag the accused out back and put a bullet in his head.

The caution extended to some of the local contractors and interpreters that were supplied to us during base improvements in our area. Sgt Ackers and I had the clearances and classes to be able to use the Cellex machine. This box enabled us to capture information from cell phones. That info could then be cross-referenced with information from other captured phones. The enemy had been shipping professionals in to fight us, so no wonder some of these guys had the training they did.

Ackers created a new SOP (Standard Operating Procedure) that required any of the contracted locals and personnel to hand over their cell phones at the ECP location before the day's work began and they would get their phones back at the end of the day. We scanned everyone's cell phone as soon as we got them and found several videos of our guys casually talking to the interpreter. He was asking sensitive questions but in a way that wouldn't seem suspicious in conversation. The interpreter followed the same format that a lot of our agencies use when creating commonalities and building rapport with the target source. Before you knew it, they were talking about night vision capabilities and how we use thermal vision to see like the predator. Damn it... this guy was good.

The face of the young soldier we pulled in to talk to about the incident, with our intention of opening his eyes on how he had compromised information without even realizing, was beyond terrified. The look turned into disbelief and then anguish as he felt responsible for a casualty-producing IED that hit us the week prior. Anything he had mentioned was information the enemy already held on our capabilities. It wasn't even pertinent to the situation, but he didn't see it that way.

We were going to hammer him much harder about the incident to drill it into his head, but this kid was way harder on himself than we could have ever been. It was never meant to place blame in his mind, but the realization of just how brutal the consequences could be for a slip of the tongue put everything into perspective. We reported it and we never saw that interpreter again... such was life in the Arghandab River Valley.

The Move to COP Johnston

There was so much that I hated about COP Ware, but the biggest thing was the fact that we were right with the "flagpole." This meant that the guys were busy to the point of exhaustion. The constant race to improve on our position within the valley before fighting season set a breakneck pace that interrupted any sort of routine that used to be your sleep cycle. It was bad at times in Helmand, but nothing like this. Your existence just floated between duties and sleep with your only time of solitude being when you had a bowel movement. That wasn't even comfortable to do until they brought in a trailer to replace the trench that was dug for leaving human waste. There was a satellite communications array now, a chow facility, and even a shower trailer, but none of extra facilities was an even tradeoff for the op tempo we had to maintain. It was agreed that 1st Platoon would replace 2nd Platoon at what was now considered COP Johnston and 2nd Platoon would rotate into our duties on COP Ware. I think they were suckered in with the promise of showers and a cook.

Good luck with that! They could have the burn pit that was blowing smoke into your face as you stood in one of the guard positions from trash and various gear we would burn. The other lucky duty position needing completion after the outhouses were constructed was the constant battle of burning the human waste that was generated on the COP. The toil included a JP8 fuel jug and a long stirring stick to ensure a nice even burn of the poop soup being made as the black smoke billowed from the cutoff 50-gallon drum we would store underneath the outhouse to catch the solid waste.

There were plenty of those additional duties that I knew the guys wouldn't miss that came with the larger outpost. Chow hall duties, setting up additional tents for the support units when they arrived, trying to keep the rats out of your gear, unloading pallets of supplies when the next sling load would be flown in via Chinook, performing guard "tower" rotations, attending briefings, and actively patrolling with our squads whenever 1st Platoon would have a patrol. It was possible to be running missions one to two times a day depending on the purpose of the patrol. I think we were all a little burnt out from COP Ware and needed a change of scenery.

The aforementioned shower trailer had only been at COP Ware two or three weeks when we loaded up to clear the road and begin the transfer process from Ware to Johnston. When we arrived there was a mad scramble for a good bunk and I justified taking the far end of the tent so the person on TOC duty could bang on the wall and have me fix whatever commo equipment had broken in my brief absence. We had to go through the entire wiring of the outpost when we got there with one of the HHC guys, Kyle Weber, because we realized that the entire COP had been wired backwards. A lot of the electronics the guys from 2nd Platoon had plugged into the outlets had been acting up or ceased to work after too long as the phase was off what it should have been set. I'm not an electrical engineer, but the existing foreign wiring that had been there was the main culprit and it left the task of figuring out the situation to a few of us that had minor electrical skills.

This debacle led to me getting to know one of the replacements by the name of Sgt Barry Pilcher who had met us right after we left Helmand. Battalion had sent some guys in to replace the ones who were wounded or had disappeared during mid-tour leave and just not come back. One kid from California just disappeared and we never saw him again. Another shot off his own kneecap in an "accidental discharge" when home on leave. Harris ghosted us after the stress of killing those Taliban attackers outside of Lashkar Gah. It was signs like this that had me wondering how bad the situation was… what was I shutting out along the way? What was I desensitizing myself to? Was I crazy or a sociopath to adapt to this environment?

Barry was an Oklahoma kid that claimed he was a Texan because it was his place of birth. He was as southern Midwest hillbilly as they get and he fit right in with a lot of the backwoods southern residents of the States. One positive trait rednecks possess is they usually know their way around a motor and makeshift trailer wiring. Between myself, Barry, and Weber, we made improvements that allowed the system to work without it being a fire hazard at least. Generators are a weird thing and the progression from operating a simple 5k Army generator to a 50k Generac was another. I vowed to learn how to properly care for and use a generator after that because of the knowledge value it provides within a disaster area if you ever find yourself in one.

Because he came from a family of backyard mechanics, Barry turned out to have some basic knowledge in welding and a bit of mechanical prowess. Some of those skills only come with possessing a bit of life experience to go along with it. My favorite soldiers were the farm kids because they were already acclimated to hard work, they were tough as hell, and they had a good amount of common sense that came with them. The foundation for kids that grew up in farming communities prior to their military service is a damn good one that will work to their favor.

After the wiring was sorted, we realized the air conditioning unit that powered the climate and ventilation in the two Alaskan tents we were housed in was not working. There was no way to get another unit or a repair, so it just ended up blowing hot air around the living area which we supplemented with some fans that were sent forward by my family. They held a large roadside tag sale and the proceeds from it purchased some stuff that we could use in our current spartan environment. Most everything that came in was distributed evenly, but Weapons squad would internally get the first dibs, to be succeeded by the other squads within the platoon via the trickledown effect. Some hats were made up for the platoon that were based on some artwork that Doc Shultz scribbled onto paper in his off time. We also received a dozen "just add water" pancake mixes sent forward and I put those aside because there wasn't a way to cook them just yet. Not properly anyway. Maybe the Afghans would let me use their frying pan one day if I shared some of the hotcakes with them. They were friendly enough.

Because I was issued a few tough boxes full of sensitive items that needed to be locked up, along with all the other assigned gear in my possession, I managed to acquire an entire top and bottom bunk area while living on COP Johnston. It probably left the impression that I was an asshole because the space was at a premium. However, no one showed any hate towards me at COP Johnston other than the occasional spat. Maybe it was just because I had found a way to integrate into the hustle needed around the outpost or maybe because I would fix computers for the guys and bring in new games for their now jailbroken PSPs. The job of an RTO is considered a bit of a nerd gig anyway, but it allowed some access on COP Johnston as I was able to stay fairly squad neutral because of the position. However, at some point, I started to shut myself off to getting to know any of the new guys because they just hadn't been seasoned yet and were too new to be considered one of the guys.

A group of us had received orders from the Army immediately after we departed COP Ware and I had some that were sending me to Fort Lewis after we returned to Bragg. I needed to figure out how to make it through the current battle we were engaged in and drop off a Special Forces packet with a selection date before human resources could transfer me to Fort Lewis. If I transferred posts before it could arrive at selection, it would cause a wait of another year before I could re-apply. At that point, I would be deployed with the unit out there and facing the identical situation next rotation. Fortunately, I secured a December selection class that left the day after Thanksgiving with an end date 10 days before my report date in Washington State. It was motivation to pass because clearing Bragg and making that move in a 10-day time period is impossible. If I could acquire a class date using a satellite phone and intermittent email from a battlespace theater 10+ years ago, you have no excuse these days if you say you can't attend the tryouts.

Because we had no attachment in the position, I fell into the place of a "tech guy" category and the guys from my past still refer to me as an IT geek, even though I am far removed at this point. There was a saying that I dumped on the guys when they would ask if I could fix a piece of tech, whether it was the military equipment or personal. I would jest and spoke as if I was communicating with in a Neanderthal: "YES! I make box work." After reimaging and tuning up SFC Hill's personal laptop (he was promoted around the time of the move), I gained the benefit of having a blind eye turned to some of my antics.

I had a minicomputer with me that I had purchased during mid-tour leave. It was loaded with a form of Linux operating system because I had wanted to attempt to learn coding as we were deployed and promised that we would have more free time as we became established in the area. All of the IP and MAC addresses that were designated to the 25B (IT technician) that was attached to us on COP Ware were posted on the side of one of the network stacks in the satellite array control rack. I assumed that everything went through a single hub for this slice of the theater, so I replicated his MAC address and changed some of the network permissions for Facebook usage on our node of communications. I doubt whatever I did affected anything, but the next day, all of the computers within the Afghan theater were able to log into Facebook over the NIPR network and our 25B disappeared. I swear there is no possibility of my actions resulting in those coincidences. I hope not anyway. From what I understand, he didn't want to be there anyway.

COP Johnston was a weird place because it had originally been an ANP station that consisted of a connex thrown on an elevated rock with a few Hescos strategically placed around the perimeter. We had no real guard towers except for some rickety stands that 2nd Platoon had built when they had arrived. It allowed someone to fire a machine gun off the Hescos while standing on a supported scaffolding construction. They made perfect secondary guard tower positions after the full-sized towers were constructed by contractors.

One perk was realized immediately as we no longer had to burn our poop; the locals provided a porta-potty service that would empty the three blue units directly behind the ECP. It was a strange occurrence to watch a septic truck roll up to a combat outpost and take care of the produced waste for the week. The other intelligent act was moving the burn pit outside of our walls to stop the smoke from blowing into the faces of everyone on the place. It would float around the base of one of the towers and the ECP location, but it was better than breathing it in all the time.

Imagine a station within Afghanistan that possessed 28 US troops and five Afghan police officers existing on a slight hill outside of boomtown. Villagers would pass by all day and we would offer a friendly wave sometimes. Sometimes, we would have to shoot off a pen flare that was placed in the tower with us or point a green laser at them if the locals were acting suspicious or became a little too curious. For the most part, they never bothered us, and we didn't bother them either. We occasionally utilized the local "Uber Eats" and a local kid would drop by once a week to bring us pitas and flatbread for a few dollars. It was enough to feed a squad of Afghans for a week and we would devour it in one sitting in less than 30 minutes.

The situation of standoff was accepted by most of the locals. The area was dangerous enough to warrant the high need for security in case the enemy wanted to drive a Vehicle-Borne IED (VBIED) up to the front gate or next to a compound wall. The area was not a friendly one and there was a main road that could supply a threat in the form of a large vehicle laden with explosives. Thousands of cars passed by there daily without a checkpoint to slow them down. Police checkpoints dotted the hills all over the area, but the officers would rarely leave the wire, smoked hashish throughout the day, and sometimes were just Taliban spies. They would even occasionally shoot at us as we moved through the valley while going past the grape field areas. The ANP weren't great shots though… so I'm not sure if that was a plus or a minus. You would hear the various zips and pops and would need to stand tall and wave for a second for them to realize you weren't a hostile.

COP Johnston possessed the one police commander from the area that was considered to be any good. He was an Afghan commando that dropped his commission within the commando forces to serve with the ANP in an attempt to root out the corruption issues that plagued the inside of the organization. When we had first gotten there, he had handpicked men with him and was a great resource. His guys weren't the best, but they were loyal and would still come out with us without getting in the way. That was about the best you could ask for if you were stuck in this neck of the Wild West.

Nearby the commander's hut, the interpreters were set up in a GP Medium tent that was on the far end of the COP along with the police that were assigned to our location. I don't know why the Afghan interpreters had a propensity to be named for Italian fashion houses, but we also had an "Armani" in the mix along with other Americanized names the troops could easily remember.

The families of the interpreters would hear of events within the country and warn their kids to either take a break from the job for a season or switch unit assignments if possible. After the move to the Arghandab, and we began to have a lot of trouble getting any quality interpreters assigned to our area of the country.

The squad leaders were put in another tent across from the Afghans, on the top of the rock we were on. Two Alaskan tents that were set up facing each other served as the housing for the rest of the troops consisting of the lower enlisted and their team leaders. Lastly, a wooden shack that abutted the left side Alaskan tent served as the communications area with the platoon sergeant and lieutenant living out of bunks in a rear sectioned-off area in the shack. The radio equipment was right next to where my bunk was at the far end of the tent. This enabled whoever was on TOC guard to bang on the wall for me to fix communications if they failed at any time. The communications situation was so shaky within the valley that we had constant interruptions due to either equipment failures, the wind knocking out our peer-to-peer antenna, or we had a briefing to attend.

The other nice part about COP Johnston was being integrated into the TOC guard rotation as opposed to being in the towers. The job was no breeze and the shifts where different than the towers, but damn, it way better than the brutal tower shifts. While it could be a boring task to sit in a guard tower for six hours at a time, base protection was a necessary evil while operating out of COP Johnston. We had a guy with us serving in one of the other platoons that had been on an outpost when the 173rd was overrun due to a sentry falling asleep while on guard. The Taliban cut the sleeper's throat and proceeded to let the rest of the assault element into the outpost. Not something I wanted to happen to us. Being hemmed up for nodding off or bringing a book on guard was a better alternative to being dead. It's about perspective. War isn't pretty, nor its tactics sometimes… but damn it was a steep learning curve.

The last thing you would ever want to do would be to miss a detail that led to an attack or fall asleep. The sergeant on guard (SOG) would rove around and talk to guys for a little bit to try to keep them awake, but there was a balance that needed to be maintained and four towers plus an ECP on top of patrolling would grind on everyone. You would find yourself creating narratives for people in your head or masturbating to stay awake during the long shift. Yeah, the secret of the infantry on guard… when you have tried chew tobacco, stories, songs, talking to yourself, cycling between cleaning weapons, and everything else you can imagine, you will still start to drift off as your body fights you internally for sleep. There is less shame in the SOG coming around and catching you with your dick in your hand than letting yourself drift off.

Most everyone was pretty discreet about, it but damn, I wouldn't want to go anywhere near those towers with a black light. The shine would probably instantly blind you. One such indiscretion was that a former guard sentry had forgotten to grab tissues or whatever his method was of getting rid of the mess. He grabbed the first thing he saw when the moment came and beat off into a bag of "Squincher" drink powder.

The government has all sorts of products that resemble the civilian name brand, such as Gatorade. It's akin to entering the dollar store and seeing generic versions of the products. It never quite tastes the same, but it gets the job done good enough. Think about that the next time you buy "mil spec." The environment was so hot in the towers that they would place a bag of drink powder mix into each tower so you could put some in your canteen or Nalgene bottle while you were slowly dehydrating in the heat of the day. The salt could help replenish what your body craved… electrolytes. This kid forgot to remove the damn bag with him and the next poor bastard apparently loaded up on powder on his shift. The joke went on that something in the water tasted funny as he called up the SOG to ask about it just as the offender realized what he had forgotten to take with him when his rotation ended. I don't think the bags of supplied electrolyte powder were ever touched after that incident was made known.

The squad leaders took on the task of rotating as the SOG and checked on the towers along with occasional TOC shifts added in. We had to run missions the entire time, but the amount relaxed a bit and allowed us to get a little bit more sleep time to regain some of our sanity. Maybe it wasn't that there was more time, but that you could count on the structure more with fewer people to deal with. Even with that small additional bit of time, it seemed to be always interrupted with something that needed to be accomplished, someone needed something, or there was a task that needed additional guys.

We had finally gotten the wiring straight on the generator when it started to act up. Something within the voltage boards had malfunctioned and it wasn't providing electricity anymore. It was probably because of the backwards polarities and preexisting wiring that had been used up until that point. All of a sudden, a second huge 50k generator arrived and was placed right next to the first one we had… and it was just as non-operational. What we needed was a generator tech, but what we had to work with was some redneck ingenuity and trial and error. Either way… we made it work because we had to.

In addition to the large generator units, there was a little Army 5k generator running the TOC area. A purpose-built piece of equipment for the Army can be some truly rugged stuff. If they were priced the same as something from Home Depot, I wouldn't hesitate to buy a leftover generator unit from the government. They come with phases, plugins, a Faraday cage, and will run forever on just one tank of whatever fuel source you have on hand. That generator took so much abuse from the elements and was only down for 10 minutes the entire time we were stationed on that hill. It had been used heavily within Helmand province as well because of the need to maintain a communications presence separately from the supplied local power source. One of the duties was filling up on fuel every shift to make sure of constant operation, but that was all part of shift duties that were divvied up among the various positions. The essential "chore list" needed to be done in a timely and orderly fashion or your situation would quickly spiral if the delicate balance was interrupted.

It's something incredible to watch a group of 28 soldiers dropped into the middle of a tense situation that requires a massive amount of attention to detail and come out just fine. These guys shouldered the burden of responsibility that far surpassed anything that anyone their age would normally be expected to and they excelled at it. The cohesion and rapport built within the walls of those Hescos were bonds that would last far beyond the time spent there.

The other interesting aspect in these situations is the realization of just what it takes to successfully run a small village or town in an apocalyptic situation. You might think that you have all the information down by watching "doomsday preppers" or *The Walking Dead* episodes, but you'll never know exactly what it's like until you are there yourself. There was a large whiteboard where we would have to report the numbers every morning that included what supplies we had on hand. Re-supply would only come once a month and would be sling loaded in a bundle that would be dropped in the field outside of COP Johnston. It wasn't too much different than having to offload the pallets from COP Ware, but we had to set in our own security because there were no walls. We had to be quick enough to get everything loaded up before someone could take some shots at us with their weapon of choice.

Murphy will happen. Rats will get into a food connex or the water bottle supply that you were given was tainted by being left out in the sun for a month. The water source you receive while operating as an American soldier in a large-scale combat zone is usually a plastic Dasani bottle that arrives in massive, shrink-wrapped pallet form that sits out in a desert field or flightline that is open to the sun. This particular batch didn't just have the typical cancer being leached into it due to the low-grade manufactured plastic, but it also contained E. coli! The water situation got bad that month and it was to the point where we had to ration its usage.

The human waste management system on COP Johnston had its own pluses and minuses as the blue plastic huts are just as conducive to heat there as they are anywhere in the world. We didn't have to burn the waste, but the 120-degree weather would create a venerable sauna out of the units. Walking into one, even at night, was a real experience. If you dared to use the shack with your uniform on, you came out looking like you had gone swimming.

A huge concern was voiced over the porta-potties because while on a previous deployment, this very unit exposed a ploy where the insurgents of the region kidnapped the septic truck driver and held him for ransom with the demand of money for the return of the driver and truck. At first, they refused… but then the waste began to pile up. It became so bad within the walls of their compound that the men pooled their own money together just to get the damn septic service up and running again. Funniest use of tactics that I have ever heard of, but effective. Thankfully, we never experienced that, but there was talk of explosives being outfitted to the truck… so we ended up having to clear it every time it came by to offload the sweatboxes for the week.

Bathroom habits were something of a nuisance to deal with when you had different walks of life and nationalities living together in such close proximity. We ended up needing to have segregated "bathrooms" because of how the culture of the area would utilize the restroom. These porta-let units were made for Western culture and had the standard raised seating area. In most countries within that region of the world, they squat to relieve themselves. This required a bathroom stall that is basically two sections for the occupant's feet and a hole in the ground. This does not translate when using an American porta-potty. Afghan nationals would stand on our toilet seats and created a river of waste coating the interior of the huts. There would be dung up the side of the wall, toilet paper left all over the place and trailing out the door, and the area would never be clean after they left. It led to us having to assign one of the units a separate bathroom because of the conflicting hygiene standards. Just another one of the challenges we faced while working hand in hand with the foreign forces.

The situation regressed to being without showers again, but if we had some extra water lying around that wasn't drinkable, such as the E. coli stuff that now filled the rear storage area, we could load up some solar shower bags that were sent out and have a hot shower within 20 minutes due to the sunlight. I was only granted that luxury once during our time stationed on COP Johnston, but the experience was glorious and not one to ever be forgotten. SPC Cannon was nearby manning one of the lower wall security points and harassed me as I lathered up in a little in the makeshift shower stall that consisted of two plywood sheets.

Life's little pleasures are more recognized after experiences like that and you start to enjoy the simple things that life can afford you after going without for so long. I know that I have the ability to live through just about any situation life could ever throw at me after life in that area, but why the hell would you ever want to when you can push yourself a little bit, and live better than royalty of a period only 500 years ago. The fact that we live in an age of convenience and comfort became very apparent.

At some point, a group of SeaBees traveled through to survey the area surrounding the outpost in relation to the town to calculate if they could engineer a way to enlarge COP Johnston into a size that could provide a truly fortified posting that could support operations within the valley. They couldn't believe the conditions we were living in and stated that they hadn't seen anything this austere in quite some time. I had thought we were doing pretty good considering where we had come from. Almost a month before we left, we were sent a shower trailer, a freezer connex, and a bunch of other improvements that had the bleak scene of COP Johnston looking up. There was even a portable kitchen on a trailer brought in for the cook that we had attached to us to use. He hadn't don't much of anything up until now... and would need to be yelled at even more often now that his excuse of not being able to prepare a hot meal without resources was no longer valid.

One morning, I woke up the cook early to help me navigate firing up the griddle on the trailer to surprise the guys with some breakfast of my own doing now that I had a way to cook things. Breakfast was finished and being doled out right in between a guard rotation and a patrol that was coming back from a long night They were beat. Those containers of instant Bisquick came in handy after all and I had found a pound of butter from the cook's supply and was determined to use enough of it to drench every hotcake that came off that griddle that morning. That's pretty much my signature pancake... enough butter to cause your system to go into shock. There's nothing better than getting something so unexpected when you are going through hell. Simple pleasures.

Other hilarious memories at COP Johnston involved a few of us in weapons squad raiding the freezer to unload an entire 5-gallon tub of Ben & Jerry's ice cream between a few of us armed with metal spoons that we had stolen from the DFAC (dining facility) back in KAF as we rolled through at one point. We cut the lock that the cook had put on the freezer as we were fed up listening to his micromanaging of the food sources. He was an E4 that acted like the soup nazi from *Seinfeld* with anything involving his field of work. His concerns were valid seeing we might take advantage of accessing the food supply too frequently if given the opportunity, but he hadn't been there with us for very long.

Most of Bravo Company together for a rare moment while staying at the ANCOP located in Lashkar Gah, Helmand province. (Supplied by Kyle Weber)

Linking up with Afghan National Police counterparts to provide training along with the intent of further international relations with the Afghan populace. The shells of vehicles at the bottom of the hill are a grim reminder of how dangerous it was to travel through Helmand province. (Supplied by Hector Trujillo)

Getting ready to carve the turkey and serve the troops Thanksgiving dinner at the ANCOP facility in Lashkar Gah. Shown right to left are 1SG McAlister, CPT Adam Armstrong, SPC Chris Wiesner, SPC Jason Johnston, SPC Joshua Leeson. (Supplied by Hector Trujillo)

Sweeping for landmines off the highway in Helmand province.

Half of the bridge caved in on the MaxxPro MRAP vehicle while crossing over the canal. The road infrastructure in the country was not meant to handle the size of the equipment we would travel in. Vehicle rollovers had a high possibility of fatalities. (Supplied by Kyle Weber)

Sgt Allen Thomas (right) overlooking the highway along with Sgt Tyler Anderson (left). (Supplied by James Lee)

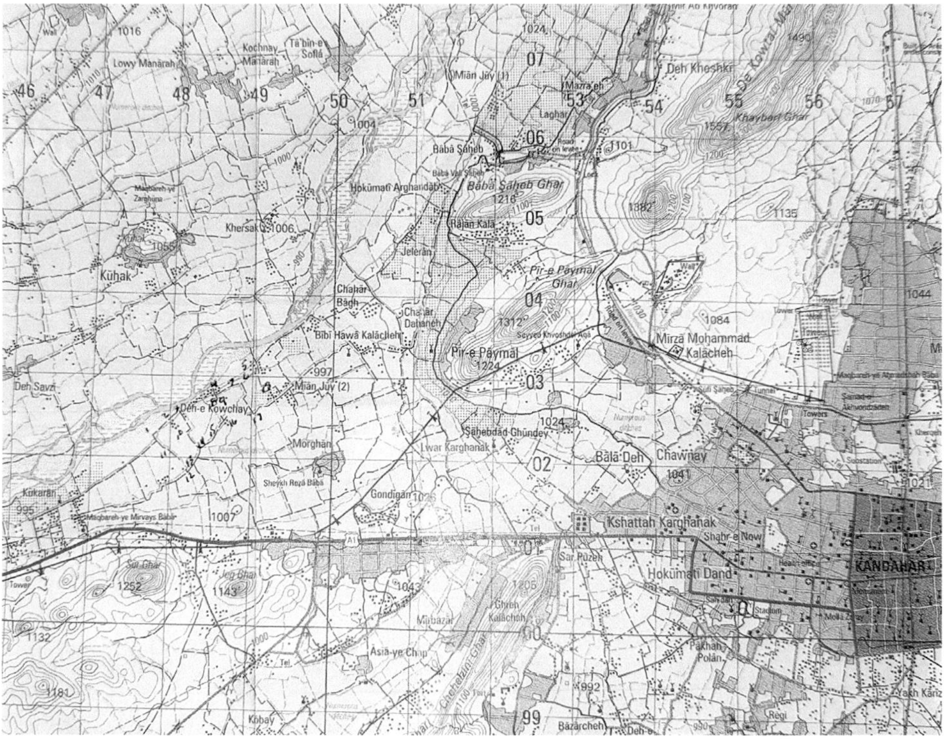

The typical sight of the living conditions the Afghan police were afforded by their government funding. (Supplied by Hector Trujillo)

Even in such a small area of operations that was roughly a 2.5 mile square, you would find landmines throughout the Arghandab in what was estimated by LTC David Flynn and his staff to be as densely as every 200 feet scattered throughout the region. (Map supplied by Mathew Hill)

The view from the front gate of COP Johnston. (Supplied by Lyle Pressley)

View from the rear of a Chinook helicopter as the tail gunner watches the Arghandab River Valley fade away in the distance. You can recognize the mountain in the center frame along with the river to the far left. (Supplied by Zachary Morton)

1st Platoon systematically clearing one of the surrounding towns after arriving in the Arghandab River Valley. (Supplied by Mathew Hill)

The upper roads in the villages above COP Ware needed to be kept clear as it was vital to maintain a constant line of communication to reach higher command further off down the road that they would clear in the opposite direction. (Supplied by Kyle Weber)

We had to sleep whenever and wherever we could at times. If we had an hour or two of time, it was best used in getting a nap because you didn't know what the next hour would bring. (Supplied by Mathew Hill)

SPC Rudy "Doc" Ponce hamming it up with SPC Joshua Simas while getting a minute on a combat patrol through an orchard during the winter months. The camouflage pattern is UCP-D which was a test variant we were fielded in an attempt to better conceal our position. Simas is wearing a Thor III dismounted CREW system which caused other issues altogether. (Supplied by Mathew Hill)

Sgt Scott Brunkhorst getting ready to leave COP Ware on a combat patrol with other members of 1st Platoon. You can see the fabric of the Hesco barriers flapping in the wind as they had nothing in them and were essentially a giant façade around the outpost exterior. Pictured from right to left are SPC William Ross, Sgt Scott Brunkhorst, and Sgt Barry Pilcher. (Supplied by Mathew Hill)

Doc Way fording a canal along with other members of Bravo Company. We would vary our patrol routes to mitigate risk and one way to slip under the watchful eyes of the enemy was to use the canal systems that flowed throughout the valley. As long as you had overwatch pulling security, you would be able to follow the streams for a while before needing to exit due to depth or current strength that day. (Supplied by Lyle Pressley)

The walls throughout the valley created challenges of their own. You couldn't follow the road due to the landmine activity. However, you couldn't just walk over the landscape either. Sometimes, the enemy would rig the walls with explosives as well, so you had to choose your path wisely. (Supplied by Kyle Weber)

Examining a command wire set to detonate a nearby IED. Spotters would lie in wait and watch for the perfect moment to trigger a blast for the maximum desired effect of death, dismemberment, or disillusion. (Supplied by Lyle Pressley)

A view of COP Johnston from guard tower 1 which was located above the entry control point. (Supplied by James Staples)

View from guard tower 4 that was just opposite of tower 1. The town of Morgan is on the hill to the right portion of the picture frame. (Supplied by James Staples)

C.O.P. JOHNSTON
IN
HONOR
OF
SPC JASON M. JOHNSTON
K.I.A. 26TH DEC 2009
B co 1ST PLT 2-508
P.I.R.

B co

DAMN the VALLEY

1ST PLT

SGT JAKE
(DOC)
5 AUG 2010 SCHULTZ

The sign that was hung outside of the TOC on COP Johnston. Artwork was done by Sgt Jake "Doc" Schultz during his stay with 1st Platoon. (Supplied by Chris Wiesner)

The lineup of boots outside of the Alaskan tents that served as the main living quarters on COP Johnston. Guys would leave their wet boots there to dry out after they came back from a patrol and pick up their second set on the way back inside the tent. The rotation would go on and worked well as long as you shook out your boot to ensure nothing had crawled into it during the stay outside. However, as soldiers would be hit while out on patrol, their boots would remain on the shelf outside to be joined by other sets that were either drying for reuse or discarded due to breakdown from the elements. (Supplied by Mathew Hill)

The 3rd Platoon MRAP that hit an IED and ejected SPC Michael Verardo out of the turret during the rollover. Ultimately, everyone was declared fit to return to duty as the newly designed protective measures within the vehicle had done their job. (Supplied by James Walker)

COP Brunk I was established in the town of Deh-e Kowchay to restrict enemy movement throughout the region. It was clear that this particular town housed the main body of problems we were dealing with at the time. 2nd Platoon was tasked with securing the area and manning the outpost while the other platoons would perform interlocking patrol movements in conjunction with their efforts. (Supplied by Lyle Pressley)

The rubble of COP Brunk I after the Taliban used a suicide bomber driving a VBIED with 1,000lbs of explosives rigged to explode in it. The outpost was a total loss and over half the men of 2nd Platoon were sent to KAF to be checked out by the flightline medics. The cover picture is the flag being unearthed during the aftermath and restrung over what was left of the outpost in a clear message that we would not be leaving the area. (Supplied by Lyle Pressley)

Members of 2nd Platoon sitting on the riverbank while coming down off of the adrenaline high that the VBIED incident had caused. (Supplied by Lyle Pressley)

Casevac UH-60 Blackhawk landing on the riverbed in the Deh-e Kowchay area. (Supplied by Kyle Weber)

Rooftop where SPC James Staples and SPC Chris Wiesner fired from after getting attacked with a pineapple grenade tossed at us while settling into a patrol base. Apparently, the neighbors weren't too friendly. (Supplied by Chris Wiesner)

2nd squad preparing to leave on a combat patrol from COP Johnston. (Supplied by Hector Trujillo)

The view from Antenna Checkpoint ANP station. The police on the checkpoint had a position that wasn't too far off from the Deh-e Kowchay area, which made them a little jumpy. They would occasionally shoot at us as we would cross the fields below their position. (Supplied by Hector Trujillo)

Sgt Jake "Doc" Schultz sharing an MRE with a local while attempting to explain the concept of the food the American soldiers brought with them. (Supplied by Mathew Hill)

Lt Vincent Demarest talking with a group of locals on the streets within the town of Morgan. (Supplied by Mathew Hill)

Sgt Sanchez and PFC Martinek taking a break in the water tank holding area located on COP Johnston. The temperature would remain approximately 20 degrees cooler here and was considered a welcome temporary escape from the normally inhabited areas. (Supplied by Mathew Hill)

Journalist Bill Neely taking the 150m run on the small stretch afforded us on COP Johnston. We had a makeshift "gym" area with a few TRX straps and various weighted equipment we would use on occasion. There wasn't much room, but if you wanted to get stronger, you would find ways to make it work. (Supplied by Mathew Hill)

Former members of Bravo Company 2/508 showed up en masse to a pilot program dubbed "Operation *Resiliency*" that was developed to reconnect soldiers in a peer-to-peer support function. (Supplied by Lindsay Hart)

The cook had been attached to us from somewhere in HHC and showed up eager to do a job that just didn't exist for him yet. He was also a POG (Person other than Grunt) and we didn't trust him to go on patrol with us or stand guard. He wasn't in shape to be doing so anyway… he wasn't obese, per se, but he wouldn't have made it on a 1km movement through the conditions we were forced into constantly. Because there wasn't much for him to do, he quickly became lazy. So, when the kitchen showed up and he was expected to have hot chow up and running the very next day, he got to experience a slice of "situation black" like I did.

After that, it's no wonder that he went and locked up the food connex and held onto the key like it was part of the nuclear access code system that included the fabled red button. The guys on the COP would not have emptied the pantry given the chance, but the Afghan police would have been on it like locusts in a heartbeat. We had received replacement police at one point that were not anything like the original crew the ANP commander possessed previously. The cook was bullied around a bit, not because he was any less than us, but he would bitch about the situation he was in while not having to experience the same level of suck that we did outside of the wire. I realize that all the jobs, support or not, are relevant. An infantry soldier signs up to do what they do as well as a cook doing what they do. Both are needed and relevant jobs, but both are different in their challenges. Still, he took a lot of crap from the guys on the posting.

Some of the guys looked pretty emaciated at times during our time on COP Johnston and the outpost always reeked of the alcohol that was being secreted by our bodies. This wasn't from ingestion. This was muscle breakdown as the body wasn't getting proper nutrition and your system would burn an insane amount of calories per day. You could graze on food all day, which is the best method if you can, and not gain a pound from it. The reason you want to graze is allowing you to have a fuel reserve if the ability to eat is hampered by a 12- to 24-hour period where you get stuck in a fight.

Family from back home would send out four giant protein jugs a month that would arrive with the monthly mail drop. It only came periodically, so I would always have at least two 16 sq in boxes arrive every time. The guys would look for them because they knew something would probably be handed out to the squad. Everyone was extremely honest about respecting their relative areas within the living areas. When you are living in close proximity to one another all the time, there is bound to be friction, so it was kept at a minimum through a type of code that translated to trust.

One of the strategic things about Johnston was the ability to have clear communications throughout the valley, whereas you would lose touch with COP Ware somewhere in the orchards between it and the nearby town of Deh-e Kowchay. The other strategic importance was serving as a cork that plugged access from the main road across the river. TOC duty in COP Johnston was critical because it had the ability to relay anything needed from patrols within the region to either COP Ware or the HQ unit that resided on the mountainside.

There was a strange peer-to-peer antenna that resembled some of the modern Ubiquiti wireless antenna systems that can handle providing a broadband network using point-to-point routers and access points. There was nothing like it that I was aware of, but what I did know is that the box needed to be in near perfect alignment with the receiver to work properly. A slightly audible high-pitched chirp would sound every so often to verify signal lock. The interval ranged from an almost constant tone with a good lock or intervals up to two seconds the further off target it was aimed. Speeds would be a full 200kBs for one minute and then the wind would kick up and you were knocked off lock. One of those frustrations we needed to deal with because it was about the only way of receiving outside information from the world back home. You would only have one 10-minute call via intermittent satellite phone coverage per month, and even then, sometimes you just didn't want to talk to anyone. We set up two computers for the guys to use and there would be a rotation to use them every so often which made the TOC a good spot for some company.

Another battlespace surveillance equipment piece brought out was something they called a RAID tower that possessed a wild array of camera technology onboard. The visual technology was perched on a 150ft collapsible tower that could see via night vision, thermal, and visual over the distance of a mile. Monitoring the tower became the job of the TOC and sergeant on guard as you could keep an eye on local activity during the nighttime, which was when they would lay in ordnance. This, combined with the various OP positions nested in the mountains, gave us a decent view of the larger open areas. It didn't have the ability to cover everything, but it helped us establish some of the local patterns we couldn't see otherwise, and follow up with an investigation of any suspicious activity. A huge blimp that hung over the skies of Kandahar had the same capabilities but at a massive scale with arrays that covered miles of the sprawling desert city. Very much like some of the traffic camera blimps that are in urban areas around the United States these days.

Patrols from Johnston

In assuming responsibility of COP Johnston from 2nd Platoon, we needed to learn new patrol areas within the section along with the inhabitants living in the villages. It was a smaller area of operations that overlapped with the patrols of the other platoons, but it had challenges and benefits of its own. For example, we were now nearby a bazaar and could sometimes stop by a local cigarette vendor within the village we were adjacent to.

The only cigarettes we had available locally were these godawful creations called Pines and a Japanese brand that was slightly less awful by the name of Seven Stars. We only convoyed to Kandahar on one occasion in the time that we were there, so my carton of Camel orange smokes were long gone. I don't know why the packs were yellow or orange, but they came from a French store that was located on the boardwalk within KAF. It was the best you could find in the way of a decent cigarettes. The locals didn't even like their locally sourced addiction and would "trade" me for cigarettes occasionally. While diminishing my personal supply, we would sit and talk for a brief time. I knew those guys were ripping me off, but it might come in handy down the road as it humanized you to the people that lived within the area.

During a presence patrol near the bazaar one day, one of the locals that had traded smokes with me back at COP Ware recognized me as we were moving through town. "WOOSH!" he yelled from a distance as he approached our patrol, coming from the opposite direction. He alerted us to some activity down the road from us, but as with most information we were handed, it just made us a little more aware as we moved through. Who knows the real intent or motive behind the warning, but if anything, it could be that he had been trying to look out for us. That was an occurrence that hadn't happened before.

Hard Right Over Easy Wrong—March 12

Specialist Josh Feeback was behind Zach Morton as 1st squad was being shown the various areas that 2nd Platoon had encountered the last few months on patrol. He didn't understand a lot of what was going on and was just following the guy in front of him. He found that he would drive himself nuts if he started going down the rabbit hole of questioning the tactics of his leadership. He saw value in some of the procedures, but others just seemed off. Why were both of the SAW gunners bunched together in the patrol movement? It was just one of the strange behaviors during the patrol that day. SFC Frazier was pointing out the questionable areas while directing Sgt Ackers about the particular nuances they had faced in Deh-e Kowchay up to this point.

Frazier was in the process of signing over the mounds of equipment stored at the COP Johnston location. Anyone that has done any government work knows that ultimately, someone has to be responsible for all this equipment. Somewhere down the line, an obscure piece of equipment with a serial number will be asked for and it won't be produced. At this time, the company or battalion supply will dig into their records and magically produce paperwork that shows exactly who is responsible for paying for said item. I saw plenty of guys get hit hard in the pockets for one thing or another over the years. When you are responsible for and signed off on about $9 million of government-owned property, you tend to get paranoid about making sure that each and every thing on that list is accounted for. I had my own stack of hand receipts because SFC Hill had sub-signed it all over to me. At which time, I broke everything down by squads and had all the squad leaders sign for it all.

Feeback just kept getting a funny feeling. They had fanned out into wedges in the fields when he was used to walking in a file due to the dense orchards. He had learned not to ask questions though… his team leader had made sure of that. SPC Simas could be brutal at times and would expect his team to listen for the command and execute immediately and without question.

Simas' unrelenting attitude towards immediate and unquestioning obedience could have been from his past experience in the military. He had been on the invasion of Iraq along with 1SG Mcalister and had seen his own fair amount of firefights in the past. Even though he was only a specialist, he had been around long enough to be able to pick up the demeanor of a sociopathic NCO with a penchant for punishment. Feeback remembers the time the team was forced to do pushups in the hot sand to the point that he had developed blisters on his hands after the sergeant on guard had found a book in the guard towers after his shift. He had tried to interject but was shoved back into the earth with the rest of them. There was no talking to Simas when he was like this, so why bother… just put up with the abuse because it would eventually pass and he would be smiling again within 10 or so minutes.

As they moved onto the roads, Feeback's uneasy feeling got worse. His head raced. This place was littered with mines. That's why they had moved through the orchards the way they did. Were things different over in the COP Johnston area? 1st Platoon had only been there for a few days and the surrounding area was a different reality than the patrols he had run out of COP Ware. There had to be a reason though because Frazier had been out here for months while 1st Platoon were sucking wind with the high op tempo the commander had them running out of COP Ware.

Suddenly, a portion of wall blew up about 5 feet from Feeback and tossed Morton in the air like a rag doll. It was like a movie scene as Feeback woke up, his ears ringing from the blast. His brain was following a reboot procedure that others had described to him after they had been in a blast a few months ago. His senses were slowly coming back online as the body of Zach Morton came into focus.

Morton was on the ground and covered in blood. Feeback had to get to him. He didn't think he had been hurt himself, or at least not badly, so his sense of urgency to start looking over Morton was growing the more he became aware of his surroundings. That's when James Staples and SFC Frazier arrived on the scene and went into trauma mode as they needed to figure out where the source of injury was.

Everyone had been rocked by the blast fairly heavily and there were various fragments of metal embedded in the guys that had been hit. A four-inch-long flat metal fragment was lodged in Morton's back and blood started pouring out of the wound when SFC Frazier dug the chunk out of his back. As they were plugging the hole in an attempt to stop the bleeding, Morton wasn't looking so good and his breathing became heavily labored. His lung had been punctured and they couldn't seal the wound to stop it collapsing.

SFC Frazier started heaving and throwing up as an effect from the blast that had just gone off in close proximity to him. Even if you aren't physically affected by the shrapnel of an IED, the blast can be just as destructive as the shockwave hits you like a punch to the face from a professional boxer. It's essentially the same thing as your brain bounces around in the skull cavity that houses it. This is what causes traumatic brain injuries that can plague someone the rest of their lives even if there are no visible problems.

The helicopter finally got there and Morton was as white as a crisp bedsheet when they loaded him up. They had been losing him and needed to get him out of there right away. No one else had been seriously injured, so they gathered up all of Morton's equipment that had been left behind and headed back to COP Johnston. The company got word later that Morton was going to be ok, but would be joining the growing number of troops being sent to Walter Reed.

Down the River

Operating out of COP Johnston now, we would no longer patrol past COP Ware into the villages in the northeast, but we would follow the river further into the area of a little town by the name of Deh-e Kowchay. We nicknamed it DK because it was easier to pronounce. Every time we would venture into the area, things would happen. It was further away from everything else we patrolled up to this point and was set right off of the river. In this particular town, it seemed as if the religious leader was the one to hold the power and influence in the area.

After a bit of talking to the mullah (religious leader), he spoke of bad men in the area and how he no longer had a working loudspeaker to assist him in the call for prayer throughout the day. It almost always seemed that they would be playing the haunting calls five times a day and voiced in Arabic as the speaker would broadcast the need to face Mecca and bow down. Some of the people would filter into the mosque, some would just be performing the prayer ritual out in the fields where they were tending sheep or watching us. Most of the farm work would happen throughout the night due to the daytime being so hot that it was hard to get any manual labor completed. Another reason why the locals probably thought we were either crazy or superhuman.

Everyone we had come across had said there were bad men in the area, but you got the distinct feeling that DK was a different type of area than we had been dealing with up to this point. We wanted to put forward a show of good faith, so we supplied them with a battery and wiring to get the loudspeaker system running and operational again. That lasted about a day… and then the materials conveniently disappeared. It was a pretty stupid gesture on our part, but at the same time, how much more damage was that particular bit of wire and battery going to do in a land where landmines were as plentiful as the pomegranates on the trees but always in season?

Activity within DK was pretty overt and plentiful, and you couldn't trust the people living there until you knew who was who. This started a series of patrols that began to uncover weapons caches in the surrounding areas, a survey of the town, endless Key Leader Engagements (KLE) and finding a rather large Russian rocket in an old man's backyard.

Lt Demarest was on patrol when we came across a hunched-over little old man crossing a field. He looked ancient with his leathery skin heavily worn and lined with the signs of aging in an austere environment such as this. We started to bring the interpreter to the front of the patrol when the man spoke to us in perfect English. It turns out that he had studied at Oxford University in England and returned to Afghanistan to live out the rest of his days in his home country. After a brief discussion, the lieutenant scheduled a follow-up meeting with the gentleman and we moved back to COP Johnston via the large open areas to allow for quicker movement with less risk.

Later, we would return to visit the old man after a walk through town to the far end before the road that ran parallel to the river went off around a bend. DK held a bit of a humbling and strange atmosphere. It always seemed to be very quiet when we came into the town, there were never any kids out, and a lot of leftovers from the Russian era were strewn about the area. One of the compounds inside of the village was using an old Russian heavy drop supply parachute as an awning to shade an open area pavilion that overlooked the street. The town was a maze of high walls and steel-gated entrances that limited movement greatly while moving through the town. This was going to be a different kind of challenge as the sense of being unwanted hovered thickly in the air of the town of DK.

Beware the Ides of March, March 15, 2010

That morning, as we were getting ready near the ECP for the patrol, James Staples saw Sgt Lee stepping off with his team that morning. "I feel for you guys. Stay safe," he mentioned to Lee as they left the gate. He knew they were heading into trouble because anything within the DK area was bad news. It had been proven to be that that way in the past and was following a trend at this point.

3rd squad was supplemented with elements of Weapons squad and other bodies that would fill the necessary gaps for the mission that was to take place in town. Cannon and Ross would be providing heavy firepower with the 240 as the gun team and we had procured an Afghan policeman that day to help cover any language barriers with the locals, as Gucci would be involved with the key leader engagement that was scheduled by Lieutenant Demarest during a portion of the time there.

As we departed the backside of the town of Morgan, Lee was on point with Specialist Brandon Watson handling the mine detector up front. He spotted two kids from the far end of the field watching us from the cover of some bushes. He instructed Watson to keep moving as he traveled back through the patrol to let Sgt Thomas know what he had just seen, and what he thought was happening.

"Well, let's just take a peek then," Thomas said as he raised his rifle to peer through his ACOG sight, which provided a bit more magnification to investigate. It was as if the kids instantly knew the jig was up as they sprinted away, behind the walls in the direction of the town we were headed. "Damn... I guess it's gonna be one of those days then." Thomas stated.

When we got to the end of town, there was a "T" intersection with the compound where we were to have the meeting just off of the corner by about three houses. Lee set in security and as the machine guns were providing cover of the high-speed avenues of approach, Demarest, Martinek and I found the old man and were invited into his little compound to talk.

As we came into the courtyard of his compound, there was a huge Russian missile resting against its nose cone on the ground with the body, fins and all, standing intact against the far wall. After a brief discussion that offered bringing out EOD to dispose of the projectile, we sat down, and he brought over a platter with hot tea for everyone to enjoy along with some Afghan cheese. What was a meeting in Afghanistan without chi anyway? No sooner than we had taken a sip, there was a boom that shook the compound walls. We immediately jumped up and flowed out into the courtyard to see a flurry of commotion as the team leaders were getting their guys reconsolidated and attempting to get security in place after the initial scramble after the blast.

Ackmehd the Human Sacrifice

Lee had just adjusted Specialist Jordan Flake after thinking he was just a little too far outside of the security bubble for his comfort. Accounting for everyone in the team, keeping them in an effective position, and adjusting to the situation continually was all part of his job as one of the fire team leaders. They had just added Pilcher to the squad in the position of team leader and they weren't quite sure what to think of him yet. This area had proven to be dangerous and they needed to know that he could hack it out here. He had been sent forward from the rear detachment company for Battalion but held previous experience from the Iraq invasion serving with 1/504. Still, this was Bravo Company.

Three or four locals had come through that been friendly enough, all with smiles and very compliant in allowing themselves to be searched before moving further into the town. Lee was heading back to Sgt Thomas in the middle of the position to let him know where everything was set in and to take a minute to light up a smoke. Thomas had let Lee know that there was some intel chatter on the radio about possible suicide bombers brought up by the COIST team member back at Ware. He had just gotten back to his assault pack when he heard Flake say, "We got another one up here."

"Damn it," Lee muttered to himself as he figured that he wasn't going to be able to take a break here. The Afghan policeman with them was in position with Flake, but it was necessary to have two guys to search someone properly as the additional soldier would continue to pull security. He was moving to Flake's position when the Afghan police officer started to shout. Lee started to run towards the yelling as he was lifting the mini thermals to his face to see if the man's heat signature would betray the signs of wearing a suicide vest on his person.

As the ANP charged his AK-47 to fire, the man went to his knees with his hands on his head as a sign of surrender… and was silhouetted by a bright red flash accompanied by a cloud of thick black smoke. Flake saw the man's rib cage flying through the air as the rest of his body was strewn about into the surrounding landscape. The pressure plate that provided the bomb detonator was integrated into some sort of knee pad to allow for the deception needed to close the gap with the target.

Lee was thrown backward and onto the ground and remembers thinking to himself about the bomber, "What an idiot!" Here he was, unharmed and on the ground. His bell rang but he could still see Flake right where he just was and seemingly unharmed as well. That's when Thomas started to scream.

I came into the middle of the position along with Demarest to get the situation report to send up to higher and there was Sgt Thomas, on the ground within the security bubble along with Will Ross holding his shoulder, but still facing down the road in a security position on the gun. Thomas wasn't looking good. Once you know the shade of death, you'll never forget what it looks like. It's not something that frightened me, but it was familiar and something that gave me an immediate indication of just how bad the situation was.

Communications in the valley were messed up due to multiple factors within the area. But DK was right on the edge for our radio capabilities even with the long whip extended all the way. Motorola Talkabouts would have reached the distance needed, but the high-speed encrypted channels that the military required couldn't reach out and get us the help we needed. We were on the backside of the village and I could barely get a signal out. I had to sprint back to the compound we had just come from to call the medevac for Thomas and Ross.

Were there Taliban maneuvering on us? Should I have taken another guy with me? Was the old man behind it all? Would I run into a trap when I re-entered the house? It was a two-room walled-off area, but the enemy wasn't stupid and here I was raising a long whip over the far wall of the place. After the message was sent and confirmed, I returned to the scene where Thomas laid and now looked ashy while Doc was trying to save this 250lb bear of a man that was now fighting for his life on the ground while bleeding out.

Lee had left the center position to assist the policeman that had been at the apex of the blast and was roughed up pretty good. He had shrapnel everywhere with little flecks of metal creating wounds all over his body and face. He had two major wounds as well because the ball bearings the vest had contained had blown a hole in both his left shoulder and his left thigh. Both areas that have major implications for bleeding out if you don't take care of them quickly. Lee was running on pure adrenaline at this point as he stripped off the man's gear and clothing while trying to take out his own personal IFAK tourniquet, forgetting the medical bag was already on his back. He was rattled for sure.

Gucci had moved over to assist and saw how badly the man was injured. He grabbed up the police officer's AK-47 and went into a systematic flurry of action as he yelled at onlookers who now stood in doorways. The actions of the Taliban and the sight of his hurt countryman had driven Gucci into action, and we saw a side of him we hadn't seen before. He had always kept his cool in the past, but he was more like a lion after seeing one of his brothers in such a state.

We started to look around for places to create a safe LZ, but it was cramped on this end of town and we couldn't cover what was down the river from us or across from it. The landing zone would either be the riverbed, where we knew we could land but wouldn't have security, or in a flattened off area adjacent a compound where we had effective overwatch. PFC Martinek and I had to clear a landing zone area while the others pulled security, worked on keeping Sgt Thomas alive, and continued to adjust to the situation. Martinek and I found ourselves zigzagging in a search pattern across a portion of land belonging to a highly volatile area in a war zone that was littered with landmines. Thankfully there weren't any in that particular spot. It would be a tight squeeze, but the area still fit the dimensions of a landing area for a Blackhawk. The pilots that responded to the medevacs were incredible and we had no doubts of their abilities as they had proven them on multiple occasions already. The only issue we could see was the inability to cover the far river side if someone decided to shoot at the chopper from the opposite riverbank.

At some point, I went to check on Flake. The scorched ground in front of him was an immediate and grisly reminder of what had just happened right in front of him. This was a kid just out of high school that had joined us mid-rotation as a replacement and had been thrown into the fight without the benefit of attending the prior training cycle or the events that had built cohesion and resiliency within the ranks around him. Lee had just gone over him briefly and tried to reassure him it would be OK, but Flake was terrified.

"You all right bud?" I said as I approached him, and he responded in a shaky voice, "He just up and exploded." As I got to him, I realized that there were pieces of body, blood, and scalp on Flake's person along with something on his shoulder. It was a piece of the bomber's ear! I brushed it off as I looked him over, making an excuse that I was just making sure he wasn't hit anywhere else. "What was that?" he said as he turned towards me and his eyes started to make their way down to the remnants of what was once a piece of human but now just a hunk of charred flesh on the ground. I tossed my assault bag on the ground next to him, covering the ear in an attempt to spare the kid any additional details of the ordeal that were going to haunt him later. "It's nothing," I reassured him as I continued to perform the blood sweep. "You have water?" I asked him as I brushed off a hunk of scalp off his lip area that had burnt, crispy hair follicles poking from the charred flash. "Yeah, I'm good." I remember staying with him for a minute or so before moving back and moving on to another task because you can't just leave someone alone after a traumatic event like that. You have to try to bring the elevated emotions down a notch or they are liable to create more harm. I'm sure I needed to have a smoke at that point as well.

Lee was on the radio with Seamus 66 when they called that they had seen movement in the orchards and there were three men moving towards our position. "Oh crap, here it comes!" thought Lee as he was readjusting the men again along with checking everyone over once again. He pointed Tyler at the sector he was covering and let him know that if anything came within 100m to kill it without question. It didn't matter what it was... KILL IT.

QRF was on the way, but if the approaching element was anything significant, we could be in a bad way really quickly. Pilcher came back into the center with Thomas' gear and handed the fighting load carrier vest (FLC) to Lee stating, "OK, I guess you got the juice now. By the way, you might want to change your magazine." Lee looked down and saw a large chunk of his Magpul PMAG magazine missing and rounds clearly visible through the damage.

Taking the moment to reset and take a breath, Lee looked at his assault pack that had been sitting next to Thomas when he was hit and realized that it had holes in it. He opened it up to grab a bottle of water to find the one on top empty... what the heck, he didn't have any empty bottles yet. It started to dawn on him that his bag had been punctured by the ball bearings that were in the bomber's vest rig and had blasted through the very spot he had been about to sit down in before the commotion started.

Doc started to flip out after about 20–30 minutes because the helicopter still wasn't there. At this point, he had performed three separate needle decompressions to keep Sgt Thomas breathing and the situation wasn't looking good. We would normally have the medevac helicopter on station within 15–30 minutes in our area and we were starting to get really worried we were about to lose Thomas due to the long wait. After about 45 minutes, we heard rotors. We already had Thomas and Ross prepped and ready to go, but we had been waiting in this area far too long.

There is something to be said about the professionalism and urgency at which special operations move as opposed to some of the regular army counterparts you find on the battlefield. We could immediately tell this was an army crew, as their performance on the objective was a far cry from that provided by our normal PJ crew. The pilot landed in the riverbed and we had to readjust again as they were outside of our established security bubble. The medics then dropped Thomas multiple times as they fumbled towards the Blackhawk to load the casualties. Someone was watching out for Sgt Thomas that day as he would live through the night and face the enemy another day. We almost lost him right then though. In fact, we were told he flatlined in the helicopter on the way to the flightline hospital triage at Kandahar Air Field.

That night, we were to run recon and surveillance patrols out of that area with 3rd Platoon providing security while we attempted to show the town that we would not be rattled so easily. Things were different in DK after that and took a developing turn because the commander refused to take a hit like that lying down. Captain Armstrong now moved 2nd Platoon from COP Ware into position within the town of DK. We had finally found the hornets' nest, the tiger hole, or whatever you call the enemy's territory in which he felt ballsy enough to send human sacrifices to take more of us down. I'll give the enemy one thing; they were determined to figure out a way to stop us from continuing to operate within the area. Too bad they didn't study up on the 82nd Airborne. They would have realized it would have been much better just biding their time in hiding or keeping a low profile until we left. However, now it was done. They wanted a fight and they weren't going to dare face us in a direct engagement.

Up until now, it had just been landmines laid in everywhere with very little interaction that involved us vs them in a "fair" fight. Sure, we knew there were insurgents operating in the area as we had assisted in snatch-and-grab missions, arrests, and people we brought in with us after they popped hot on the HIIDE system. However, it was like fighting ghosts. We were walking through minefields with no purpose. You want to know how to demoralize an army? Lay in as many random booby traps as possible and watch as the opposing force hits them one by one, never finding the source, but losing guy after guy and have them wondering whose turn was next.

When you make the enemy tangible, as well as show that he is a true asshole that would sacrifice their own like that, you light a fire that cries for vengeance in the name of the fallen. You want to cut down those that did this in a hail of bullets and ordnance dropped from on high. There are rules on the battlefield and we definitely upheld the moral high road in these cases. However, things happen that skewer your sense of morality and sometimes your view changes when you've seen someone used as a human sacrifice. It makes one angry… furious, seething with hatred for those that would stoop to such levels. One is pushed toward the envelope of falling to the enemy's level of morality within a valley that only a few cared about at the time of their occupation.

The Arghandab Triangle—March 30–31

With everything that was happening within the valley, we were sent more replacement new guys. Still, we were only 28 men up and down by one or two at a time here and there. It had started to divide up the squads again as guys would be injured and sent to the rear and the new guys that replaced them would be largely at the mercy of their internal fire teams for buddies. We stopped wanting to get to know any of the replacements, which is a bad sign because the occurrence is talked about in just about every Vietnam book I had read during my life about soldiers dealing with the worst areas of the country. Not the correlation you ever want to notice while serving within a war operation.

We had been on an overwatch patrol in Deh-e Kowchay and had been keeping an eye on things while the push into the area was being planned and prepared. We wanted to keep the small foothold we held while simultaneously letting the enemy know we weren't going to let him defeat us that easily. It wasn't eventful, other than the chain of events that was set off during our route back to COP Johnston. Private Shane Betts was the last in the order of movement of the forward team with SPC Cannon walking right behind him while carrying the 240B as weapons support by fire. Everyone was accustomed to walking in each other's footsteps, whether they realized it or not, but someone who was on one of his very first patrols wasn't acclimated to that point yet. He wasn't accustomed to how to move, how to recognize everyone within the platoon while operating in the pitch-black nights, how to step in different environments, or really what he was doing at all.

That kid had to be the luckiest person in the area that night as the land mine that was meant to take off his foot had been buried by its emplacement team just a little too deep. Walking just slightly off of the footsteps that lay in front of him, PV2 Betts hit a toe popper in the path that half the squad had just passed right over. The mine essentially broke his foot and knocked him over. However, the screams he let out after were louder than anything that had been emitted from those that had been hit prior. I came up to Doc who was looking him over in the dirt. "How bad is it?" I asked him as I waited to send up the full report. "You're not going to believe this… everything's there!" Me and Doc started laughing and then our humor quickly turned off as we hissed at him to shut up as he was acting like a pussy and had just received his ticket out of this hellhole before he even had a chance to experience any of the suck.

This was the spiral, the disengagement that I had referred to earlier. Betts wasn't human to us or at least, we didn't really treat him as such. I've heard it said before that a person's worst day of their life really is the worst thing that has ever happened to them. With the occurrences we had been exposed to up to this point, it's not surprising that it was just another day for us. While for PV2 Betts, it was his worst nightmare come true. Anyone in that situation would have been terrified, anyone in their right mind anyway.

Once again, we found ourselves in the middle of a grape orchard clearing an area for a chopper to land and take our boys off to the hospital for recovery. It only added an additional hour to the night, so it wasn't all that big of a deal at the moment.

SFC Hill took 3rd squad and moved to the explosion site for the site exploitation the next morning along with EOD, to verify if there was a new method being used to lay in mines that we weren't aware of yet.

I'll be Gone Till November

Sgt Lee woke up to SFC Hill yelling for the sergeant of the guard and he knew immediately what was happening. Pilcher, now his team leader, yelled from the tent that the squad was already up and the guys were getting spun up to go out. They had gotten pretty good at the routine by now and everything was staged and ready to go at the end of your bunk because you never knew what was going to happen.

Lee knew Hill was getting torqued up and the longer it took to get the guys out of the ECP, the more flak he was going to get from Hill. He didn't blame him, he wanted to get out to the guys too, but he didn't want to make a wrong step getting there. Once they made it through the town of Morgan, the squad beelined through the muddy fields that were experiencing an irrigation rotation as the farmers worked the fields that night. Bombs don't go boom when they are wet, so it was a safe bet.

The link-up happened just as the medevac bird was taking off with Betts aboard and Lee started working with Ackers and Hill to get security set in so they could begin to rotate a small rest cycle before the morning came. They had been called out unexpectedly and sleep was something that was in short supply those days with the amount of patrols and activity that had been happening. Once again, they found themselves sitting on an IED site for an assessment.

The morning arrived and they received word that a detachment from 3rd Platoon would be bringing EOD out to them by way of escort from Sergeant Alejandro Jauregui's squad. It was going to be another mashup of elements as Captain Armstrong would be moving along with SSG Brunkhorst for a mission in the DK area. It's no surprise that almost immediately after the element split off, Brunk's squad found an IED and needed to bring EOD back to the location of the patrol so the commander would be on time. The assessment with 1st Platoon was going to have to wait.

As they waited for Jauregui's squad to finish up, Armstrong wanted 1st Platoon to hit the area immediately surrounding them with a metal detector. Lee grumbled about it but he told SPC Watson to get the mine hound unit up and scanning. The detectors were OK when they worked, but you had to have some experience on them. Sometimes, the things just wouldn't want to work right. This is why veterans groan when they hear the word "mil-spec" being advertised.

Lee was getting annoyed with the entire situation at this point and he just wanted to get it done so they could get back in for a few hours before it was time to go out again. "I've got it!" He snatched the metal detector from Watson and started fiddling with it while beginning to sweep the field. There was a washed-out bridge structure ahead over the canal and Lee didn't feeling like getting wet today. He knew he needed to get to the other side, but he didn't want to get another set of boots soaked that morning.

He could jump from the support pylons that were still in the ground without an issue. Perfect! He balanced onto a concrete portion of the crumbled bridge because there was no danger there. Can't set an IED into concrete... right? Lee checked the area and then told Watson to keep an eye out because he was going to cross the canal first. He aimed for the next pylon and jumped. BOOM!

Pilcher was the first to get there and popped over the edge of the canal. "What's going on?" he asked Lee as he surveyed the scene in front of him. Lee couldn't make sense out of any of it. He didn't see any blood, and everything looked intact, but there was a horrible pain coming from one of his legs. Something wasn't right... he couldn't put any weight on it, and it hurt to move.

"Don't send anyone else over. The main charge didn't go off and something isn't right. My left leg is fucked," Lee pleaded as he tried to half-hobble, half-swim in a canal full of horrible-smelling water and sewage. God only knew what else was in there as Pilcher pulled him out onto the other side and heaved him up the embankment. He put Lee on his back in a fireman's carry and walked him about halfway to the area the guys had marked off as the medevac landing zone when Hammer had to take over. Lee wasn't a big guy but at about 170lbs plus another 50–60lbs of gear on him, he was an exhausting thing to hoist on your back and carry across a muddy farm field.

Doc Ponce was out there and was stumped by the injury as well. He couldn't tell what was broken or shattered inside the leg without an X-ray, so he just immobilized everything with a SAM splint and molded it to the leg so it would offer some sort of protection. The medevac showed up just as the night before and loaded James Lee onto the chopper for his ride out of the valley that morning.

1st Platoon had lost two soldiers within a 24-hour period now. Hill was reconsolidating and yelling at Hammer to get the squad together as he was going to take the lead to get them back in to COP Johnston after EOD arrived for the site assessment. The word was that Sgt Jauregui was bringing EOD to Hill's position now because the bomb that Brunk had found had been a hoax IED. There had been a bit of an argument about it because as EOD was stating the setup was a clear hoax, something wasn't right. This was something new and we had never seen a tactic like this before.

Edinger

Jauregui was getting severely annoyed at this point. What was going on? It seemed like every step that had been taken that day had gone wrong. When did the dominos stop colliding with one another?! When was this hell going to end? He yelled to the guys. "We're headed back to Brunk and we've gotta haul ass." In a hasty movement, they turned the patrol around and went right back towards the way they had come from. They were essentially the personal safety detachment for the EOD team that had the job of disabling the bombs that seemed to be all around us. Jauregui's squad went back the way they had come, but not every step was the same.

Just a few inches off to the left or right led to Specialist Nick Edinger instantly losing his foot in an area that EOD had just cleared. Their methods had proven to be completely useless in the valley that day. The bombmakers were true masters of their craft. Where they had failed with Lee and Betts, the setup proved to be extremely effective when everything had dried out as in this particular instance.

Jauregui was still in the vicinity of Hill's location and needed to get Edinger back there, NOW! As if reading his mind, Hill came running to them with Doc Ponce. As doc started to immediately triage Edinger, Hill took a good look at Jauregui as he was winded and having trouble trying to speak to call up the medevac. "Chill the fuck out, motherfucker. Take a breath." That was all it took and J snapped back into it. Sometimes that was all a guy needed was the prompt to take a pause and categorize the massive flow of information his brain was pushing out at that moment while his adrenaline was coursing through his body.

After the medevac was sent up and they moved Edinger back to the HLZ, Jauregui still had to travel back out to Brunkhorst's last known location. They were moving back across the fields when Tiemen found a tripwire. So, EOD marked everything off and they routed around it… and then they found another tripwire. This process was repeated once more, but after finding the third tripwire, all movement came to a halt.

They quickly realized that every possible move ended in more guys hitting bombs. They hadn't confirmed anything yet, but they were pretty sure that Brunkhorst had been vaporized. J called in to COP Ware and Sgt Ledet answered the call, letting them know they were bringing another EOD team out to their location with some more C4. "If you hear a boom, don't bother sending anyone. We've got so much C4 in our bags that if we hit anything, we're all toast."

Back at Johnston

Once again, we reset our gear and got ready for the next day because we knew we would be right back out there. I was on TOC duty when we got the call early that morning from SFC Hill that Sgt Lee had just hit a toe popper that was immediately off the area we were just in. The exact same malfunction of an IED had just taken Sgt Lee out of the fight as well, but he was going to be fine as he even still had his foot. You could hear Lee chuckling in the background over the radio as he was probably grinning through the pain, knowing he was to be stateside again soon. Ice cream and Walter Reed hospital was in his near future, to join everyone else within the wing that was starting to brim with members of our battalion. The real cost of war.

SFC Hill put in an order to everyone within the patrol base to stop any movement and as the sun came up, it revealed that they were in the middle of a minefield. The entire region was a minefield, but this was something different. There were tripwires, ranging flags, and signs of disturbed earth everywhere. I can only imagine the feeling of dread experienced at that moment. No one had any idea how we blindly crossed that field that night, but it's a damn miracle that we didn't hit anything else as we had cleared that landing area along with the movement back to COP Johnston without incident.

The patrol was holding in place as EOD was moving to them along with another squad that traveled from COP Ware through the orchards towards DK. At this point, I was in the TOC full time because the situation had gone to full alert and everyone was either in the towers or with body armor and equipment on and ready to roll as a quick reaction force.

There was a huge boom and I thought to myself immediately that there was no way EOD had made it out to Hill's location yet. I had been getting ready for the coming patrol and was in the section of the outpost that housed our "fresh" water supply that had been trucked in to provide a water source for the shower connex that was on its way shortly. The temperature stayed about 20 degrees cooler than anywhere else on the compound due to the amount of water held in these large holding tanks that acted like a buffer to the ambient temperature. The plywood surrounding the structures insulated everything from the sun and there was a type of cooling effect due to the water temperature staying more constant during the day. Someone had even put a few cots in there and guys would come hang out and watch movies or just bullshit in the space at times. The wooden walls of the water facility flexed with the shockwave from the bomb that someone had just hit.

I ran back to the TOC to see what was happening and you could hear SFC Fox over the radio calling for Brunkhorst… no answer. Jauregui got on the radio and told Fox that he was closest and could move back towards their position to find out what had happened.

Where is your Blackberry?

I was in the TOC as everyone was rotating between guard shifts and sleeping in their kit as they waited for the call to come that we were heading out. Most of COP Ware was empty at this point because the good majority of the company was all over the battlespace. Demarest let me know I was heading out with LTC Jones and his PSD (personal security detail) to link up with Hill at the original blast site where Betts had been hit the night before.

The sheer number of losses and urgency of the situation had triggered an instant response from the battalion commander and he had to see for himself what was going on within his battlespace at the moment. This was going to be interesting as

I already knew how tense the situation was at the moment. Hill was never one to care about pleasantries in dealing with the officer side of the house and would pipe up to give that answer that no one else in the room wanted to say. He would tell it how it was even if it was abrasive. However, run something by him on a day like this and you were bound to experience some friction.

We left with 2nd squad and made the link up with Hill. I stuck by Hill as the rest of the guys that we had brought left to link up with the 3rd Platoon elements and join the careful search for SSG Brunkhorst. We were headed back to COP Johnston when a member of the Lieutenant Colonel's security detachment came up and whispered something to Hill, which led to a torrent of screaming.

"We ain't going back for no God damn fucking Blackberry! Are you kidding me? We're out here losing guys left and right and you can't keep control of a sensitive item! You go back for it, motherfucker! Fuck you!" and with that we started hauling ass on our route back through the mud fields on the way back to Morgan and COP Johnston.

"Uh, why are we walking though the fields? We're falling back out here. Why aren't we on the road?" came a squawk over the hand mic on my shoulder. Oh God… why?! Can't they understand that they are in our battlespace and have no clue what they are doing out here? "Go ahead and take your chances on the road then!" Hill yelled, not bothering to even use the radio at this point. He muttered under his breath "I hope you get blown up" as we continued the blistering pace back to Johnston.

That day had taken a toll on everyone in Bravo Company. There had been reports from guys within 2nd squad that they were doing hands across Afghanistan while looking for any of Brunkhorst's remains in the surrounding minefields. They were given trash bags, but there weren't enough to go around as the remains were recovered. Pieces of Brunk were put into assault bags, rucks, cargo pockets, and the supplied trash bags as they performed a double-arm-interval search in an area where any step could lead to yet another casualty. The grass had a slick black coating to it and someone realized that it was residue from the "pink mist" effect that the guys from the infantry refer to when a body part or person was vaporized with a form of explosives.

After that incident, 1st Platoon worked as a bit of a blocking position in assisting with the move into DK. There was no going back now. The Taliban wanted to ramp it up, but we were more than willing and hadn't given an inch of ground yet. The increase in intensity could have also meant another thing… our efforts were being noticed.

The 82nd Airborne mentality is well known for an occurrence that happened during the Battle of the Bulge during World War II. Whether it's fact or just a really clever piece of propaganda, the marketing heads at division put it on a poster. It reads, "Well, buddy, just pull your tank in behind me. I'm the 82nd Airborne, and this is as far as the bastards are going." In reference to a paratrooper's response to a retreating tank unit asking their current position on the line during the historical battle. The Taliban hadn't faced this type of determination and resilience before and damn if we weren't about to show it to them.

Should I Stay or Should I Go Now?

After those three days, there was a halt and regroup pause to the push and the tempo changed within the valley. Instead of the constant patrolling and duties, things became more paced and methodical because we had to change our methods if we were to survive. We had to be careful in moving forward because at this pace of loss, we would end up being relieved early, just like the last unit that was here.

Questions were posed asking for the removal of Bravo Company from the area. Could we handle it? Families of members of multiple companies had written the battalion command and the scandal surrounding the removal of the previous commanders was causing rumbles throughout the ranks. Armstrong and Mcalister were pulled aside by LTC Jones to discuss the situation and after finding his focus wavering while on patrol, Armstrong determined that the IEDs were doing the exact job that the enemy was intending for them to do.

The psychological distress and creation of terror that was generated from the losses could easily make things worse and turn the entire company into a liability if the situation escalated any further. The squeeze was from all angles and the enemy was a master at creating the absolute worst situation within the moment. This sentiment was expressed within the form of a letter and sent as a response to the situation. It was then quickly forgotten as the battlefield situation required every bit of the commanders' focus and resolve. The battlefield politics occurring above them at the time could not play a role in Bravo Company's responsibilities or the consequences of the conflict would spill over into catastrophic results on the ground.

So, battalion supplied us with more dog teams, EOD attachments, and a mortar platoon along with some other assets. Bravo Company was regarded as the disciplined one by LTC Jones and he trusted that the commander on the ground knew what he was doing. Cpt Adam Armstrong was one of the few commanders focused on the task at hand instead of being sucked into the vortex that involved the politics in the removal of the previous command.

Work was put in to push engineers and troops into the DK area and 2nd Platoon patrolled the area and assisted in security while the base was established. I never got to see the interior of Deh-e Kowchay again other than moving among the outer orchards that were to the east of the town. From what I was told, they were initially using one of the buildings near the center of town in proximity to the compound with the Russian parachutes.

There were a lot of nights that we would be either watching the RAID tower or heading on foot to the ANP compound to the south of DK to provide overwatch and provide an alert if anything was moved in significance to the rest of the company's position. There was a lot of chatter now because we were now actively disrupting enemy operations and the people within the villages of the area were now talking with us.

It was interesting to see the 82nd operating in elements of 10–14 men when conventional army will operate at an easy 50+ men per operation. Those were the sizes of some of the Ranger regiment elements that passed through on the way to perform a hit in the town of Gondigan that was southeast of our position. Regiment also had a Chinook go down just off the river and we ended up watching the shell of the aircraft until they sent a "recovery" team which just blew everything in place with a whole lot of explosives. Why recover anything when you can just blow it up? Right?

Watch Your Step: TSgt Pauli's Story

Technical Sergeant Gregory Pauli was one of the Air Force EOD guys on the ground for the day Brunk was hit and had a good idea of what was going on here. The bombs weren't anything out of the ordinary, or even complex in build, but the tactics being used were ones that had been rarely seen before within the EOD community. The insurgents were masters at hunter/tracker techniques and would use the environment around them in ways that funneled the guys walking the ground into a trap.

Sometimes, they would cut tree branches to create a natural pattern of light that psychologically brought someone to walk in that direction as if pulled by a magnet. You had to realize what you were seeing before you could fight it. The numbers of kids that had a past in hunting were dwindling within the Army and it wasn't a skill that had much attention given to it these days. It was all MOUT (Military Operations in Urban Terrain) villages for door-to-door clearing and running battle drill ranges. The bread and butter that our infantry and combat arms was used to.

Pauli had seen it progress since 2001, when he first joined. He had seen how the military had started to operate more efficiently and improve upon its training, but he had also seen the enemy adapt to the various tactics that American troops had thrown at them.

He determined, along with Captain Armstrong, that DK was the stronghold within the region and there was an IED belt that surrounded the town as well as peppering the ground of the area within. Anyone would have to cross the belt to gain access to the area. This usually meant crossing two or three IED sites before getting within the outer cordon of the mine belt. Then you had to deal with the bombers that would don an explosive vest to trigger themselves into a deadly threat.

On top of that, the Taliban would be watching and would send out teams to lay tripwires as a nasty surprise when you turned the patrol back around to make your way home. This is one of the reasons the infantry teams would attempt to never overlap patrol routes or cross back the way they had come in from. Every movement had to be deliberate and necessary, and it was a maddening task to try to accomplish correctly, because when you didn't, the risk factor was exponential.

A lot of what initiated that day would be the same failed tactic that broke the foot of John Warzinski, one of the other EOD members. You could just be a half step off of the guy in front of you and you would disturb the earth just enough to set off a charge that someone had missed along the way. The enemy hadn't figured out the exact charge amount yet for the homemade PMN mines and they would just end up breaking someone's foot instead of taking it clean off.

But the largest factor that troubled Pauli was that the hoax mine that SSG Brunkhorst had set off had been set up in a way that was meant to take out the entire EOD exploitation team. If Brunkhorst hadn't gone in there to make sure the situation was safe, it would have been his teammates that would have come back from that call in body bags. He wasn't happy about what had happened out there, but it showed him exactly what they were up against.

This enemy wasn't like a lot of the ones he had seen in the past. They weren't sloppy and they were consistent. In the past, he watched the various ordnance and traps placed to take out US personnel. It was usually a mixed bag of different techniques learned during their training, but this enemy was consistent and tactically sound. We weren't just facing a cell that was on the train up, but one that had an advanced tactical background and the discipline to "bake the recipe" consistently every time. We were up against someone who took their job as seriously as we did.

Battleshits

On a village patrol operation within the town of Mian Juy, there was an eventful afternoon while settling into a patrol base along with 2nd squad. There had been a fair amount of activity surrounding a specific group of compounds that wasn't inside the limits of DK, but just outside the southeastern edge of town. We had interacted with a particular homeowner that had offered us refuge and information anytime we were in the area. It was a friendly open door.

In a compound just down the road from that position, Sgt Musil had just set the squad into a security posture with Specialist Chris Wiesner on the rooftop along with Specialist James Staples manning the 240B machine gun. Wiesner was armed with a 40mm grenade launcher that had names of the fallen and insults aimed at the Taliban scribbled onto the tops of the grenades in the ammo belt. The rounds were fashioned much like the bomb rounds you see being loaded that are emblazoned with angry messages meant for the enemy with hopes they read them in their last seconds before becoming another piece of the landscape. John Culp had moved some of the guys into buddy teams around the compound and was setting in security while Musil moved to take a much-needed bowel movement in one end of the open courtyard.

Sgt Musil had come down with a bad case of dysentery. Well… another bad case of dysentery. It was an unavoidable issue within the country, but he had gotten sick a few times already while we had been deployed and the current version of the virus he had manifested in the form of food and water flowing through his body just as fast as it went in. Yet another problem for the modern-day warfighter. You need to be able to handle all of the stressors that the environment will throw in your way while getting no form of regular sleep while insurgents that want to see you dead are stalking the surroundings or watching from within the villages. Not a friendly situation and your cortisol levels are through the roof at all times as survival instinct is almost always fully switched on.

It was approximately 10 seconds after I had called in our location and situation when we heard something cracking across branches as it flew through the tree line along the eastern wall of the compound. Hammer was peeing into the corner of the compound when he saw the grenade spoon separate from the main body of the charge just before it was knocked around the corner. Thunk… BOOOOM! A pineapple grenade had just been lobbed towards the compound we were occupying with the intent of catching us with our pants down!

"Jesus, fuckin'… Fuck!" Musil screamed, ripping up his trousers as liquid feces was still running down his legs. He tossed his armor on in one smooth motion that defied the very laws of physics. Staples immediately turned the gun in the direction of the grenade's origin and held the trigger down, attempting to lay suppressive fire faster than they could take him out. He couldn't see at the angle he was positioned, so he hoped for the best and braced himself as he shouldered the 240B and stood up to a heavily braced position. Rounds were zipping around him and the foliage was being cut apart as weapons barked from both sides of the conflict. You couldn't see anything through the heavy foliage between the two compounds which is probably what saved Musil and Hammer from becoming grenade fodder that day.

Wiesner had locked a 40mm grenade into his launch tube and yelled to Hammer, "Am I good to fire?!" "Yeah, fucker… FIRE!" Hammer screamed back at him. Wiesner turned and fired, but the fact that he hadn't shot the M203 for a long time showed as the round went over the intended target… way over… way, way over. It was one of those moments when time slows due to the amount of adrenaline that is flowing and the near-death experience that created a vortex of slow-motion pockets here and there. It was as if the entire battlefield was made aware of that first round going off as the distinct tube launch sound echoed throughout the air.

Everything went silent, and it was as if combatants from both sides had stopped firing to watch where that first round would hit. Like an ESPN broadcast, you saw that sizable round travel like a golf ball going up, up, up in a high, northeastern direction over everyone's heads and land somewhere outside of the other end of town. After the explosion in the distance, the mad minute continued as the extremely frustrated and red-faced Chris Wiesner unleashed a torrent of obscenities as he found his mojo and proceeded to unleash half the grenade belt in cyclic fashion into the offending compound where the grenade originated.

I'm on the radio with COP Ware already and they are asking if we need assistance in the firefight. I yell across the compound to Musil, who is stacking Hammer, Ager, and Doc Ponce along with Sgt Clayton's fire team along the compound wall in preparation to flow into the main street and assault the adjoining compound to clear the threat. "We need help on this?" I hold up the hand mic to let him know where it's coming from. He motions with a slicing motion across his throat, and I nod to acknowledge. "We're good. I'll let you guys know the sitrep when we get into it more and if we'll need anybody out here."

On that, Musil sees me key the mic and set it down for a second, and motions as the guys flow out into the streets to assault whatever it was that had snuck up on us. They came in hard and fast. As Hammer and Musil were up front, they hit the first door and it opened to the outside orchard behind the place. Ager flopped onto the ground as he came through and Hammer had to pick him up by the drag handle to get him back into the stack. Bobby went into the first little room inside the building and as he cleared the short room, Hammer split right to the next door. As he approached, an older man cowering with two little girls hugging his legs materialized in the doorway.

That split second, Hammer had a decision to make. He could guarantee this guy had been involved in what had just happened, but to what extent? Someone had just tried to kill all of us in the compound next door just a few seconds ago. Did he have explosives on him? Were the girls human shields? Was he justified in his actions to shoot? Should he just pull the trigger and continue to pull as he dropped this piece of shit to the ground? It wouldn't have been the reaction of most, but Hammer did the one thing that kept him from ending that guy's life right then and there. He punched the guy in the chest with the muzzle of his rifle and screamed at him to get the fuck down while they cleared the rest of the place.

There was a hiding spot in the room's wall that was filled with Taliban money we confiscated during the search. It was really fiat currency at the time in most of the country anyway. There were blood trails leading out of the compound and we were told by other villagers that we hit at least one of them pretty good and possibly another. Supposedly, these three had decided to pay someone off to attempt to surprise us. It had almost worked had it not been for a tree limb blocking that grenade arc that day.

I'm not sure what became of the family, but I know they went on to live another day when most soldiers would have gunned them down for being an accomplice to the enemy. Did they have a choice in this instance? Were they just strongarmed from the beginning and taken advantage of because they were the weak? What I do recognize is the entire livelihood of the family had been in the courtyard during the firefight and the scene afterward was not pretty. Everything lay dead and the ground was slick with blood. Among the casualties were a full-grown cow along with some goats, chickens, and a dog. Probably the least deserving of this type of death, but a grim example of what happens during a war.

Tarps

Another incident not too far from the same area occurred as I was patrolling with 2nd squad and Sgt Musil. There were two Afghans shaving their bodies over a set of tarps in the field under the cover of some surrounding trees. This was the preparation before donning suicide vests to blow themselves up in a kamikaze type of death minus the plane. They made the mistake of going for their AK-47s that lay on the ground next to them and fired a few rounds our way. We must have caught them by complete surprise as we had never seen anything like this before, despite the method being prevalent in the area.

We were in the middle of an orchard when shots began ringing out. One of the guys immediately turned and ran in the opposite direction of the gunfire. Hammer grabbed him by the collar and yelled directly into his face to get on line with the others and return fire. He shoved him towards the direction of the incoming automatic weapons fire and he moved via bounds into position with the rest of the assault team.

It surprised me because it wasn't a soldier that I was ever worried about. He was a little weird and quiet, but he had seemed to be squared away. He knew his job and all of the required learning, did the training without complaint, and had arrived from the 18th Airborne Corps LRRS unit. They didn't usually send screwups to LRRS. You never know how someone is going to react until you put them in the heat of the moment. It's one of the valid arguments that the Special Forces continually bring against the existence of the 18X program. They want (and desperately need) combat seasoned guys over there because until you have been in combat, you don't really know how you'll react to the occasion.

The combatants tossed their guns and ran. We may have winged one of them, but they were fast without the cumbersome body armor and equipment that we were required to wear. Drop in the life expectancy risk factor along with some fight-or-flight adrenaline and people will surprise you with some real speed.

The large win was that we discovered weapons and some explosives along with a main prize of over 50 detonators that could each have been used in a single bomb. That's 50-plus potential bombs that were taken out of rotation within a valley where we were finding an IED every other day. It was a good find and it slowed the insurgents' actions in the valley for a while.

After the debrief, we were breaking everything down and going into our priorities of work when the inevitable unofficial brief would go down. This is where guys would slap each other on the back or utterly harass each other with an extreme parody of what had happened on the battlefield that day. Jokes were made about Sam Hammer being likened to Scorpion from the game Mortal Kombat when he would use his grappling hook and spear his opponent and state "GET OVER HERE" before decapitating the enemy. It was being likened to the incident earlier in the day.

It could be brutal, but it was all with purpose. How could you expect someone to stay in the fight with you and have your back if he couldn't even handle himself in the most basic of functions in a firefight? I just remember questioning why someone would tuck tail and burn? What snapped in his head that had caused him to run? It caused me to re-examine my own performance. I think that everyone has a breaking point somewhere, but what determines that point is mitigated by how you handle yourself out there.

I always felt the right answer for me was to just stay focused on the job at hand. I was the radio. I was the eyes and ears on the battlefield and could get help sent in by way of more guys, air support, overwatch, and a lot of other capabilities that were available to us. That was my primary function. If someone came into my sector of fire or the need arose, then I would perform as a shooter. It was the same in Helmand while driving the truck. I was the driver during that firefight. Maneuvering, monitoring the radio, looking to see where the fire was coming from, tactical advantages we could move to, areas of cover, communicating with others in the truck, and helping toss ammo cans to the gunner for reloads.

When you break down the sheer number of tasks you should be paying attention to, it's exhausting. The ability to operate under that amount of pressure is what separates an effective and lethal soldier from one who is just mediocre. The incident made me start to evaluate where I honestly graded myself in the current environment we found ourselves in.

Brother Culp

It was somewhere around this point in time that things were looking pretty messed up. There were soldiers disappearing left and right due to all of the toe poppers and various combat injuries, but not many that had been sent out ever came back. The replacements wouldn't be around for long, so we didn't get to know them. The anxiety levels at the outpost were elevated and we found ourselves either focusing on the job at hand, improving our lives in any small way we could, or cracking jokes.

One of the comedic routines was started by our crazy Ukrainian, John Culp, who had a knack for going a bit more overboard than most. Someone had called him "Brother Culp" in a response to his newly created parodied character who was an evangelic preacher that would now come and "bless" each patrol before they left. It was only a few of the patrols that really got weird, but man, did he get into it. The parody was a strange line between irreverent and strangely accurate as it mimicked a southern Apostolic Pentecostal preacher that I had grown up listening to yell from the pulpit as I had observed from my wooden pew.

If you have attended a church of "holy-rollers," you'll know what I'm talking about. Brother Culp would go the whole nine yards on this comedy bit as he would sometimes use a canteen to spritz the patrol with his "holy water" or he would lay his hands on someone's head and pronounce that there would be no landmines that would be able to take this one's legs today. It was all humorous enough to double you over laughing if you had never seen something like it before, but the display was enough to make me uncomfortable because of how accurate his depictions were mirroring the church of my youth.

Somewhere along the line, the parody became something different though, and after a while, some of the guys pulled Culp aside and asked him if he could say a real prayer over the patrol because they needed something to calm their nerves. The wild character of Brother Culp would still peek his head out from time to time, but the event evolved into a state where both the comedy and the traditional/familiar were a warm blanket of distraction or reassurance that they would not die that day.

Taliban Turnover

A large section of the population had distrusted us, but they were beginning to open up to us more. Maybe it was the opportunity to make some side money off the Americans, but it's possible that they saw us patrolling, day after day, regardless of how dangerous it was. My feeling was that they began to see our humanity in our endeavor to provide peace within the region. We did, in fact, care what happened to these people. I don't care how disconnected you get, but seeing innocent people hurt on the battlefield does something to your soul. It changes how you see life and the harsh reality sinks in that monsters that prey upon the weak do indeed exist. The fortunate part is there are those that exist on the opposite end of the spectrum of balance. A yin to the yang if you will.

One such gentleman was a well-respected Afghan contractor from the area and would pass along information he would overhear and keep us alert to threats within the area. There were other sources in the district governor's office reporting to our battalion as well. The information would usually turn out to be legitimate, but after a tip about a booby-trapped body, we began to give him some real credit.

There was word that the Taliban were planning on rigging explosives underneath dead police officers' bodies so those who moved the body would be caught in the explosive force of the booby trap. Sure enough, it wasn't long after that a local police officer showed up face down in the middle of a grape orchard one morning. We moved to the position and called up EOD to come dispose of the possible explosives that could be rigged up under the body.

One of the local Afghan police chiefs came in and was spouting that the body needed to be taken care of immediately in accordance with Muslim law. He demanded that we let his men and the family take care of the body. We informed him of the explosives, which he denied existed. After him swearing at us up and down, screaming at us, and telling us he was the authority for the scene, we moved off the X and told him the site was fully his to exploit now. He promptly walked up to the body, had his men with him turn it over, and disappeared in a flash of light as a large charge blew up underneath the rigged body they had overturned. We had tried to tell them, but sometimes, you just have to let people learn for themselves. Rough lesson with a steep learning curve.

It was around this time that I had the stark realization that I faced the very real possibility of death out here. I faced it on an everyday basis, but as I looked at the situation and analyzed it, I realized that I was already dead. I didn't know the time, the place, or what caused me to think about it, but I realized that we were already dead the moment we had started living. It was only a matter of time until the reaper caught up.

Maybe this is a sick way to look at it, but I find it very freeing. You realize just how important every day you are given is to live. If we are headed towards the inevitable, it's already known what the end result will be. It has been assured. So, why not live like you are truly living when you are given the gift of another day? It has made my family holidays much sweeter and the time I have with the ones I love something to treasure as the majority of us just let it pass us by, not even realizing what was just outside of our grasp.

Those that have perished before us would have wanted the remaining to live with fervor because they themselves were not given the chance to do so. The sacrifices made for our existence were apparent. It made us appreciate what we had and reflect on the little things that ended up meaning the world in the end. Pay attention through the noise and silence your world in order to listen. Simple can be complex given the context. Much like a small sound can become maddening within an environment of complete silence.

CHAPTER 8

The Booms Get Bigger

COP Brunkhorst I—July 2, 2010

The situation was currently being established within the town of Deh-e Kowchay in a joint operation that cooperated with host nation counterparts, engineering companies bringing in supplies, and a flurry of local contracting. I was in the TOC that morning monitoring the radio when the walls bowed from the overpressure of a blast. HOLY SHIT! The wooden door of the TOC slapped the doorframe and kicked open briefly when the shockwave hit COP Johnston. This was an explosives payload something over 1,000lbs and unexpected even in IED Alley.

I jumped up from the desk and ripped open the door of the TOC to see a mushroom cloud rising from the direction of DK. SFC Hill jumped up from his cot in the back. "Yeske, what the fuck was that?!" he yelled from behind the partition.

"Not sure yet, but it was in the DK area. There is nothing for radio traffic. Should I try to call 2nd Platoon at COP Brunk? I don't want to clog the airwaves if that was them." I was given the word to hold up and just wait a minute or two to see what developed while Hill went and spun the squads up. This was probably going to be another all-hands situation. COP Ware jumped onto the radio network after about a minute and asked if we had heard anything from COP Brunk. Nothing. Shit... the waiting was torture as you know in your gut that was them and it's about to get really busy around the battlespace. Within 10 minutes, we had a QRF ready to go along with All of the defense positions fully manned in case of a complex offensive.

COP Brunk Remodel

Specialist Brian Errickson was in his bunk trying to get some sleep. It seemed like the duties never ended and now they were pushed into the thick of it in what seemed to be the origin of the conflict for the area. First it was Johnston and then Morton, Thomas, and others getting hit. The patterns were becoming obvious even to the privates that Deh-e Kowchay was not a friendly area to the Americans.

Thank God their platoon sergeant, SFC Frazier, was one of the laid-back pillars of leadership within the company. The guys could relax a little bit while in between the heat of the guard towers and the buildup of yet another makeshift compound that was a "brilliant" idea of leadership. First a radish field, now someone else's house. What the heck did they pay these people in order to stay there at their house anyway?

He would see the various family members coming and going from the back corner of the compound that they retained even with the Americans there. The people had nowhere else to go for now, so there they stayed.

Errickson was a firefighter by trade and had always enjoyed helping people. It gave him purpose in life. Maybe it was because he didn't think much of his own life that he always seemed to be OK with putting it on the line for others. It became everyday life for him, and he aspired to be part of the finest firefighting company in the world. The FDNY was his goal and every day he suited up with the New Jersey Fire Department and made a call, he felt like life was worth living.

Then the day had come that a group of psychopaths had decided to crash a plane into a tower full of people within the very heart of the city, driving a stake into the very symbol of everything that was American to the world. The very concept of freedom being challenged by a militant radical group of extremists that reveled in the thought of bringing the world into a constant policed state of sharia law was insanity to him.

He remembers being packed into one of the city buses that the NYPD commandeered that day to bring as many emergency personnel into the city as they possibly could. There had never been a day like this before in the nation that anyone that he knew could remember. "They are about to take down building seven," came a cry from someone on the bus. As he looked around him, he could see the steely faces resolved to do their jobs in protecting the citizens of this country, but Brian could also see the burden on those men and women as well, because so many of them had come to work that morning without kissing their loved ones or saying goodbye before they left. They knew in their hearts that this could be it. The very present reality was telling them that this very moment held their very existence on this planet in question. Yet there they were...

He closed his eyes and allowed a bit of relief to wash over himself... was that... yelling? BOOM! A brick dropped square onto his face... WHAT THE FUCK!

As he fought his way back up from the blackness, Brian found himself taking in everything that was swirling around him. How long had he been out? What the hell had just happened. GOD DAMN IT! WHERE IS MY WEAPON AND KIT!

With no idea how long he had been knocked out, fighting dust in his lungs and trying to come to his senses, Errickson was starting to come to. He found his SAW, body armor, and assault pack, which was always loaded up with ammo for the fight. They had just been hit with something... but what the hell was it? Who was hurt? Was this going to be a complex attack?

He joined Cruea, Garcia, and Marsh at a spot in the wall that was breached wide open and the perfect target of opportunity to anyone who wanted to flow into the compound and start shooting them up and laying bursts of automatic fire into their bodies. "Holy shit guys! HERE THEY FUCKING COME!" someone said as they saw figures coming down the road at speed.

They lit up the alleyway with a ferocity to counter anything that dared challenge them that day as their brothers lay under the rubble behind them. With no idea of the full extent of the damage behind them, they only knew one thing: kill anything that came advancing on their position at this very moment. No idiot other than a terrorist would be running toward the source of an explosion this big anytime soon.

"OH FUCK, CEASE FIRE, STOP SHOOTING!!! CEASE FUCKING FIRE!!!" boomed SFC Frazier as he yelled with everything he had to implore his men to stop dealing death towards the figures that had stopped advancing on them. "God damn it! That's 3rd Platoon, fuck, THAT'S THIRD FUCKING PLATOON!!!"

In a quick exchange, they yelled over to the figures crouching behind cover. Thankfully, no one was hit either. The platoons didn't blame each other either, but holy crap if some of those guys weren't almost cut down in a hail of friendly fire during the incident. Everyone immediately put it aside and focused their attention on the scene behind them. Good God...

The entire compound had been flattened and people that were missing were still emerging after being uncovered from the rubble. This was a task Errickson could do. He had dug others out before during his time in the fire department. This was his sole purpose and existence right then and there and this is what he knew how to do and do well.

Training and instincts built in from years on the job kicked in as he started to move into what had been the barracks areas and methodically, but swiftly, began the process of extracting the bodies of his fellow soldiers. All while hoping and praying that they would still be alive.

One after another, the men were removed in various positions throughout the compound. All had been buried alive and some were not doing so well. Specialist Lucas Cullum had been heard screaming underneath the earth, but was silenced as dirt began to fill his mouth and the soil and rocks started to bear down on his body, slowly crushing him and causing his breathing to shallow. In the nick of time, SFC Frazier, Skowlund, and Jacob frantically uncovered him and began the process of triage.

All over the compound, it seemed like the bodies were being unearthed from underneath piles of rock and remnants of material that were original or had been built into the outpost as a fortification improvement. Errickson moved with the shaken but able-bodied guys that were able to uncover the others. When they finally had everyone accounted for, he started looking for what to do next. Someone stationed in an airborne unit excels at understanding there is always something else to do during a moment of crisis, so start looking for that next task and get after it.

Oh my God... he realized in horror as he approached the collapsed portion of the compound towards the back end. The kids... He began to dig with the others.

Body after body, they began to come across the little ones, now limp in their arms. Those that they had come to protect had become casualties of war all because they were caught in the middle of the fight.

The people within the valley just wanted to live. Here we stood, defending them from the constant state of fear that was imposed on them from those that preyed on the weak within the towns and villages of the area. The realization came that although his brothers in arms would live to fight another day, they would now live with the reality that they could not always provide safety for the civilians they were there to protect.

Back at Johnston

I'll never forget hearing Sergeant Simon Miguel's voice come over the radio about two minutes after the blast. They had been out on patrol when the blast occurred and he had climbed up on the roof of one of the compounds with his manpack radio to call for help. The OP worked as their relay for communications coordinating the reaction efforts to come from COP Ware and getting squads out there to assist. The enemy had driven a VBIED close enough with enough explosives to level the entire village block. When you consider how much abuse some of the mud hut walls could take, 2nd Platoon had been very lucky to make it out of there that day. SPC Chad Stewart was on the observation team stationed on OP165 that day and ended up relaying to command while we awaited the call to get us on station to assist as well.

We heard of guys being buried in the rubble and they were digging people out of the blast radius. Two people were vomiting up mud from the dirt they had swallowed during the incident and were lucky they hadn't perished in the tomb created by the blast. This is when the picture featured on the cover was taken as the platoon was uncovering portions of the remains of their outpost and one of them was snapping pictures of the damage. In the spirit of those that had inspired our national anthem, the guys lifted the American flag that had previously flown over COP Brunk from the debris as dirt, dust, and stones were falling off of it. It was an emotional picture that summed up our experience in the valley as we were constantly hit and would have to refit, regroup, and be right back at it hours later.

Dissenters and Pacts

Our resolve was hardened with each hit that we took in the valley and it only made us more determined to stop whoever was trying to break us down. We itched to take the fight to the enemy as we heard firefights daily from across the river. Charlie Company was getting the full opposite treatment that we were when it came to enemy engagement. The enemy wouldn't go near us with any direct-action attempts because they knew we would run through them and the losses wouldn't be worth the attack. Instead, they played it smart and dug in, only operating covertly to lay in ordnance and slowly dwindle our numbers while working on crushing our spirits. It was working on some of the guys.

Certain troops were refusing to leave the wire because of how petrified they were of losing a limb or what they thought of as a normal functioning life. Attitudes like that would start creeping through the ranks like a cancer and it was something that needed to be stopped right away.

James Staples was getting ready for one of the daily patrols when he noticed one of the guys was missing. He headed back into the tents to figure out where he had gone. Damn joe was always making life hard on him. Easiest shit in the world… right time, place, and uniform. Just had to suit up and walk around. That was exactly the problem.

His missing guy was sobbing softly on his bunk with his head in his hands. Staples was now taken aback. He thought that maybe the guy had left his batteries or something, not this. He had to make a decision on the fly how he was going to approach this. "Do I really have to go out?" The soldier turned his head with bloodshot eyes and tear stains running down the dust that covered everything. "Fuck yeah, you have to go out! All the other guys are down there already waiting on your ass to go out. Why the fuck do you think you're special? You think they want to go out either? Fuck, I don't want to go out… you know why the fuck I'm out there, you motherfucker!"

James was heated, but the feelings of the other kid echoed some of his own. He just couldn't show it because he had others depending on his strength to hold it together in the situation. Could he hold it together? He felt bad yelling at him, but he also knew that sometimes the training instilled in these kids took over. The reaction that the Army had placed within his psyche to "get it done" when the situation got rough took over and the kid mustered the strength to throw on his armor and grab a rifle while heading out the door.

We would make agreements with the guys we could trust on the patrol that if our wounds hit to a certain degree of disfigurement, to just let us die out there. I was personally OK with my legs being gone, but if I lost my arms, that was it. Doc was told to either make sure it was painless or if it came to it, don't let me hold the team back.

At this point, I'm sure the Afghans were convinced that there was no way we were going to leave the area. They had seen us bleed alongside them in a country that breeds generations of warriors. This type of bond is important. You can't fake something like this. When you can stand tall and hold yourself to a moral code when no one would blame you for going berserker on the villagers, you gain the attention of the population.

The Patrol that Went Wrong

I didn't accompany 2nd squad on many missions, but I remember wanting to go out with their squad for a few reasons. They never hit any landmines in Bobby Musil's squad. They were always careful to never retrace steps, not travel where there had been much patrol activity, and they always took the hard route.

It helped that they were always postured hard. 2nd squad was known as "anger squad" for a reason. It was likened to releasing a bunch of angry hornets upon the valley whenever they left the wire. There had only been one planned ambush attempt during the grenade incident and that had not ended well for the Taliban. Looking right and doing the right thing at most all times makes a difference out there when the enemy is constantly watching. They aren't stupid and will seek out an easier target if given the opportunity because it means they can live to die another day as well.

Being stoked to leave the wire with them, I somehow ended up forgetting to pack the ANCD. I want to say we had just departed the ECP when I realized it wasn't in my pack, but I decided that the fallout from making it known would bar me from the chance to go out alongside anger squad again. So, I stupidly kept my mouth shut.

Let me break down exactly what just happened in that moment. When in a combat zone at that time, you will either run a cryptological key or use frequency time hop for those units that were still behind or needed to sync radios on the fly. The ANCD is a data transfer device that holds the cryptological keys for the radios to function during the week. It's a sensitive item and if the enemy gets their hands on a unit, the entire campaign theater will have to change their frequency crypto keys right away. I knew right where I had left it, but I didn't have it on my person to reload a radio in case anything went down while on patrol.

Not a big deal because there were so many backups. I had a manpack radio, a Harris 152, and a Motorola for the guard towers. The squad leader had his handheld MBITR radio along with ample spare batteries. If a radio was running low on battery power, you just swapped it out before it died and you wouldn't lose your frequency settings. All the batteries had been charged, tested, and verified as good to go during the pre-mission checks.

In a freak occurrence mid-patrol, Bobby's radio goes out and loses fill. So, I have everything programmed to be the same in my radio so it's not a big deal. I hand my radio to him and get everything situated to keep pushing forward. I just continue mission using my manpack as the radio source. Plenty of radios to go around and we were having to run multiple frequencies on this mission.

About 30 minutes later, the radio I had handed Musil went bonkers as well and died completely. I swear the universe was messing with me at this point and that's when I revealed that the ANCD hadn't made it out on patrol with us. I tried a slave cable sync, but that method didn't work either. It was decided that we needed to make our way back, but in a route that would minimize danger and have eyes on our patrol element via one of the towers as we came back across the terrain.

Murphy would show me, yet again, that he wasn't done messing with us because the 117G manpack went completely dead during one of the river crossings. Great. Nothing but an unencrypted Motorola that communicated to the guard towers, but most likely had the enemy listening to the traffic coming across it. I know we listened to their radio and cell calls all the time. I had done river crossings the entire deployment without an issue, but something shorted out or water had leaked into some orifice on our communications source because that thing was dead.

We received word that air assets were going "black," which meant that we no longer possessed the possibility of getting air assets or casevacs while we traveled back to COP Johnston. We hunkered down into a position next to one of the creek beds as we waited for a dust storm to pass. These dust storms would inherently mess with operations on the battlefield of Afghanistan because nature's elements would just refuse to cooperate with the mission timelines that had been set forth.

We eventually made it back to COP Johnston, but not without me having learned a valuable lesson. Backups on backups on backups… and don't try to hide something that could be a damn detriment to the entire unit while you are out there just to save a little face. You won't in the end… in the end, you could possibly end up getting people killed.

Meant for Us—July 13–14

It was probably due to better relations with the locals that we received the tip we were on the target list for a VBIED attack. We attempted to "red team" the situation and think of all the possible ways the enemy could come at us. Ultimately, SFC Hill just cut off the road that traversed the front of the outpost and forced any local traffic to go around the entire field perimeter outside of the village. The distance was only an additional 700m or so and any foot traffic could still pass by without any issue. It proved to be the right move as within three days, someone probed the wire in the middle of the night.

1st squad was just coming back from a patrol in the town of Morgan when Sgt Ackers heard some radio tower chatter about a suspicious vehicle on the road. It was one of those smaller motorcycle carts that had a utility truck-type cab on the back end of it. They had come from the main town area and seemed to be confused as they approached the newly pushed-out blockade of concertina wire and traffic cones. The driver stopped short of the serpentine and sat there for a few seconds. It looked like he had been accustomed to the route and had not expected to encounter the blockade that lay in front of him now. Chris Wiesner was in the guard tower that overwatched that section of road and had been watching all of this unfold. He retrieved his green laser to attempt to direct the cart around the field.

When the laser light illuminated the razor wire in front of the driver and motioned along the new path of travel, the vehicle performed a quick K turn and went back into town. It wasn't until later that we realized the significance of the situation.

Overall, it was a quiet night. The patrol sat outside an area of ruins on the outskirts of town after strolling through the middle of town earlier. We just waited for a bit while watching the nighttime activity under the stars. The patrol only lasted about three hours and was meant to shake up the established patterns a bit. It wasn't too much past midnight when we headed back to COP Johnston for the night to hopefully get some rack time before the next day under the desert sun. We were inside the entry control point and Ackers had started to do the after-action review for what had essentially been a boring night. That was when the sky lit up and the aftershock hit us.

Tracers started burning through the sky and the tower facing the bazaar on the main road started screaming of incoming rounds over the radio. I would have been terrified too, as those damn guard towers were just a metal shack placed on stilts, out in the open. There were some bulletproof areas, but no one trusted the rating so we had placed additional sandbags behind the outer walls as well. I preferred the low position of the secondary towers along with the fact that they contained all the heavy crew-served weaponry that had been pulled from the trucks. Most of your body was behind six to eight feet of Hesco barrier filled with dirt and sand that would shield you in a fight, not the few inches of sand within the bags that were in the higher towers.

"What the fuck was that?!" Ackers said to me. "You got anything?" We headed to the TOC as he told his squad to stay in full kit and top off on water while we figured out what was going on. COP Ware was already on the radio with SFC Hill and they were just as baffled as us. Hill was damn near begging Captain Armstrong to unleash us to respond to the fight down the road and move to the contact position immediately. The commotion was coming from the direction of the ANCOP facility that was in the Gondigan area. We were told to hold tight until further instructions came down about how to respond to the situation.

After what seemed like forever, SFC Hill joined us at the ECP and supplemented the patrol with some of Weapons squad in case the situation turned into a large-scale firefight. Things had quieted down at this point and we were pretty sure we had missed any of the action. Everything pointed to the Taliban rerouting the ordnance that was meant for us and using it against the Afghan prison or the police checkpoint that was down the road. We had only stopped by that prison on sporadic occasions and hadn't worked with any of the ANP from that particular station. Essentially, we were going in blind.

We took the road and ran to what we hoped would be a release for the pent-up anger that we held towards the enemy that operated in our area. It wasn't the uncontrolled hellbent anger that would get people killed, but something much more focused than that. This was the chance to unload our pent-up aggression combined with solid tactical training combined with a few thousand rounds to cut down those responsible for our fallen brothers up to this point. It was a downright murderous run and I loved every minute of it.

The walls rose up on either side of us as we all ran towards the commotion. You couldn't see a damn thing on either side, and it was essentially a gauntlet, where someone could have placed an effective ambush or a bomb if they had wanted to take a large-sized element out. When we turned the corner, the scene that unfolded in front of us was surreal. The once-pristine white wall that stood about 30 feet high now had a massive, blackened smoldering sore gouged into the side of it.

Fox Company had been coming through the area and were caught in the middle of what was a complex attack that breached the walls of the prison compound. A donkey cart laden down with heavy explosives detonated itself against the ANCOP walls in the adjoining road that traveled the rear wall. Once there was a hole, the attack led to a suicide bomber detonating himself after he ran inside of the breach. Men armed with AKs, RPGs, and grenades began to attack and crossed the threshhold as well. Our towers had seen the tracers from a team of guys led by Lieutenant Scott Haran into one of the guard towers to repel the attackers.

The huge issue was that no one had been in the towers doing anything to stop the attack. The Americans had been requested to stay out of the towers by the Afghan police because the ANCOP barracks were underneath that particular tower and they didn't want the Americans in the tower or coming through their barracks at night. During the day was fine and the tower was staffed, but nighttime patterns of life led to rumors that there might have been some weird goings-on in the Afghan barracks during the night hours.

By the time we arrived, the action was over and we were getting radio chatter that medevac birds were inbound. Hill yelled at me to get the long whip out for comms and we started assisting in bringing the Blackhawks down into the graveyard across from the prison to get the wounded out of there. The scene was eerie as the red smoke floated around the Afghan grave markers and the wounded were loaded up. I don't even remember how many we put on the birds as Ackers and his squad pulled security and provided a perimeter.

Afterwards, SFC Hill approached what was left of the northern wall of the prison. There was a huge gaping hole there now with smoke and smoldering ruin coming from within. Hill started yelling "friendlies" as we came through the wall to try and assess what exactly was going on. SFC Hill and I entered the compound and linked Ackers up with the 1/508 element that was currently pulling there. What you saw when you came through the hole was a section of tents that had been completely blown over and across the courtyard. These tents had held troops in them at the time of the blast and had been tossed a distance of about 100ft. An AC unit the weight a few hundred pounds was up on its side like it had been flicked by a finger on the hand of God. We hadn't even known this size element had been here, but damn, they had just received the full effect of the Arghandab that night.

We came through the hole and headed to the far right which was where the battalion command TOC was housed. As we entered the building, there were 10 or so huge screens against the far wall with over half of them only offered static snow while others were pouring with information, showing BFT (Blue Force Tracker) graphics of troops in the area, TAC chat, and ISR imagery. Different portions of the floor were slick with blood because some of the troops had brought Lieutenant Christopher Goeke into the TOC as a sign of respect for the man who had just died. The wounded had now been emptied from the casualty collection point and it was starting to quiet down. At this point, they had people directing everything so there wasn't too much for me to do while Hill was briefed by Lieutenant Colonel David Oclander on the scene and what we could assist with.

I had been directed to help out with anything I could in the CCP or with radio equipment while staying nearby. Because all of the urgent trauma cases had been taken care of, I ended up checking over a kid who had been caught in the middle of the situation. He was clearly shaken as he spoke in a tearful broken voice about Staff Sergeant Sheldon Tate who had shielded him when they had jumped into the bunker together. Tate had been killed but this kid had made it out. Sometimes, that's just how it is.

The 1/508 element that was there thought that they were receiving an incoming rocket attack because of how strange the initial explosion was. So, like at Kandahar Air Field, some dove into the bunker along with some interpreters. The others also poured out of the tents and into security positions as fast as they could. The Taliban had hit in a complex and well-coordinated attack. As they entered the hole that was created by the VBIED in the wall, they unloaded with grenades, RPGs, and random AK fire to accompany suicide bombers. The guard towers hadn't done a damn bit of good because there was no standoff from the road that ran right alongside the wall. The Taliban knew right where the bunkers were and came through randomly spraying bullets into the bunker and raining death on anyone that had sought refuge within.

I listened as the traumatized kid poured out his story about the guy that had died on top of him and had kept him from certain death. I was numb to the losses at this point and more interested in what had happened, while also frustrated we weren't allowed to assist earlier to cut the perpetrators down in a fury of hot lead and hate.

This was the kind of warning that you need to look for because this is where you ride the edge of your humanity. When you become dulled to human loss and decide to process those emotions later, this is something you will take away with you for life. It's a survival mechanism and something that changes perspective of your place within the universe. At this point, we were more primal than I have had the chance to explore again. It was wonderfully simple and at the same time, more complex than most would ever want to face.

On one end, I wanted to yell at the kid for leaving his weapon behind when the attack started, but on the other, I understood that wouldn't accomplish any good at this moment in time. That's not what was needed. He would judge himself far more harshly down the road than I ever could. It was safe to say that the majority of the guys from Bravo Company were more upset about not getting to the scene in time to unleash hell upon the enemy. This was coupled with frustration about the lack of security that was allowed by the superiors in the situation. Bunch of heartless bastards… and exactly what was needed in that particular part of the world at the time.

The takeaway was to always expect the worst and never trust another entity to pull guard to watch over your own. We were offered guard duty services multiple times by the foreign nationals in Helmand months earlier, but we had still maintained our own. If anyone ever offers to have their men pull guard, put your own in the towers alongside the force you are fighting with. Ask them to have their men "train" yours in their proficiency or to have show us how they pull guard. A cross-training with your men alongside the allied troops would put their ego at ease. Ultimately, it was determined to have been an inside job as the towers didn't open fire on combatants that breached the walls during the incident. They had also found an Afghan police counterpart pacing the lengths of the tents and equipment that was housed within the walls of the ANCOP.

The other question was why didn't the police outpost on the opposing hill catch the enemy in crossfire or move to assist their brethren when the initial attack occurred? The questions of operating within that valley began to severely blur and you needed to break the situation down to what was right and true in the face of the moment with the information that was in front of you. Afghan troops were starting to appear more and more undisciplined and the more prevalent appearance of hashish being grown or smoked among them was a major concern. They really didn't have our backs if it got down to the brass tacks and there were less and less men that you could trust to not side with the enemy if things got really ugly.

Life in the Continuation of the Suck

At this point, the mission within the Arghandab was mainly focused on establishing a proper presence within DK and solidifying our grasp in that area. The amount of missions blurred as any "free time" you had was eaten up by necessary tasks. You needed to be focused and catching up on episodes of whatever show your friends had brought back with them from their mid-tour leave rarely took precedence.

SPC Adam Voelker had this huge chest of novels he kept at the end of his bunk area like a giant library for our time there. He was always picking something up and I think there was a bet about how many books he could finish in the time we were there. There was an X-Box that had shown up that we paired to a TV some of the guys had stolen from the walls within Lashkar Gah. Stuff would trickle in from here and there and we had a continual community pile held within a tri wall container between the two Alaskan tents where anything was up for grabs.

The squads didn't associate with each other much unless the guys served together in another squad or platoon previously. It made for little gangs that rolled together and were fiercely territorial about their areas within the tent. I was able to enjoy a bit of neutrality as I had been in two different squads as a machine gunner and would cycle through the squads during the patrols as needed because I was the RTO. I got a "pass" because the guys knew I could acquire things and I was good with electronics.

SFC Hill gave me a little slack at this point due to either exposure to my methods or the fact that I was being utilized heavily within the domain of 1st Platoon. One of the best compliments I ever received in the Army was said in response to a visiting command member. They asked some sort of question about the operation of something at the COP and Hill's response was something along the lines of, "You'd have to ask Yeske over there, the kid pretty much runs the damn place."

There was a running joke that I was from a vast fortune of money and was only doing this stint in the military as an adventure. Harris had given me the alternate nickname of "Billions" and it stuck only to reinforce their whisperings of an unclear backstory. So, I played into it and would occasionally call for my imaginary butler "Jeeves" for various pieces of kit or to pick up the patrol site because we were about to move out. The other side of the joke was to play a sort of knight's squire for Hill and either provide the desired piece of equipment or clack something together behind Hill as he walked. It was intended to portray the scene from Monty Python's *Holy Grail* where King Arthur is on an imaginary horse and the fellow behind him knocks some coconuts together to make the sounds of hooves as they skip along. Someone would always attempt to add some strange contribution to the atmosphere to attempt to take the edge off.

The one other time I ever received any validation from SFC Hill was on patrol one night. We had stopped on the backside of a hill while waiting it out on one of the zero dark stupid hour patrols when he decided to risk a cigarette. Technically, he didn't smoke anymore, but since the day Johnston had died, he would occasionally light up. I carried extra smokes because of this… maybe a bit of a suck up in that regard, but the technique had saved me from another "situation black." I was told that I had been an absolutely horrible joe, but once they started pouring on responsibilities, I turned out all right. It was his way of saying that I was heading in the right direction and it actually gave me a bit of hope that I might stand a chance during my next progression of my career as long as I made it out of here.

Maybe it was also a bit of that trust that earned me the right to carry a hand grenade in my kit. A grenade isn't something to get scared about except when the area had a lot of walls to climb over, and things would get caught on your kit and pull on it. That's why there is a method of taping the pin on a grenade in a particular way and storing it within a closed pouch. I had a pouch that was specific to that purpose on my kit but had only held a can of Copenhagen up until that point, which was also a patrol necessity. Firstly, the grenade tape is one small strip of masking tape that is just meant to be an additional safety measure as well as providing a stabilizer for the ring on the pin to stay in one position. If you do it correctly, the pin won't slip out of its position and the ring will be easy to grab and pull, even if you are fumbling for it, which will be the case for most.

Hill's father had spent his career as a Green Beret serving with various units within the Special Forces for a span of 20 years. He had ended his career as a master sergeant and I imagined that his son had wanted to follow a military path of his own instead of following in Dad's footsteps. From what I gathered during our training cycles, which was then reinforced with a combat deployment, Mathew Hill was in exactly the role he was meant to play in life. He was a conventional army warfighter, but in the best of ways. When it came to the infantry's true task of getting down and dirty with the enemy to accomplish the mission, there was no one better for the job. I knew he had seen some action in Iraq prior and there was talk of Bosnia at one point in his career, so I gathered that he was serving in the military prior the towers coming down. Whatever the case, he sympathized with my case to make another try at the Special Forces route and didn't give me too much grief about it, unlike the majority of the rest of the company.

A lot of the struggle to get there was filling any of my down time with tasks that needed to be accomplished to get to where I wanted to be in the military. I knew that I wanted to head back to the Special Forces Selection and Qualification Course, so I had to stay in good shape for that as well. Not many were motivated to do additional workouts on top of the strain induced from being on patrol, but there were guys who helped out in putting together some sort of makeshift gym area. It consisted of vehicle tow bars and TRX straps that would be combined with 100m sprints that ran the back side of the COP.

A short stocky redhead by the name of John Kenney had joined us at some point and was always willing to throw heavy things around the yard. I would find John Meier and Adam Voelker back there sometimes too, but again, you had to be careful about stressing your body too much because of the environment and constant op tempo. I was having four jugs of protein sent in a month to supplement the food there to try to stay in shape. A lot of the guys had leaned out and started to look like their clothes were hanging off of them like bags. If anywhere has a challenging enough terrain to toss your body into a state of eating itself, it's Afghanistan.

One patrol led us through the orchards at night and we halted after a few high wall crossings. I questioned what was going on and someone whispered that Meier had a bad fall off one of the walls and had messed his shoulder up. I didn't fully realize what had happened until later, but he had fallen off the top of one of the walls and landed face first into one of the small streams that trickled through the region. The weight in the bag of the assistant machine gunner forced him underwater and he couldn't breathe for a while before Voelker realized what was happening and fished him out. I called for a medevac helicopter while Meier argued about leaving the battlespace. One of the new guys, Watson, magically developed a scratched cornea condition and offered to take John's place on the helicopter out of the valley. Watson ended up being an alright guy, but I know that I wasn't the only one to question his dedication to the unit over the incident.

There were philosophical conversations between the guys involving thoughts on death, events that were happening back home, regrets, good memories, jokes, and everything else in between. Somehow, the battlefield has a way of bringing about a census of all that you possess in your life and rearranging the importance of how things measure up with your newfound perspective. The real fact is that not many of the trimmings do matter. It's just that. The real substance is from within and the raw experiences life has to offer.

A healthy dose of this came from an attachment by the name of Sergeant Jacob "Doc" Shultz. Shultz was an E5 medic who was, quite frankly, burnt out by the time he arrived. He did not care the least bit how he looked, acted, or was perceived, but he always put forth a professional effort when it came to his job. We had needed an additional medic because Ponce was getting worn out as well due to being so overworked at this point. Doc Rudy Ponce was an awesome guy, but he was out walking on every patrol because you were required to have a medic with you due to the IED threat; it would grind anyone into the dirt.

Sgt Shultz had come over from Charlie Company and brought with him an air of comedic relief along with some illustration skills. Now we had another competent doc on the scene and our chances of survival were better. It didn't hurt that his "bedside manner" was a comedy routine in of itself. He had the personality of a battleground philosopher who would one day be an aspiring journalist or war reporter. Everyone expected him to show up as such one day. Maybe it was that I drew my own parallels to his resemblance of the character Matthew Modine played in *Full Metal Jacket* as Sergeant Joker.

One of his memorable contributions to our reflections on life and human behaviors was his intervention in the "most epic way to commit suicide" conversation. His version involved a bungie jump coupled with shortened piano wire that was fastened around the neck with his hands glued to his ears. That way, his body would bob over the overpass after the piano wire decapitated him during the jump and his headless body would be left holding its own head as it dangled above the passing cars, spraying everyone with gore that was pumped out of the dangling body. We laughed about that sort of thing at the time. It was really dark humor that you became familiar with as your time developed within the ranks. Maybe the idea was if you can't laugh at death, then your experience with it is going to be much more horrific when it comes for you.

Doc knew he was a necessary asset and his worth among us was high, so he took advantage of the leverage. We were heading out on a three-day blocking position mission and he showed up at the last minute wearing white running sneakers. SFC Hill was furious, but at the same time, didn't care enough to delay the patrol another few minutes for a pair of shoes. Shultz looked about as ate up as the interpreter and maybe that was the plan. He was damn good at his job, so did he really need anything else other than his knowledge and the lifesaving equipment that he carried with him in the bag on his back?

Another asset that had been attached to 1st Platoon was Sergeant Jason Spottedhorse, a fires NCO who assisted us along with PFC Martinek. He was a giant Native American from the Kiowa tribe who had a gentle heart but a wild spirit. My job got easier as they integrated him into the patrol rotation in a supplemental RTO role because we were all cross-trained in the radio equipment, channels, and etiquette needed for operations in the valley. He just had more capabilities and experience than I did in the craft. Someone had pointed out a pattern that if we had more than one manpack radio source on patrol, such as me and Martinek, we would get hit almost every time. It was so much so, that superstitions and fears stopped having us put onto patrol rotations together.

Every day would bring its own challenges and the next day was always sure to bring more. We would catch word of someone else catching a bomb or being involved in an IED incident, or we would just be told that the situation called for us to take down our ability to communicate with the outside world until further notice. This was so they could ensure the family of the deceased would find out through official channels first instead of catching a tweet or social media post about it.

The odds were that you were almost certain to step on a landmine within the area and it was just a matter of when. We were joined by reporter Bill Neely from NBC/ITV news for a short time on COP Johnston to produce a segment on the area because of the sheer number of bombs we had been finding, along with the jab about General McCrystal being removed from command. We were quick to be annoyed and disenchanted with the task of lugging around a reporter because it increased our chances of being hemmed up for something that we did wrong. There were stories circulating of people going to jail for doing their job, but someone, somewhere wanted to make an example of them.

We softened towards the reporter a bit after hearing how he had been kidnapped by the Taliban while in Kandahar a few years ago and had no love for the insurgents we were fighting against. It put our minds at ease a little, but we were still wary not to say the wrong thing at the wrong time. A bunch of us were interviewed by Mr. Neely along with his videographer, Daniel Demoustier, who was along for the ride. The sight was comical as the subject being interviewed was being watched by the squad leaders, who were looking over the video camera, ready to pounce on you for any words that could be construed as derogatory towards your purpose in

Afghanistan. I understood, and so was one of the few the command team on the COP allowed to be interviewed.

None of the interviews were ever used and the two-minute-long final snippet found its way onto YouTube at some point. It still exists mixed into the web of cyberspace along with some of Mr. Neely's career videos that are posted on the NBC servers. Not everything produced that covered the war was seen by the public and things are different these days as cell phones capture battlefield moments better than on-scene news cameras have been able to in the past. One opportune moment occurred when Specialist William VanDerSlick had a hilarious slip up while being filmed during a patrol.

Slick was an older guy who joined after an incident had him leave the police force he had served on for many years and rejoin the military after a massive break in between tours. If I was considered old at 26, then he was freaking ancient. When he showed up, I thought it was a joke that we would be toting grandpa through the minefields alongside us. After some more digging, we found that he had been in the Marines during *Desert Storm*! I guess they really will take just about anyone into the fold during times of war.

There's a moment in the video where you see him slouched over. You won't catch the audio as the voiceover from the reporter is blaring over everything, but if you could, you would have heard the words, "I just hope I hit a fucking mine already." I saw it happen as the cameraman had been looming around like a shark in an area we were experiencing difficulty moving through. It's all a game to them. Slick chuckled as he realized what he had just said was immortalized on film and might come back to haunt him later... you're welcome, Slick. That uttered sentiment was the feeling of the majority of the men stationed on COP Johnston. Their hopes had gone from never wanting to hit a mine to praying that it would only be one of the versions that took a foot or minor extremity.

As the conflict became a war of attrition, the feelings on the outpost changed. The unit before us was driven to the point of turning their frustration and anger onto the civilian populace, but we hadn't stooped to that level, and we never would. I honestly think that was the real battle within the Arghandab: continually doing the right thing in the face of everything that screams to you that it wasn't worth it to stay on the path of the righteous. By this time, everyone in the platoon was tight enough to know better than to talk if an incident like that happened and would cover our asses, but thankfully, no one attempted such an indiscretion.

Day after day, we continued to trudge through that valley, waiting for the inevitable.

The Rumor Mill

A few of the men were scared to continue patrolling and would invent injuries, illnesses, and other reasons why they couldn't leave the safety of the outpost.

Everyone was scared to some degree, but when you let that fear take hold of you is when it becomes an issue. A healthy dose of fear can keep you in check, such as the version that arises every time I jump out of an aircraft. I was always double and triple checking my equipment, looking around me, watching the other people for problems, and seeing what the aircraft crew faces and reactions said. I liked to be one of the last out of the plane because I was able to see how the jump was going and how the follow-on mission was destined to go.

Occasionally, someone would need to come off patrol rotation for a few days because the situation in their head was so overwhelming, they couldn't focus on the job at hand. An occasion that happened to Barry Pilcher after his wife told him she wanted a divorce one night over the satellite phone. He started to get into his own head really badly about it and realized that his obligation fell under keeping his team alive and he was out of focus.

It took some balls to talk to the platoon sergeant about a situation like that in an area where he needed everyone to pitch in heavily to make the operation work, but SFC Hill put him on double tower guard rotations for a few days so he could figure it out. Pilcher was back on patrol within three days, but the rumor mill had painted him to be one of the guys that refused to leave on patrol. The guys weren't the same towards him after that. Soldiers can be downright nasty to each other in a war zone if you let dissention grow.

They didn't have the decency or ability to let someone know they couldn't handle it and to get them out of there. I understand that some guys that just can't cut it. You are better off without them weighing you down out there anyway. There is a difference between scared of your reality and a chickenshit coward. I applaud the statement offered by Col Beckwith that states, "I'd rather go down the river with 10 studs than 100 shitheads."

There is a story in the Bible that talks about a leader named Gideon taking on a much larger military force than his own and God telling him to put the men that had showed up to a few different tests. The tests whittle the fighting force down—but they were already outnumbered and it seemed like a suicide mission to be cutting their numbers before the battle even began.

Around 32,000 men showed to fight, but they were told if anyone was afraid to stay back. The element moved forward with 10,000 men. They were further whittled down after stopping for a rest by a river. The men that drank from the river in a particular way would be the only ones chosen to go forward into the battle. When the number was down to just 300, Gideon was told by the Lord that he had the right number to attack the enemy. Needless to say, they prevailed and went on to win the day.

This is a concept that is echoed within our own military these days as you are already set apart by volunteering for service and being chosen as eligible to serve. If you are in an airborne unit, there is another sense of pride, because you were required to volunteer to serve there as well. There are other units in the service where you need to volunteer additionally along with a physical and mental selection. The process is supposed to uncover those that can handle the more difficult battles to be fought.

There is a quote from Heraclitus that states, "Out of every one hundred men, ten shouldn't even be there, eighty are just targets, nine are the real fighters, and we are lucky to have them, for they make the battle. Ah, but the one, one is a warrior, and he will bring the others back." How true this sentiment rings and how difficult it is to try to look at oneself objectively to see where you fall along that spectrum.

Among those feigning injury to not go on patrol were the plain suicidal folks. One of the cooks at COP Ware fell along that spectrum as he openly talked about cutting a specific nerve in his hand that would get him discharged from the Army along with the warzone he was stuck in currently. I don't know what his problem was because he wasn't even going out on the patrols with us!

Bad Boys

On a patrol to the village of Mian Juy, the Mullah offered for us to stay in the mosque that night and run our patrols out of there because it would be a safe place. It was a huge indicator that the attitude toward the Americans had changed. Talk to anyone of the Muslim or Islamic faith and they will tell you that a mosque is a sacred place of worship and where people are ok to enter them, it would be highly unlikely to be invited into the mosque in a time of war to originate combat patrols from to kill the assailants that were dragging villagers out of their houses to beat them in the middle of the night.

We refused the honor as we already had plans drawn up for that particular stay and didn't want to heighten the enemy's hostile attitude towards the villagers any more than it had been already. Things were changing in the valley, but the cost was high.

A particular compound near where we had gotten into that firefight after someone lobbed a grenade over the wall at Musil's squad now housed someone who had come under interest. We geared up and headed in that direction. We ended up bringing the particular homeowner back with us along with another guy to COP Johnston for questioning after they showed up as a "person of interest" in the HIIDE biometric system.

Between the biometrics systems and the explosive chemical detection swabs, we would have our hands full in "police" work throughout the region. One of the large issues we faced was that the nitrates that were common to the farms of that area as fertilizer usage would also be used in formulating homemade explosives. Who is to say which ones were just trying to make a living and which were mixing up a home brew designed to end our lives.

The Afghan police chief put the suspected men under arrest and we held them at the ECP inside the guard shack until some nondescript vehicles showed up to haul them off. It made me wonder just how many people disappeared in a country that size during the Afghan conflict and how easy it could be to just "disappear" someone living in the United States with our capabilities.

Shenanigans

The pace at which the operations were run throughout the valley was blistering, but sometimes the situation slowed enough to where time allowed for occasional frivolities to be enjoyed. One such was the shared TV shows, movies, and pornography the guys all had. One of them would bring back a virus after they mass dumped everything on to a hard drive from back home and then they would start plugging it into everyone's computer to share the new files they had brought back with them.

I ended up wiping a lot of the guys computers clean in between my TOC guard duties because of the widespread system crashing problems. There wasn't all that much to do on TOC guard anyway, so sitting and watching a computer while it re-images isn't all that rough and it gave me some favor chips to cash in on later. I didn't have much time to watch anything because the time just didn't exist in my world, but my escape lay in music. I would listen to a wide range before I drifted off into sleep as I attempted to just decompress from the constant noises of war around me.

A small sense of complacency and breakdown of discipline started to pop up from time to time. Discipline is something that keeps you alive in combat situations, so it's dangerous as hell when soldiers begin to let their guard down. There was some talk of someone smoking hash in one of the guard towers and another that someone had slept with one of the interpreters. PNN is a hell of a thing, but you couldn't rule out that these were possibilities.

One of 1SG Mcalister's big things was uniforms. It wasn't really about the uniforms, but it was the principle of discipline at the lowest level. If you start letting the standards fall, that's when you run into problems that go way beyond not wearing the collar on your IOTV. In the situation we were in, you were constantly being watched. They know exactly who you are, they know your habits, and they know the job you hold within the squad. At one point, I was told that they were gunning for me because of the backpack radio… whatever. I never lost any sleep about it.

In modern-day warfare, there is the invasion of "the cool guy." The one who strives to look like a character from the *Call of Duty: Modern Warfare* series. This is not what they want in a conventional unit. They subscribe to the old-school Roman philosophy of how things should be run. Individual units are dressed in uniform so as to give the feeling of being overwhelmed by the legions. You should not be able to tell any soldier apart from another at a glance as the intention is to remain uniform. It's a different battlefield, but the solid reasoning remains within the soldiering bible.

When we heard some of the guys starting to talk about the guys from 2nd Platoon in the DK area going out in baseball caps with no armor, we were flabbergasted. That would never happen with us, but I think after the house was blown down, their sense of caring much ended at a certain point. The reasoning they had wasn't terrible. Body armor did nothing except complicate your injuries sustained in an IED explosion. The battle casualties we had up this point all entailed limbs being blown off or worse. I would have relished the idea to be able to move around unencumbered by armor. That was not the case on our end, and we never really knew if the rumor was even true.

What I know for fact is one of our very own "uniform infractions" was called out over the net by a brigade CSM as we moved through the bazaar near Gondigan at one point. We were on a patrol near the main highway when I got a call over the radio about our damn sleeves being rolled up. An overhead surveillance drone wasn't being used to check our surroundings for enemy combatants... no, it was being used to watch us for rolled sleeves in 100-plus-degree weather. Yet another warm fuzzy feeling that our "protectors" from the echelons above were looking out for us.

At some point, 1st Platoon was tasked to come escort 1SG Mcalister to battalion headquarters on the mountainside for a promotions board. We couldn't believe what we were hearing. Diverting resources that were stretched thin so you can hold a dog-and-pony promotion board for the general staff around you. I can understand the need for ceremony and tradition, but in this case, I'm sure that kid wanting his stripes would have been just as happy having Mac come by the tent and punching it onto his chest one day. It was another one of the occurrences that had us wonder if command was out of touch with the situation entirely. It gave the feeling of being disposable.

I had my own experience that gave me an excuse to not leave the wire towards the end of our time in the Arghandab. Somewhere on patrol, I broke my right big toe. It was pretty damn painful when I would first wake up or during the times on patrol when we were sitting still. The throbbing would be radiating from the tip of my boot and up my leg. What could you do though? There was nothing that could be done other than to tape it to the toe or toes next to it and drive on. I had lasted up until that point on the radio and I knew I could do a better job at it than most that were still there, so I continued to walk on it and ignored the pain because it was better than being a coward.

Lieutenant Demarest's Sweet Addiction

As time pressed onward, we all found our little distraction or slice of happiness to offer a slight interruption from everything going on around us. Lieutenant Demarest was getting hit with taskings day after day, all while trying to pore over patrol routes, come up with new ways to get around the valley without getting blown up, cover a radio shift rotation, find time to go out on patrol, and deal with the delicate balance of morale that was teetering on a thin line. His vices led down the path of sugar. Why not? That delicious little ingredient was as potent as cocaine and could flood the brain areas with a tickle of dopamine from time to time.

Staff Sergeant Smallwood had noticed the uptick in sugary snacks being consumed by the Lt and started to give him grief about it. After a few harassing conversations, there was a wager made that Demarest would resist any of the delicious snack-based treats for a month. This included anything that came from an MRE or would otherwise be found around the COP.

COP Johnston had been improving over time and was getting a little extra attention after the SeaBees had come through and realized just how spartan the living conditions were. We received a freezer connex brought in by one of the engineer units that had dared to travel down our road along with some pallets of snacks like beef jerky, girl scout cookies, and O'Doul's beer. There were some five-gallon containers of Ben and Jerry's in a freezer connex when it arrived and some of the weapons squad crew had already attacked it en masse when we cut the lock and claimed one of the canisters as our own.

By now everyone had heard about the bet and wanted to get a chance to prod the leadership in a good-natured way. Someone had made signs and posted them all over the outpost as a "reminder" for the good Lt that stated, "Don't touch those cookies Vince" on them. Anywhere you would pan your vision, there would probably be a sign visible. The hygiene area where you brushed your teeth in the morning, the "prison gym" area behind the vehicles, the cook's trailer that was on central the hill… and of course, the TOC had them plastered everywhere.

It had been a particularly rough night and as the Lt studied a report as he was planning for a patrol the next day during his late TOC radio guard shift, Sergeant Jason Spottedhorse came into the shack with a set of cups. As the Lt looked over, Spot sat down next to him and whispered to him in a hushed tone. "Hey, I got something for ya."

As Demarest turned his head, his eyes widened as he saw the spoons peeking out of the cups and just the very top of two different flavors of ice cream noticeable from his vantage. In a desperate strained whisper, the Lt almost frantically told Spot off. "You know I can't do that?!" In classic Spottedhorse style, a wide grin came across his face with a twinkle of mischief in his eye. "No one ever needs to know. I won't tell nobody. Not a word."

Between a rock and a hard place, Demarest looked back at the poncho covering the doorway to the rear area of the shack that sufficed as the TOC. Behind the poncho and some plywood that had been tossed up was the sleeping form of SFC Hill and his own bunk. He knew that Hill and anyone else in an NCO position knew of the bet he had with SSG Smallwood. Still…

He reached out his hand and to Spot's delight, took the cups and squirreled them away behind some of the radio equipment. Damn it, he needed this. Every bite of the sweet cream-based treat was like heaven, and he was able to finish it off without anyone else being the wiser. With a look of gratitude and an unsaid thanks later on, he nodded to Spot as they came off duty, ready for some much-needed rack time before heading back out to patrol our area of operations.

Later that day, after a combat patrol, the Lt was headed back up to strip his sweat-laden gear off to start the cycle all over again. He was exhausted. The sheer number of things that needed to happen on an outpost that only had 28 men to man it continually was terrible and was taking a toll on everyone. Not only that, but he had lost his wallet on the patrol and he and Captain Armstrong had spent 10 minutes looking for it in a creek bed while having to halt all movement. It was embarrassing and his ego was feeling beaten as well. He had just finished the AAR and was going to finish the debrief report so he could just get a few minutes of solace before it all began again.

As he headed up the dusty hill, a jeering SFC Hill and smirking SSG Smallwood stood atop the highest point of the apex, holding two cups in their hands with spoons still in them. Oh... damn it! "Think you wouldn't be found out, huh Sir? Could have at least not been a dirty bird about it!" They cackled like the hecklers from the Muppets as they wanted everyone on the COP to know about the Lt's transgression.

He had messed up! Spot had kept his word, but out of all the habits to have gotten him caught, it was leaving a small pile of trash that would collect near his bunk that he would regularly empty when it got to him. There would be no end to hearing about this for the final month we would be living there. Just like it stated in the Bible that Lieutenant Demarest carried with him into the war zone, your whispers shall be shouted from the rooftops. There was no privacy on that COP and the few moments of solitude you would get here and there were short-lived as proximity made any sort of secret absolutely impossible.

While stripping off his soaking wet boots and socks, he felt something bundled in his lower pants leg. Vince knew exactly what it was, although his pride required him to suffer yet one more blow that day. Sure enough, his drenched wallet flopped out of his lower pants pocket into the sand of COP Johnston, as if karma was mocking him for giving into his craving.

Burgers and Brass

We had gotten the word that we had a reason to go into Kandahar for a quick trip and be back within 14 hours. It would be like a holiday on COP Johnston because they would need to cut any patrols for the day as we wouldn't have enough men. It was also highly likely we would hit an IED on the way out. I didn't care... I was happy just to get a change of scenery, even if it was just for a few hours. I was tired of the same old sights and welcomed the road to Kandahar with promise.

Navigating traffic in a foreign country is unnerving; navigating in a foreign country during a war is another; navigating in a war through an area where the enemy likes to drive vehicles packed with explosives up to you is an entirely different ordeal. They are also really good at blowing up stuff in every manner possible in this region of the country. Roadside bombs, bombs in culverts, directional charge bombs, or one ever growing in popularity, the EFP.

The EFP is something that was initially developed by oil drillers in America and even used as a weapon back in World War II. These guys figured out how to put together a home brew version that used a brass disc and rendered anything with armor useless. It would also fragment when it hit the inside of the vehicle so that it sent enough shrapnel bouncing around to shred any of the occupants inside. Not a pleasant way to go and easy enough for the Taliban to make or source from Iran. At least it's better than burning alive... right?

Whatever the case, we made it to KAF without too much trouble and I think the gunners only had to draw down on people two or three times. Most of the traffic could tell we weren't there to play games and left us alone. It was pretty incredible to see the streets of Kandahar and I would love to go back at some point to actually visit the city. It had just as much activity, if not more, than New York City, but it was dirty, gritty, and had a primal feeling to it.

We rolled into the gates and parked just off the boardwalk to drop the Lt off so he could take care of whatever business they needed him for. We had to leave some guards, as even in Kandahar, you don't dare leave your equipment unsecured. The new guys were on it, but we made sure they were rotated out so they could get their squads' shopping lists taken care of. Everyone was given a list from someone within their respective squads because the group on the trip was a hodgepodge of guys from all of the squads there. The trucks weren't even fully manned for the trip because we were taking guys back with us, but we still looked heavy rolling up.

That's when we picked up some of the new privates that they sent us like the kid named Private Ryan Hammers. These jokes exist all over the military within the small pockets of humor throughout the ranks. He was a short, stocky little kid that the guys compared to the animated penguin in the cartoon *Madagascar*. It was a fairly accurate description as his behavior currently matched the character as a brand new private with nothing but space between his ears to fill with knowledge. Hammer hated him, and because they tossed the new private to him, he "downgraded his name to "ball peen" because there was no way that he could live up to the name "Hammer" even if there was no relation or resemblance. (For reference, a ball peen is a small, delicate hammer used in work such as soft metal jewelry).

Two incidents occurred in Kandahar that I vividly remember. I can only attribute the first to living in primal human conditions around only men for so long. I discovered I could literally smell a woman from about 100ft away. I know you may think it's in my imagination, but I'm not the only one who experienced it. It was like a built-in sense that was noticed after just being around just males within a high-stress environment. I thought I was nuts, but after another guy said something about his experience as well, we both had a laugh over it.

The other memorable experience was the fobbit that tried to impose their will onto a bunch of crusty-looking specialists. The uniforms we were wearing were dingy as hell because they were used daily without any method existing to wash them for weeks at a time. With the fact the uniforms were disintegrating on our bodies as they were exposed to the elements, sweat, scrapes, and everything else we encountered in them, we looked like a bag of smashed ass. On top of that, we were wearing an experimental camo pattern that was a deviation of the ACU but had brown patterns integrated throughout to assist with blending into our environment. A lot of money was wasted in the decision to field the ACU pattern of camouflage as I think the only environment it's good for would be a rock quarry. All because the Army didn't want to pay for rights to use the multicam pattern at the time.

A female E6 felt it necessary to try to get in between us and the camel burgers that were being served up at the boardwalk Burger King that night. We were in Afghanistan right around the heyday of what was turning into a circus on the boardwalk at KAF. They even had a TGIF starting operation as we were leaving the country. Being screamed at to come back after we had changed wasn't the right way to approach us about it. We literally just looked at her and went back to talking like she didn't even exist. She went storming off with her boots stomping and nothing ever came of it. Even if there had been, it would have been worth it… small victory, even if it was disrespectful as hell. We just, quite frankly, weren't in the mood.

We were there all of two to three hours before it was back on the road for the familiar sights and sounds of the valley once again.

Retribution

They had gotten the call! Intelligence had created enough of a picture with the amount of evidence collected on the HIIDE and BAT systems, combined with the bomb site exploitation materials, to verify a targeting package on the IED emplacement team that had been operating in the area and plaguing the movements of Bravo Company as they operated throughout the region. It was wheels up in Kandahar and the ground elements moved in to create blocking positions that prevented egress from the insurgents.

1st Platoon was moving with Sgt Ackers' squad to the Afghan police station at Checkpoint Antenna, to remain there until the mission commenced. Lieutenant Demarest took both Sgt Spottedhorse and SPC Martinek with him, acting as a primary and secondary fires controller and RTO. This one was sure to kick off with some action as they had been called in by the task force that was operating within the area to perform another outer cordon mission for them.

They were at an intersection with the company commander, Captain Armstrong, when the A-10s came on station. They had gotten a visual with the bomb emplacement team setting in a charge right then under the cover of the surrounding trees and the group had been joined with another high-value target within the region. Did the men in the orchard even know that there was instantaneous death hurtling down at them from above in the form of massive rounds supplied from the main cannon the pilot rode atop within the cockpit of what was dubbed the ground soldier's best friend?

The orchard where the group was attempting emplacement went up in smoke as the trees exploded around them and there was nowhere to hide during the bombardment that fell from the sky. The bodies of the human occupants of the same space were mutilated as they were pulverized by both hot metal rounds passing through their bodies, and the debris from the destruction of everything else within the area. The precision engagement system that was part of the A-10C variant assisted in delivering the 30mm ammunition supplied by the GAU-8 Gatling cannon at a rate of 3,900 rounds per minute.

Helicopter blades were heard slapping the air as they were now visible and quickly closing in on the target area. A pair of choppers came in fast and immediately opened up, expertly coordinating attacks from multiple approaches as the fields of fire intersected with the areas the A-10 had just hit with its main cannon.

Between the work the A-10 had done and the helicopters making short work of any other targets on the ground, the last of the insurgents fell into a ditch just outside of the initially impacted area, no longer able to move any further as his body's functions shut down one after another from the loss of blood.

2nd Platoon moved in to assess the site and collect any of the evidence that remained along with the EOD team. After getting the full picture of the charge being laid into the ground and the site the Taliban had chosen for the bomb, they realized that it was identical to the methodology that had killed SSG Scott Brunkhorst earlier that year. "Isn't karma a motherfucker," thought the EOD team leader as he came to the realization that these were the guys who, up until now, had been their nemesis within the valley. As their bodies were catalogued and bagged up, a sense of satisfaction grew within the guys even though they hadn't been the ones to have pulled the trigger to end the existence of the scourge that had plagued them for so long. They wouldn't be bothering anyone anymore, that's for sure.

Kids

A troubling occurrences happened after Doc Ponce and Shultz had created a makeshift casualty collection point in the event we had another attempted base attack or if we had to assist a unit that was hit heavily in the area. It was mostly some camo netting covering two stretchers with IV stands and some equipped tough boxes nearby. Preparation and having an area staged for whatever you might need it for was a good

75 percent of risk mitigation as it was. When it was prepped for a future event, we trained for it, discussed the possible outcomes, and you cleared it with the others to make improvements or implement their good ideas. Some worked... some sucked.

We got a call from the ECP "tower" which was a MaxxPro Vehicle bristling with weapons blocking the entrance to the outpost. "Hey guys... there's an old guy down here with a kid... get Shultz down here now."

The older Afghan gentleman was carrying his child or grandchild in his arms and was soaked in blood down the front of his robes or kurta. He was going off on how the kid was playing in the fields and that he hit a tripwire mine. Someone mentioned that he said something about it being one of ours. I know the Taliban plays disturbing psychological warfare messages and terrorizes the villages in all sorts of sick ways, but this was a new low.

The only possibility of it being something of the sort would have to fall under some of the special projects equipment that they will use sometimes to trick insurgents into picking up "free ammo" when in fact, it's a booby trap or rigged. This happens with AKs that blow up in the face of an enemy combatant, a tracker buried in a piece of gear, or ammo that cooks off or doesn't fire right. All special operations stuff that could be used to discourage and dishearten an enemy. I knew they were using ground sensors in the area to track movements that combined with drones and our RAID tower, but who knows to what extent the full operation went.

Whatever the case, we tried to get this kid airlifted back to KAF for treatment because that was his only hope. Our medics were down there desperately trying to get the kid patched up as we requested air assets or any available medevac. They couldn't spare the fuel for the airlift of the local child as it was spread too thin already with multiple units out on mission at the time. We were told to let the man know he would have to take the boy in himself.

With a heavy heart and tasked with having to essentially tell him the child was going to die, someone had to go and tell this relative, this father, that there was no way his child was going to make it. Someone broke the news to him and with a response that haunts me to this day, he calmly said "Inshallah" and picked up his boy, who was now at death's door, in his arms and walked out the front gate carrying his bloody body. I still cannot understand being so desensitized to the loss of life in an area where it was a daily occurrence that another one wouldn't be coming home for dinner that night.

Tactical Camping

There comes a point when you have been blown up enough that you just don't care any longer and you want something to kick off so you can put a face to your enemy. This wasn't a fight like we had in Helmand. This was something else. These were tactics that were designed to break us down and leave us so demoralized that we lost our bearing and control over our actions. If it was any lesser of a combination of men there, they would have had us, but whatever the special sauce was or the degree of intestinal fortitude that was shown in the Arghandab was incredible.

SFC Hill scooped me up for what he said was an "overt" mission that night and we were going to be staying in the thick of the orchards near the town of Mian Juy near the objective where Bobby had the grenade hucked at him. I asked him what he meant by overt and a wicked smile crept across his face. He told me that it was time to entertain and he was rolling out the red carpet as an invitation. No wonder we were bringing 2nd squad and Weapons along with us.

We patrolled heavily in town that day and let it be known that we were going to be there throughout the night. There was a sense of unease in the town, but there was always a lot of tension because they knew our presence would probably bring about a disturbance that night. No one knew just how or when though.

As the sun started to set, Musil set up a loose patrol base perimeter and we started a campfire in the field we were in. It was right at the edge of town and outside the walls of any of the compounds. You could probably see that fire for miles around that night... and that was the point. There was no noise discipline and the guys told jokes, hooted and hollered about things they had seen up to this point, talked about the dirty deeds they had done on their own mid-tour leave, or just enjoyed some cigarettes without the threat of having Hill go situation black because of the danger of having a lit target illuminating a nice head shot opportunity if one wanted.

As it got darker, the fire died down and Hill had all of us move into the adjacent compound. We set security into our new patrol base with machine guns on either side of it and overwatch from the rooftops along with coordinated eyes watching the area from the RAID tower back at COP Johnston and our 3rd Platoon on the observation point at the mountain cave.

The test of nerves was the true battle. The bait was set and there was nothing to do but wait. To most, the tension would have been maddening, but to a bunch of tired paratroopers that had been continually blown up, we did what we do best before the action... we went to sleep. We had security in place, but it is still amazing to me that we could fall asleep in such conditions.

You can tell which guys are infantry on a parachute jump because they are the ones that are quiet and probably asleep as the C-130 takes off. The extra 10 minutes of rack time before the adrenaline hit and the follow-on mission can be critical on some of these events. It's the personnel other than the grunts (POGS) and admin guys that are hooting and hollering as the jumpmaster goes through the jump sequence motions. They are the only ones who want to be jumping while the infantry soldier knows that there is an accepted casualty rate for the airborne that is all too humbling when you calculate yourself into the odds for survival.

I woke up with a start at about 2am. Something was wrong, but what? I had heard stories of Taliban cutting soldiers' throats in the night if they were able to sneak up close enough to an element. We even knew someone that had been with the 173rd when the Taliban breached their compound walls and they ended up in an all-out hand-to-hand fight to the death. The stakes for sleep in the Wild West are a little different than your average point on the globe.

I decided to not wake Hill or Musil and took the chance to relieve myself and then check on the sentry points. I approached the building where the gun was on the roof. "Pssst… pssst?" I whispered. Nothing… "Hey?" I said a little louder. "Mmmmmm… yo," he replied in a groggy tone.

"What the fuck, dude… were you sleeping?"

"Uh… yeah. I kinda racked out. Shit." he replied as he started to shake the sleep off.

"God damn it man… you know how bad we would have been fucked if you let someone by… right?!" I'm pissed now.

"I'm sorry, man. I'll be alright," he said back.

"You need a dip or anything? You better stay the fuck awake. I won't say shit, but damn it man. Fuck! I'm going to make sure Kenney is up too. Don't cap my ass," I tell him.

I slowly crept up the line and approached the opposing end where John Kenney was stationed on the SAW and pointed in the opposite direction of the gun, ready to take on anything that might hop the wall of the opposing compound or come down the road. "Hey man?" I whisper, but a little louder to him as I am still a bit pissed at the other guy.

His helmet pops up from the buttstock of the weapon. "Yeah?!" but it's disoriented.

"Fucking A, dude. Were you asleep too? Fuck!"

"I'm sorry man… I just floated off for a min," Kenny said. These guys are genuinely beat at this point, but damn…how bad is this going to be or how bad could this have been? I'm worried now. Was my sense that woke me up trying to tell me that our security was down or was it that someone was watching us and planning an ambush? Could you imagine how bad that would go?

"Hey man, I'm going to check the perimeter. Don't fucking shoot me," I tell him. "And don't fall the fuck back asleep." What happened next was probably the dumbest thing that I did in Afghanistan. I went back over to where the gun was and crept outside of the wall using him as overwatch. It wasn't a terrible thing to do, but what if someone from the rest of the crew woke up and wasn't aware of what was going on? Or if there were, in fact, eyes on the patrol I would get gunned down outside of the line that had the safety and security of walls around it. Too many factors that could leave me dead hung in the balance as I left the bubble.

I rolled along one side of the wall that contained the open field and the orchard and went right to check the alleyway to our north. I peeked out and checked both sides of the road to find nothing but the stillness of the night. I listened for a moment and strained to hear anything that might be moving towards our position as we slept. Nothing.

I came back through the opening and popped back up to talk to the sleepy ranger for a moment. He seemed much more awake now and I didn't get the feeling he was going to let that happen again. "You good? You need me to stay up here with you for a bit?" I asked him. "No, I'm good to finish the shift. I'm sorry, man. Fuck, I can't believe that happened." He was genuinely sorry about it and knew all too well how it could have ended or the repercussions if he were to be found out. "Happens to the best of us," I said. "Just don't let it happen again, damn it."

That was it. I came down off the roof and went back to sleep leaned up against a tree near the middle of the compound we were in. Within minutes, I was out and woke up to the warm sun coming up over the horizon for yet another wonderful day alive on this great planet.

CHAPTER 9

The Beginning of the End

The Relief

Word came down that around August that we were getting another unit coming in to relieve us. The company that held the valley was being replaced by a mixture of troops in the size of a battalion consisting of the 101st Airborne along with a combination of artillery (which was no good in that valley due to civilian populace constraints) and infantry. We didn't want them going through the same hell and we also wanted to try to goad the enemy into coming out of hiding so we could get a chance to take a few out. We asked the commander if we could slap on their unit patch and run patrols for the last month like that to help ease the transition, but the commanding officer wasn't about to let that happen.

We had been hearing firefights across the river that involved Charlie Company almost daily at this point and we were begging to join them for a chance at retribution. It probably pained them to say no, but we had our own battlespace to attend to. As much as Charlie Company was having a rough go of it, we had our own part to play in the area. It just gave the men something to grumble about that wasn't the everyday gripe.

With word that our replacements were due to occupy the outpost any day now, there was a necessary "base improvement" that needed attending to. SFC Hill snatched me as I passed by one day and instructed me to grab a rifle and a few additional bodies to provide overwatch. We met him at the ECP as he was standing there with a rattle can of spray paint in his hand. "Just to make sure these fuckers don't try to change the name of the posting. We owe Johnston that at least." I cracked a smile as SFC Hill and our makeshift PSD meandered outside of the safety of the walls to emblazon the front visible entrance with the words COP JOHNSTON in a way the arriving unit wouldn't be able to change without significant effort. That was one thing Hill was always good about. He held the overall wellbeing of the men above everything else.

When they arrived, we couldn't believe who they sent us as a replacement. The soldiers that showed up for the fight were grossly out of shape and a severe contrast in the habits of discipline that we were accustomed to. Some of the occurrences had our blood boiling and I quickly avoided the new faces like the plague, as if their lack might affect my own chances of survival. They weren't anyone that I wanted to chum around with or get to know. It had been bad enough with the new replacements we had shipped in, most of whom had acclimated over the last few months. These soldiers were a different story. Filthy weapons, no priorities of work, overweight, and the list could go on. They were a stark contrast and it had all of us worried that these guys were going to get mauled in a short matter of time.

We held a few joint patrols to show the area, much as we had done when we entered the valley. There were not many more as our troops were trickling out of the battlespace. We were all spent at this point and were essentially checked out. It can be the time when people will get complacent because the end of the struggle is within sight, but there is still work to be done. This was the time to stay even more diligent because when you let your guard down, that's when they hit you.

Side by Side Gone Sideways

We showed the incoming guys the different areas, tried to teach them the enemy TTPs (tactics, techniques and procedures), showed them which culverts to clear (all of them), and made our best attempt to give them a chance of survival in that hellhole.

We had gotten word that the Task Force would be operating on the outskirts of our AO that day, but it was outside of anywhere we would be near. They gathered a joint patrol of ourselves and a few of the key personnel replacing us and headed out into the eastern portion of the area. It wasn't more than an hour until I started seeing an A-10 circling the mountain ranges to our right.

"Hey, you guys know if they have our position out here?" I called up to the company. "Can you check with Battalion?" "Yeah roger… yup, they know you guys are out there." "OK, thanks… out." This plane continues to circle but the pilot's flight pattern is developing into something different. I mention to SFC Hill, "I just checked with Battalion and they say the other unit knows we are out here right now, but that bird has me worried." Just as I mention it, the plane goes into a dive.

"Ah fuck… everyone get the fuck down!" Hill yells. As this is happening, I hear the massive 30mm cannon go into operation and I observe something detach from the bottom of the plane. "Shit, they just dropped ordnance," someone yells before the JDAM impacts an area approximately 500m in front of us and the cannon's massive rounds are sending dirt clods 50ft into the air as they impact the earth.

The pilot pulls out of the dive and circles back around. "Fuck this shit, we are done here," Hill yells as he quickly picks up and starts to brisky walk back the way we came. "I'm not trying to get my ass shot off by friendlies and whoever else is out here on my last damn patrol. The Rangers are going to take care of it today… let 'em have it."

Two interesting facts that I was taught that day. Number one: never get in the way of a group of Rangers on a mission. They just kill everything in their path. I'm not kidding. You are better off just backing off and letting them do their job. They are very efficient and excel at it. Number two: an A-10 has to go into a dive to do a gun run, because if it doesn't, the plane would literally stall in the air and drop from the sky. It's essentially an airframe built around a massive cannon. Very impressive piece of equipment that holds a special place in every infantry soldier's heart. Also, not something I would ever want to be on the receiving end of.

The Walk Out

2nd Platoon seemed to be stranded in the town of Deh-e Kowchay with no route for egress. The replacement units had been trickling into the combat outposts and the living spaces were becoming cramped. It had been tough enough up until now with the adversity they had faced during their tenure in the valley. Now, they were having trouble leaving because air assets would constantly flip from being available to grounded due to the environmental conditions.

COP Ware was near devoid of personnel from Bravo Company and 1st Platoon had finished vacating COP Johnston by ground vehicles earlier that day. SFC Frazier was pissed because they had already burned a route out of town that morning when they had attempted to coordinate a helicopter lift into KAF instead of chancing the multiple threats they would face if attempted on the ground. They had begun movement to the landing zone when a dust storm kicked up and delayed any chance of pickup until later in the day.

Now facing another challenge, the members of 2nd Platoon were trying to coordinate their chance to depart the region and begin the long trek home from the warzone they had occupied for the last few months. They were tired, but they still had one last mission: to make it to the safety of the larger footprint provided within the walls of Kandahar Air Field. After experiencing setbacks all day, Frazier decided to take the option of walking out to the highway and hitching a ride with a convoy of engineers headed for KAF.

A squad from 1/63 4th Infantry Division joined them on the movement that would bring them close to the area where Morton had been hit earlier in the deployment. Anything moving throughout the area of DK was risky due to the existence of the IED belt that surrounded the village, but they had no other choice as the window for departure was rapidly closing. They loaded up with everything they could carry on their backs and began the trek towards Checkpoint Antenna.

They were making good time when the inevitable happened. With one final patrol that dangled the illusion of safety in front of the men, a chain of IEDs was set off at the front of the patrol with a second charge roughly set to explode mid-patrol and kill the leadership. The charges only partially exploded but they still took the legs of Sergeant Sullivan and one of the 1/63 soldiers.

It was like the valley couldn't let us leave without one final middle finger being stuck up at us and waggled in our faces as the evacuation of more casualties had become the standard, even in leaving the battlespace. Frazier made sure to load up as many of his guys onto the medevac convoy as they would take, which still left eight of them on the ground, including the EOD team. After what seemed like an eternity, LTC Jones and CSM Guden were able to free up two UH-60 Blackhawk helicopters to lift the last of them out of there.

Bunkers and the Boardwalk

Once we hit KAF, it was a lot of waiting... which I was fine with at this point. This meant rack time, it meant some sleep, it meant a gym, it meant showers, it meant chow halls, and maybe even some uninterrupted time to myself. I must have purchased a Green Beans coffee every day and walked around that boardwalk at least one hundred times in the short time we were there. Someone saw a newspaper within the first week we were on KAF and the front page contained a picture of a MaxxPro vehicle on its side after it had been blown up crossing the set culverts we had specifically instructed to clear every time. We had found an IED in those locations every time we looked... which was every damn time we crossed it. It was disheartening and the whispers grew to anger as more of the men were made aware. There was an instant feeling that all of the work we had just accomplished was for naught.

All of the news in the few months during the time everyone was separated also started to circulate. We started to learn of the guys from the other platoons that had been severely wounded or killed. I didn't even know about Specialist Joseph Caron being killed in action on April 13 or that Specialist Christopher Moon had passed away after being hit by an IED in Charlie Company's area. I started to look around and noticed others that were missing, such as SPC Michael Verardo, SPC Jared Lemon, Sgt Matthew Kinsey, and others from the platoons I hadn't gotten to know very well over the time there. It seemed the list of the wounded went on forever and I stopped paying attention to the stories as I just wanted to focus on getting out of there in one piece at this point.

There was a newly added stain to the boardwalk as well. A large hole gaped in a portion of the covered roof area of the pavilion that circled around the perimeter. It was all that was left from a rocket attack that had originated from the backside of the mountain ranges. A female lieutenant was running there at the time and she incurred a direct hit... talk about fate. Another reason why when the air raid sirens went off, I didn't react at all. Truthfully, I didn't react at first because my headphones were stuffed into my ears, but when everyone within the building started diving under tables, I asked a kid what the hell was going on. Some wide-eyed specialist peered up at me from under the table in front of me saying something about incoming rockets.

I just started laughing and retorted that if they wanted to get me, this was probably the last way I would go. I wasn't about to go out like a little panic-stricken child cowering under a table. It probably hurt his feelings, but I didn't stick around to find out. I walked out of there to regroup with the guys in case anything was really happening at the time. The chances were extremely high that they were going to be calling for accountability of everyone soon after the threat passed, due to the nature of where we were. It was a sign that I was actually starting to think a little more responsibly after everything that I had just been through.

Pedro 66

While we were waiting to leave Afghanistan via KAF, I decided I wanted to drop by the flightline and see if the combat rescue unit that had been shuttling our wounded out of the minefields was still around. I know it didn't mean a ton, but I had to come by and say thank you. There would have been more casualties if they hadn't been on station a few of those times.

The mission of the US Air Force callsign Pedro is usually one of providing combat search and rescue to the airborne assets, yet also tasked with providing casevac in situations on the battlefield at the point of injury. Those were all my encounters with Pedro anyway. The callsign originated in Vietnam throughout the Mekong Delta when it was known for being the fastest to the recovery site and the name became synonymous with saving lives.

I could attest for their speed every time they showed up ready to carry one of our boys off the battlefield to the waiting trauma surgeons who provide care for the severely wounded before they are stabilized and transferred to Germany. Pedro had also assisted in a search and rescue mission involving a soldier that was lost in a river crossing earlier in the deployment. They had done a hell of a job out there and I had to at least let them know we had appreciated it.

Someone pointed me to one of the plywood shacks off the main flightline and I headed over. Heading up onto the porch, I wondered if I was in the right place. It was a little weird being out on the flightline without anyone yelling at me anymore. "You looking for someone?" said one of the three guys that were sitting around the room. "Yeah, I was trying to see if the guys from Pedro were here. I wanted to just say thanks. My company was over in the Arghandab and we had them on station a few times in getting our guys out. I just wanted to say thanks."

There was a little look and they all exchanged glances. The air was tense for some reason. Did I say something wrong? "They're not here anymore. Sorry," one of them retorted. "Damn, thanks anyway. I figured I would try," I said, as I turned and shuffled out the door wondering what I was going to do to kill some time before we had to report next. I didn't want to head back to the tents just yet as someone was bound to be looking for a detail or guard duty if we returned.

What I hadn't realized was that Pedro 66 went down that summer of 2010 in Afghanistan. Only two of the seven crew members survived the ordeal and had their time in service cut short due to injuries sustained. The patch of the Pedros reads "These things we do that others may live" and is a solemn reminder of just how dangerous the job is as they commit to putting their personal safety aside to serve others.

This came into the decision making even at the very end when they had been hit and the split-second decision was made to maneuver away from the troops they were coming in to save. The safest possible method for the crew to get out of the situation safely would have put the guys on the ground at severe risk if the chopper rolled after making contact with the ground in an "autorotation" landing. Instead, the pilot assessed the situation and veered to save the lives of those they had come to assist.

A controversial decision, to be sure, but one of many that were made in a combat theater during a split second of decision-making time with no visible metrics to follow on how the end state would turn out. Whatever the case, the Pedro crews were one of the best out there and our mortality rate would have been much higher if it weren't for the job that they did constantly and at the highest levels on the battlefield.

The Flight Out

When our departure plane finally did arrive, we were ready to get the hell out of there. Half of us expected us to drop right out of the sky as we had so far escaped the reaper's grasp and were never meant to make it out of the valley. Images of our plane flying out of KAF as a crack squad of Taliban sat across the mountain ranges across from the airfield were waiting for this very moment. Right when we think that it's all over and our job is complete, they are going to knock the bird out of the sky with an old Stinger missile left over from the days when America supplied them to the Mujahideen to combat the Russians. Oh, what a twist of the cards that would be. On the way out the door, to be shot out of the sky by the very tool of liberation from the former oppressors of the Soviet Union.

The pilot hammered the thrusters and the massive plane lifted off of the tarmac at an incredible pace in comparison to a civilian flight. They needed to get out of there fast and the luxury of a gentle ascent was not something they would risk—it would be the perfect moment for a projectile to be fired at a plane carrying troops as it was lumbering off the airstrip. Everyone that had made it up to this point throughout the entire deployment secretly reasoned that there was no way we would make it out of that country alive. The current state we found ourselves in wasn't reality, but some sort of hallucination or dream that we continued to exist in. We were already deceased and the universe was playing a sick joke on us in the afterlife.

As soon as we were out of range and the plane leveled out, Hill started singing a rendition of "Leaving on a Jet Plane," at first quietly and to himself... but quickly growing in decibels as others around him that knew the words began to chime in.

At the realization that the soldiers that remained in his charge were out of harm's way, Hill began to get that giddy kidlike look about him that had disappeared since Helmand province. You could see the tension drop from his shoulders as his burden was relieved, even if it was just for a few hours as we flew to Kyrgyzstan for the endless debriefs and another extended wait for return transport to the USA. His boys were safe for now. At this point, half of everyone on board had chimed in and their voices echoed about the cargo hold. Not sure exactly what the aircrew was thinking at the time, but I can guarantee that after just one look at us, they knew exactly why we were so elated and they weren't about to stop the minor celebration.

The chorus progressed into the tune of "Sweet Caroline," not surprisingly as they sing the particular song during any baseball game involving the northeast corner of the USA. One of the memories that's burned into my memory to this day that brings a smile to my face if I'm thinking about it. That rowdy group of roughnecks housed in the cargo hold of a C-17, belting out a song as the world rattled about them. The sounds reverberating within a military cargo jet, that were normally deafening, couldn't hinder the melody being produced at the moment. You could hear these magnificent bastards over it all, belting out the words with smiles emanating from the majority of us, as we were grinning from ear to ear.

Manas

After a short time, we made it to Kyrgyzstan. Other than the takeoff, the flight proved to be uneventful and we were allowed to move about the cabin as we wished. Once in the air, the mood settled down into an atmosphere that was a bit more relaxed. Even with the promise of a peaceful layover in between stops, this was still a bunch of 82nd Airborne paratroopers. As we landed in Manas, I knew some of these guys were going to have the behavior of a rabid dog on a leash as our cortisol levels had been elevated for so long.

1SG Mac eased up on us a little as we were returning from what most of the guys had considered hell and he sympathized with us. Our alcohol restrictions were lifted during our time in Kyrgyzstan but were limited to two beers only. The amount doesn't sound like a lot, especially for a thirsty group of US Army paratroopers, but two famously large 32oz Russian beers containing 17 percent alcohol by volume can pack quite the wallop at high altitude after abstaining from any substances for a year. It was a favorable approach to spend three or so hours nursing a beer while swapping stories with the other platoons. We had been so spread out that there were some of us hadn't seen the other guys within the company in three to four months. The activity was a good way to decompress a fraction before heading stateside.

There were always a few of them causing problems, however. Some were buying other soldiers' beer tickets and there was an occurrence where one of them confiscated a younger lower enlisted soldier's tickets. He stated that the soldier wasn't of drinking age yet to defend his reasoning. It was bullshit and he held no particular right to pull a stunt like that. 1st Platoon didn't treat each other like that... well, most of the platoon. There will always be that guy who thinks he is in the right and his actions were justified, whatever the case might be, because of his given right as a superior human specimen.

Narcissistic sociopaths do exist within the military and those guys should be made an example of because that behavior leads down a road ending with everyone dead. There are times you hear about when the oppressed finally snap and add to the statistics within the risk mitigation sheets that show up around command climate survey time. I wouldn't ever dream of anything beyond taking it to a fight in the privacy of the woodline, but there are those that I could envision snapping mentally and becoming a story akin to those you hear about surrounding the Fort Bragg area.

Ask the older guys about the story of sniper trail on Bragg, where a specialist assigned to the armory cried out for help and told someone that he was about to do something rash because of how he was being treated. They laughed at him, ignored him, and kept him assigned to the armory where most didn't have to interact with him. One early morning before PT, he took it upon himself to remove a machine gun from the armory and establish an ambush position off of the running trails winding throughout the forested areas on Bragg. As the various units started their morning physical training run, he opened up and killed a major while wounding about 20 other soldiers before a Special Forces team running as a group nearby tackled him from behind and stopped the bloodbath.

There are other stories that exist, but ones like this raise the question of the leadership practices in place with a high operations tempo, such as Bragg. If you served in that valley, you should be trusted to be able to maintain your composure while you put a few back with your comrades in arms after walking through minefields. You always had your minor spats with each other, but at the end of the day, it never overshadowed the mission or came in between anyone during patrol duties. Even if there was no love for a particular character, we leaned on each other to make it through and the disagreement would become water under the bridge.

The Morning After

After we arrived at Bragg, we unloaded the plane and most of the men filtered into barracks areas to drop whatever gear they had with them and crash on a bunk for the weekend. The morning after the long weekend, the entire company was conducting the morning PT formation and ready to head off on the morning run when a cannon went off at 18th Airborne Corps, signaling the beginning of the day. The problem was this had not been part of the daily routine prior departing for Afghanistan. The cannon was something new they had started firing off every morning. Some chucklehead in the rear detachment hadn't given anyone the heads up after the brigade of combat soldiers had just returned from a high-stress deployment.

The entire company of seasoned soldiers reacted instinctively and ducked down instantly, immediately breaking ranks for the moment. After everyone collectively realized what had just happened, we all quickly gained our composure and 1SG Mac kind of chuckled and said something along the lines of, "Well, if that isn't an indicator or anything!" before releasing everyone to complete PT on their own for the morning. There probably should have been more attention paid to that particular moment. It was an indicator that triage was needed and some early help may have saved the lives of some soldiers and veterans in the years that were to follow.

Parting is Such Sweet Sorrow

My career path after that deployment quickly separated me from the rest of the company. I mentioned earlier that I had received orders to report to Fort Lewis in Washington State. I further realized that it was to join the 5th Infantry Division Stryker Brigade... that's right. The very unit that we had replaced in the Arghandab that had been privy to the misery we had just gone through during our time in country. No way was I headed there, and I had never planned on doing anything other than the Special Forces anyway.

The company gave block leave for a month and I used mine right up to my selection date that required me to report in the day after Thanksgiving. It was pretty humorous because my parents had sent me a huge honey-baked ham, but it was just me having dinner at my house. My class report day was the very next day and everyone I knew was either drinking copious amounts of alcohol, with their families, or a combination of both. Nothing I needed to be around the day before I reported into a selection class. That next morning, I reported to the building for selection transport with a huge ham under my arm. I set the leftover chunk of pork down on a table that was outside along with a loaf of bread so anyone could make themselves a ham sandwich if they wanted. If there is anything I knew about reporting to any unit within the Army, it can take a good amount of time for the class to load up to leave.

The Special Forces are much better at expediting the process due to having a smaller footprint; however, we still didn't depart until noontime. Sergeant Ackers joined me for my selection class just like he had said he was going to back in the Arghandab. It was nice to have a familiar face there with me because it contained an extra motivator to represent the unit and struggle we had come from. There was a sense that we had to push each other through this next hurdle while retaining a healthy spirit of accountability with one another. Ackers had been a good squad leader and I had no doubts about his attendance at selection with me.

After my experience in the valley, selection proved to be challenging but nothing as arduous as we had faced already. The last year had proven to be valuable and I was able to have my orders to Fort Lewis cancelled. SF Branch held precedence and could play the kaibosh game with almost anyone's HR within the Army except for the higher echelons, where the air is crisp and the speed is set at a blistering pace. Other than a jump that I was called in for to keep my jump pay current, Sgt Musil kept me hidden from everything going on back at the company. Somewhere in the time since we had gotten back, Musil had taken over 1st Platoon and SFC Hill was on his way to his next assignment on Fort Benning as a black hat airborne instructor. The 82nd Airborne has a particular amount of distain for the Special Forces community on Bragg. I never completely understood it. Maybe it was the fact that a large number of the lower enlisted in the 82nd Airborne consisted of soldiers that didn't make the cut in the X Ray program. The question being posed is, why is that a bad thing? Most of those recruits are smarter on their entrance exams and better equipped physically than anything that normally arrives from worldwide assignment post basic training. It's possible the mistake was the emphasis on standards and discipline while the guys across the street would be seen wearing something other than an issued uniform leaving work after lunch every day.

After we had gotten back from Afghanistan, CSM Guden was replaced at the battalion command by Command Sergeant Major Jasper Green. CSM Green had been the Bravo Company 1SG a while back and his name was spat out like a curse by anyone in the company, usually followed with a "fuck that guy". He had a particular distaste for anything involving SF branch. So whatever the reasoning, CSM Green removed me from the promotions board after he caught word of the fact that I was heading over to SF land. I fell further from the tree when he unofficially promoted a competition during a nighttime jump operation that stated the first soldier to the Steiner aid that night would receive a coin and a four-day pass. Guess who ended up being the first person to get to the assembly area and was seen guiding the others via a buzzsaw with an IR chemlight? I hadn't even been trying either. It was probably just the fact that I fall out of the sky quicker than most and instead of taking a tactical pause, I did my job. Who would have thought?

That jump was terrible and the last occurrence of what I considered to be a jump in division. It was a nighttime combat jump from 600m onto Sicily drop zone using a T-10 parachute with a follow-on mission to be performed after accountability. At that altitude, I didn't even understand why our reserves were rigged up. It's the lowest I have ever jumped from and with a T-10, you would have about 10 seconds before you hit that ground if your main chute opened correctly. If not... I don't know what to say. I hope you figured it out at least. I've had two chute malfunctions in my time over the years in the military, and neither were anywhere near that low.

I never received anything from the event, but I didn't care at this point. The old Bravo Company was rapidly disappearing as so many had been claimed to the ranks now serving within the walls of Walter Reed, other units within the military, and those fleeing anything resembling the military in their future. A lot of the soldiers that had been on that deployment determined that they had done their time and the Army would get along just fine without their services.

The one relic of value that existed from within the history of Two Fury was the coins our previous command team, SGM Puckett and LTC Jenio, had commissioned prior us leaving for Afghanistan. There was a devil along with a naked or scantily clad female adorning the face of the coin and it loudly stated BAMF minted into the casting (meaning Bad Ass Mother Fucker). It was the most ridiculous and hilarious thing I'd ever seen, but at the same time, it was coveted by some of the troops. Some of them would have done anything for one of those coins.

Sgt Robert Musil presented me with a plaque from the platoon that has meant more to me than any other award that I've received since. It was recognition from 1st Platoon for a job well done in an area of hell that a particularly special group of ragtag mother fuckers held the line against all odds that were thrown against them. I've never met another crew serving within the military that were quite like them and I don't think I ever will. To this day, those guys will drop just about anything they are doing for one another if they are called on.

Just as quickly as I had arrived to Bravo Company, I was gone again… off to another corner of the Army in hope of better things lying within the days ahead.

CHAPTER 10

The After Effects

The War Rages On

What was it all for? That is the question you hear from the guys quite often and is an echo of other stains of wars from America's more recent history. I was never in a position to make any major differences other than in the lives and decisions made at the ground level. However, we did make a difference in the eyes and lives of those around us that witnessed our actions on the battlefield. Those we stood up for, who were being threatened and lived in constant fear every day. We did the right thing in the end. The losses were not typical and the fight was different than the one that we had prepared for, but in the end, we adapted to the best of our ability and kept our moral compass pointed in the right direction during a conflict where others had lost their azimuth along the way.

One of the gripes from men is that the tactics we utilized during the 2010 fight weren't right for the area we were patrolling. The chief complaint is that we should have been following a counter-IED mission format instead of performing a typical textbook infantry patrol and adjusting as we were attacked or learned through our time within the occupation of the Arghandab.

They aren't wrong to some degree, but the facts show that there weren't the resources available within the current levels of tactical operations. Even the coordinated effort that existed in a catalog of education programs on various IED tactics and models wasn't at the scale that it is now. The truth was that a lot of the capabilities needed were only available to those operating within the special operations community up until that point and it was still a very small organization. By the time the 2012 deployment circled around for Bravo Company, the mission information and IEDs they recovered on the Arghandab deployment were vital in supplying troops with the resources they needed when they returned. I attended a course later in my career that had a portion involving a class taught by JIDO (Joint Improvised Threat Defeat Organization) where I had a chance to briefly talk to one of the trainers. He became excited when I mentioned that I had been in the Arghandab in the 2010 time frame. I was told an entire portion of their training involves the time that was spent within the valley and the enemy's use of psychology in effective IED emplacement. Our experiences there taught valuable lessons and we essentially wrote a good portion of the training manual.

Maybe that is why the 2012 deployment was so successful in avoiding land mines while out on patrol. The experience taught within the Arghandab progressed to Samuel Hammer serving as a squad leader along with Ball Peen (Hammers) as one of his team leaders, sniffing out landmines left and right. In that one year, his squad alone had pulled up nearly 100 landmines!

It wasn't all glory though as Sgt Jauregui hit an IED that cost him his legs early on in the deployment. I was serving in USASOC at the time and was stunned to see him at green ramp standing on carbon fiber prosthetics when the boys came back in. He walked right out there and led the company back into the hangar to their waiting families after only having been in recovery for about six months. It was quite the sight to witness, and I'm honored to have been with such a caliber of soldiers during my time in service.

These things were part of the discussions I was lucky enough to have during the research for the book, when I started to understand the full extent of the picture. We don't get to see the full picture from the ground, and for a lot of the soldiers, unveiling would only serve to add to the confusion of the battlespace. The job on the ground is a tactical undertaking and one that Bravo Company had been trained well to perform. So well, that General Guy Jones stated in our conversations that he has spent the rest of his career attempting to uncover the root cause for what made Bravo Company able to operate the way they did under the stresses of that 2010 portion of their deployment.

Lieutenant Colonel Guy Jones at the time had been on the way out the door to take over command in Alaska when he had been called into the office to see Col Drinkwine for the news of his reassignment to Afghanistan. Following someone like Jenio was a next to impossible task with the caliber commander he had been combined with the amount of intensity he had put his troops through during the train up for the deployment. General Guy Jones wouldn't have wanted anyone to try to follow in the footsteps of the command pair that had brought the unit to the main effort within the Kandahar region that summer. He did the only thing he could do at the time and that was assist his ground commanders that had a better view of the situation and provide any of the assets and resources he could muster from the pool that was around him.

You don't always see the entire picture of how everything is panning out within the universe. Maybe sometimes, you just have to bleed. It's said that hard times make for hard people and in turn, hard people bring upon good times. That's the story that is published and marketed by the members of "The Greatest Generation." The situation is different now that we have access to information right within the palm of our hand. There is no glorious filter of a curtain between the public and the modern-day battlefield, as we see the situations from Syria, the Ukraine, and other conflicts from around the globe being livestreamed on social media.

There are eyes everywhere and people are starting to become aware that there is no glory on the battlefield. Only death and needless destruction. People perform glorious and selfless acts on the battlefield, yes. There are even times when they are recognized for it, but most of those who receive these high honors would tell you that they would never wish to go through that experience ever again.

Everyone talks about how "the military will make a MAN out of you" or how "you've all grown up" in the process. They don't tell you about the horrors faced by those who have served in an intense combat situation. Pictures will show examples of the faces of those who have pulled out of an intense area that was under fire for an extended period of time. Your body does crazy things for survival allowances. There are switches that turn on, and in some people, never turn off.

Such was the case with Sgt Thomas and his recovery from what had happened back on that intersection in Deh-e Kowchay. Looking back, Staff Sergeant Allen Thomas was always the guy that could make everyone laugh in the middle of a shitstorm. I remember very vividly the narrative that he would weave about establishing a bum commune of sorts in his post-military fallback career of establishing a hierarchy within a tent city inside the city limits of LA. He would then run the camp in a fashion parallel to Colonel Kurtz from the film *Apocalypse Now*. It would have guys doubled over in laughter and involved copious details of how the camp was to be established and run.

He was the most interesting DC/Maryland transplant that I had ever met. I hadn't seen any of the pictures from Thomas' youth until later, but I can tell you that the version of him I knew reflected a country boy that could strum a tune that had the ladies swoon over him or had the boys reflect on some of their times from their past. He was a barrel-chested man with a presence that could quickly take over a room if he wanted to but he was humble enough to use that ability only when he needed to. At 250lbs of muscle with a stout frame to back it, he wasn't someone that I would want to cross in a back alley. I would definitely never want to be on the wrong end of him leading a squad through a breach in my doorway during the middle of the night.

When I saw him in Tucker Gym, he was reporting to the warrior transition unit. That's where guys would go when they were awaiting separation from the military for whatever reason. You would get solid soldiers that had been wounded in action and were being cycled out of the Army from the units they were stationed to on post. The WTU would also receive the turds from within the Army. The shitbags that had popped hot on drugs or had a DUI and the Army no longer required their services.

I hope they have separated those two streams within the warrior transition unit now because trying to stay out of trouble in those units can make life a living hell. Because those in charge of the scourge need to keep order, they just lump everyone into the same category. Talking down to someone like SSG Thomas was something he didn't take very kindly to and it made his struggle during the entire situation pretty damn stressful.

He looked hollow, different from the Thomas I had known. You could tell there was a light still there, but it was different. It was struggling, but he was still there. Allen was a resilient soldier and he was trying to get some gym time in that morning before reporting back to the WTU in a few hours. We talked for a few minutes and after, I rejoined my group with the training company I was assigned to. It was just some small talk, but I noticed that he just seemed tired. I didn't know the situation at the time, but I told myself he would be OK. That was the last time I ever saw SSG Allen Thomas alive.

I was told by those I knew in the area that something had happened. Allen had killed himself. Allen didn't just kill himself. Then the news started coming fast and furious. His neighbors… Allen had gone off one night and killed his neighbors along with their dog after a shootout with another one of the surrounding houses. There was a flurry of talk and anxiety among those that had been from Bravo Company and those that had known Thomas. How could this have happened? Someone that had always been the one to make everyone laugh had just snapped like that.

Then came the news article and we were instructed not to wear our military dress to the funeral to pay our respects. The cuts became deeper when someone within the organization had stated that if anyone was seen at the funeral in their dress uniform to pay their respects, they would be subject to receive an article 15. What was happening here? This guy was a hero and they were treating him like a villain that had left a giant stain on the regimental crest of the 82nd Airborne. In my personal opinion, he belongs next to the fallen from that 2010 deployment because that is where we lost the SSG Allen Thomas that I knew. That is where we lost a lot of the guys.

I found myself opening my home in Fayetteville to some of the other guys that I had served with as they came into town for the funeral. John Meier and Voelker came in from the west coast and David Rogler met up with us at some point. We all piled into my hilariously unassuming Buick LeSabre and I drove the already intoxicated crew over to the funeral to pay our respects. It was like a family get together, mixing the happiness of being reunited with some of the guys we hadn't seen in a while with the grief of losing a member of the company that had touched so many of our lives.

The military does this weird dissociation where you can just disappear after you leave the service or become injured. Even more so when an unexpected injury takes you out of commission because no one was expecting it. In a career where the requirements are physically high, like in combat arms, it's even more pronounced because the ones still on the team can't slow down. Life will have to continue its natural path without them. It seems cold, but it's just one of those things we unconsciously do as warriors.

Separation from the service does not work well within a society where we don't have a community support system like the villages from our heritage had in place. The battles continue for our warriors who were separated from the pack, but now they are facing their troubles alone and without a support system of those who understand and are part of what makes up the brotherhood. Dealing with the isolation and providing an open line of communication is an area we need to be better in. Something that was addressed in an effort later along with David Huff.

Going Mental

Community is starting to fade both in society and the military. We are always told, seek help, talk to someone, but when you do, you are flagged as being someone with their stability in question. It will quickly bring a promising career to a screeching halt with the "problem" being shuffled out the door with a "Thank you for your service" instead of the help needed to recover from trauma they have experienced. Sometimes a guy just needs someone to talk to in confidence to process the amount of baggage that has piled up over the years.

That was my own personal case before I rotated back to the conventional army. Thankfully, I had someone that had been assigned to USASOC HR and they kept an eye out on me after I went to a mental health appointment one day. My phone rang the next day with SFC Musil on the other line asking if everything was alright currently. It was a gesture that reassured me that someone cared, even during a period when everything was crumbling around me. Someone cared enough to at least call and check up on me.

I had found myself numb... numb to everything. Existence was just that and I would be reminded daily that there wasn't anything left at this stage for me. I had to reset once again. The vision I once had was no longer an option via my current trajectory and my purpose and direction were now laid uncertain. I found myself doing things to give myself a rise. Crazy things.

Things like burning down backroads in the middle of the night after staying up and out while up to no good in the land where the capacity to get into trouble had no limit. Fayetteville is a mashup of a few wild and illicit subcultures if you know where to look... even then, you could just stumble upon most of it as a lot of guys do. There were reasons government field agents operate all over the area, one percenter bike clubs have compounds surrounding the city, MS13 has a presence, and the DEA and ATF are constantly in and out of the region.

Wherever I fell along the spectrum, I found myself heading home from work one day doing a ridiculous amount of speed on one of my favorite stretches. A souped-up 370Z I passed during the stint was now on my tail as he followed my line over the windy country road out of town and towards my house. Chances were that he didn't know what he was doing, and I could see from my rearview mirror that I shouldn't pull too far ahead as not everyone could hold the edge like this, especially on a public road.

My fears were valid as I watched him burn past me on a long straight that led into a 90-degree right-hand sweeper of a corner. His car never made the turn and went skidding into the woods at about 90mph, tagged a tree (which exploded and fell), spun like a top the opposite direction and flew back off the right side of the road after smashing into yet another pine tree. I was already past his car and spun my vehicle around to help out the other driver.

As I ran up to the scene, the car was still running and spraying fluids everywhere as the forward bumper and radiator had separated and were off in the woods. The driver was unconscious and slumped forward in his seat. It was a good thing his little souped-up car had a full cage and harnesses, because the car would have split in half otherwise. As I killed the engine, I yelled at the kid to wake up. He started to groggily fight off the haze he was in. I was moving him away from the car and onto a berm closer to my vehicle when another person showed up and let me know he had EMS on the way.

Nothing like having military members around to know what to do in an emergency. Within minutes, MPs, police, and ambulance were all there and the scene was taken care of by the time one of the MPs sauntered over to me and started to take my statement. I can't fault the MP for trying, but when you are asking someone "How fast would you say he was going?" and "Would you say he was traveling at a high rate of speed?" I know better than to incriminate someone with information that would end the kid's career. It was bad enough that he probably wasn't fully covered by insurance for everything he had in the car, not to mention what his command was going to do to him later.

"I really couldn't say... I was just trying to help him out of it after it happened." But it was somewhere around that time that I realized my actions that had been affecting the others around me as well. I needed to get in front of whatever this was. I had lost my purpose and I needed help.

Operation *Resiliency*

The commonsense morals and code that should bind together a brotherhood of men like this survives beyond their service. It applies to humanity, but in this particular case, it was a group of men that put their differences aside to lead one another through the valley of the shadow of death. This is not aging, but it is maturity. The military does a fantastic job at accomplishing that, especially in a war zone where the learning curve is significantly steeper. If you don't figure it out quickly, you probably won't make it.

This resembles the "quests" that legends perpetuate or the traditional ascension into being a man of the tribe after being initiated through a process of trials. Those who can't cut it or that the lion eats during the hunt, weren't meant to move forward in life.

It's cutthroat and primal, but it is what it is. Modern warfare has softened the image or this, but the principle remains the same at its core. Surviving trials or a hardship is part of our programmed algorithm and the process for transitioning into adulthood. The loss or softening of this process may be what ultimately leads humanity to destruction.

Since that deployment, there have been parties, funerals, phone calls, and reunions among the men. A good amount of the men that were injured on that deployment went on to do great things despite their injuries. One of the enlisted, Nicholas Edinger, competed alongside Lieutenant Derick Carver in the World's Strongest Disabled Man contest in England. The obstacles are the same ones they are accomplishing during the strongest man contests and are tough even with all your facilities. Another played with the US Olympic baseball team.

Michael Verardo's wife, Sarah Verardo, didn't let her husband's injuries hold her back as a caregiver and she became heavily involved in the non-profit sector, eventually taking the role of CEO for the Independence Fund. From there, it wasn't long before she was heading up missions to help revamp VA policies while advising presidential administrations on the matters at hand. Since its creation, they have further expanded to create sub-organizations that assist veterans in other ways than just the original mission of providing track chairs for disabled veterans.

These guys were put through the pressure cooker and found forged on the other side of the conflict. However, they still needed help and it was after the suicide of yet another that the proposed solution was a hybrid unit reunion that focused on team building-type events combined with time for fellowship among the soldiers that had served within Bravo Company during that 2010 deployment. The Independence Fund created the program in collaboration with the VA to provide a functional format combined with psychologists to help out with any situations that might arise.

Being a joint venture with the VA, there were a lot of eyes on this event because of the potential to begin to solve one of the problems that has been an epidemic within the ranks of the military. That's where a *Wall Street Journal* writer by the name of Ben Kesling comes in.

The Book (We Loved to Hate)

It was at the reunion that brought a lot of us together when an article was written about the efforts of the Independence Fund during what essentially was a pilot program that set the groundwork for what became the Operation *Resiliency* events they are providing for veterans today.

Ben was brought in to get a picture of these guys and report on how the event went through the eyes of a veteran and a professional journalist. At the time of the article, he was writing various veterans' affairs pieces for the *Wall Street Journal* in and around the DC area. It made sense and the article pulled some attention… enough attention that it spurred on someone at Abrams Books to contact Ben about doing a full-length novel based on what he had seen at the Operation *Resiliency* retreat. There was only one problem… he didn't want to write it.

After some soul searching and persuasion, he took it on and spent the next two years working on things in between travel, his family (the guy has four kids… that alone screams either an incredible wife or some serious superman skills), and the other articles he was continuing to write for the journal. People think that books make money these days… honestly, you lose money on books. The time and frustration spent in putting your thoughts into a page in a clear format in hopes that someone is listening these days rarely pans out to be profitable. Also, people don't read anymore.

He put his fears aside and started to delve into more interviews. I had briefly been introduced to Ben during the retreat, but I had wanted to make sure he talked to the guys that had been wounded for whatever article he was going to write. I reasoned that I wasn't someone whose state of being had been affected by the deployment. Once there was word that there was a full-length book on the way and he needed more of the story to tell along with a timeline, I decided to get in touch. I was glad he was writing the book because I had never wanted to write about any of it. It was something that had been in my heart to do, but I didn't want to take on the task. It was too massive and would bring too much attention if it turned out to gain traction. I even thanked him for tackling the project. His reply was, "I better get it right, because if I don't, I'm going to have 150 or so angry paratroopers gunning for my ass!"

When the advance proof arrived, I tore through it in five hours. My initial concern was misrepresentation, misquotes, and the danger of our story being twisted into something that it hadn't been. Some of the talk during the reunion had details that were a bit over the top and I hadn't any recollection of. There was talk in the background and all over social media. Not anywhere in a public forum yet, but there were concerns among the guys. One of them called me genuinely concerned that he wasn't sure what he had said to Mr Kesling over the phone and that he had been on a ton of Lorazepam at the time when he interviewed. Great…

I didn't catch much initially other than some discrepancies that didn't change the overall "feel" of how the attitudes were in the valley, but I severely miscalculated how those details would set off a chain of frustration, rage, sadness, confusion, happiness, fond memories, deep wounds uncovered again, and a flurry of heated discussion over the book's publication.

Bravo Company by Ben Kesling hit the shelves on November 1, 2022 with a volume of anticipation from the guys of the company. Some had received copies a week prior due to the distribution channels being crossed and had a sneak preview. They had been waiting with eager anticipation as they were aware of the project, but wrote it off as something that would never happen. Yet now, here it was in a physical format! I have to admit that when I received my copy, I was excited as well. I tore open the package ready to read what had been said about us… and I started to cry.

I have no idea where those tears had come from… it was the weirdest thing. I had not anticipated this reaction. Why was this happening? As I stared at the cover with what appeared to be soldiers moving through the mist and emblazoned with the name of the best place I had served in the military under some of the nastiest conditions known to man, I was in my car at the bottom of my driveway with tears in my eyes for no reason that was apparent to me. Maybe there was, in fact, something locked away that I hadn't faced yet. Maybe the emotional response was relief that someone was paying attention to what we had been through in the Arghandab other than just us.

The book had only been out a few hours when the initial controversy was stated over the channels that the guys had put in place to try to resume some semblance of communication. There was already enough chatter to have warranted a Zoom call with about 50 of the guys along with the author to try to clear any confusion three days prior to release. It ended up being a mixture of a reunion among the men and a shitfest directed at the author. I respected the hell out of Ben for taking that call with these guys as he tried to maintain that everything written was done with honor and respect towards the men of Bravo Company.

It wasn't long after that I was talking with Jared Lemon, one of the Bravo Company guys from 2nd Platoon, and he summed up the situation best out of anyone involved. He said: "All of this controversy around the book isn't even about the book. It's about our own issues that we haven't faced yet. These events are based around events that touched us to the core and every single one of us is emotional about it. That is why we are talking about it. If anything, at least it's opening up the guys to talking about it." I couldn't agree with Jared more and after having spent a good amount of time talking with Ben, feeling out his motivations and morality, listening to some of the podcasts he was on, and reading the published material of his past, I felt like his intentions were honorable. At the very least, he had produced the book we had given him with the interviews that were taken.

I tried to understand the situation myself by talking to some of the loudest voices during the onset of the rumblings. Maybe if I reassured the guys that we could produce something of our own, it would quell the storm for now… but the noise only got louder. During my concern, I reached out to our old commanding officer at the time we had been in the valley. He had been there for everything and continues to be there for the guys in ways I would have never guessed when I had served with him back in Two Fury. It was suggested at one time that LTC Adam Armstrong was a career guy, the yes man, the brown-noser… the typical things the enlisted talk about when involving the officer side of the house. Pretty sure those guys have eaten their words by now.

Actions do speak louder than words, and damn it if that wasn't the credo he instilled in his command at 10th Mountain as "Deeds, not words" was drilled into the men during his tenure there. Even with his time and attention focused on his current command, he found the time to care for a group of a little over 100 men that served under him over 10 years ago. For him, the mission has never ended even after we left that radish field before the winter season of 2010 in Afghanistan. It's another one of those "tricks" the Army pulls on you, you're never truly out after you have spent any time in military service.

It was during a brief interaction that I asked him if the knowledge of me producing a book might help calm the guys down about the matter. He thought about it for a minute. Adam was the voice of reason here and he knew the guys more than anyone. After all, he was still leading from the front in a fashion, even after all this time. What he said stopped me dead in my tracks and I went cold. "I think you might want to wait on that. It has its place, but if you tell these guys too soon, you are going to turn their frustrations towards you."

I had messed up again… the realization that instead of trying to insert myself into the problem, I would quickly become the problem if I didn't stay neutral. Word was already out among a few and damn it if I hadn't seen the signs of the crosshairs turning my way as well. Akin to the artillery guns swiveling position on the battlefield, the one in charge could easily adjust fire and focus the "fire for effect" on me. It was too late in some respects.

It proved to be a learning experience to be aware of for anyone that attempts to go the publication route. I found myself at a book release party that was held in DC during the release of the Bravo Company book. I figured that was a good way to see how the men were being presented in front of the intended audience. It would be good to see some of the guys as Mac and Jauregui would be there along with David Huff. I had arrived at the address a little early and was in my car when I heard Sarah Verardo's distinct voice in the street.

As I approached, I think Ben saw me first, but I hadn't realized that there would be another guest there. Dakota Meyer, Medal of Honor recipient, was in the trio, and after Sarah said hello, he simply reached his hand out and said, "Hi, I'm Dakota." That was it. No titles, no attention, nothing to even mention his last name. I knew exactly who he was and had actually read his book that he had written along with Rob O'Neil about two years prior with the title *The Way Forward*. I had actually joked about it because there was another project of mine titled the same in my backlog of material.

After finding out the guys were still on the way, I opted to stay outside as I wanted to go in with them and I knew Ben and Sarah had priorities to go over inside finalizing everything for kickoff time. As they headed up the steps and into the house, I couldn't help myself. "Hey Dakota, you know you stole the title to one of my own books, right?!" He turned and without skipping a beat, he said, "Well, you'll have to take that one up with Rob." Guy had me cracking up before the party even started.

About 20 minutes later, an SUV rolled up with the guys in it. I underestimated how it felt when reunited with any of the guys from the old unit and we hugged it out in the street before heading inside. The doorman greeted us as we entered… it was Dakota shaking hands and playing the role as the greeter. One of the things some of the guys had bitched about was the usage of a Marine to promote a story about paratroopers, but after meeting the guy and watching him around the guests there, he is nothing but as humble as they come with a heart that cares for others. I approached him about an instance in his book where he had talked about an abrasive moment with a panel of VA programs managers. His face lit up and he immediately wanted to introduce me to the lady who had gotten him into the room with the executives at the time. He was always bringing the spotlight to other people the entire time.

Dakota also set me straight about something that I occasionally forget. The suicides within our group had always bothered me, but it's more about the perspective. It's not up to us to understand the events, but to be grateful for the lessons and good things that come from these experiences. It's a blessing and not something to make a crutch in your life. It opened me up to doing a lot of self-reflection to ensure that I'm not heading down a path that I don't want to.

Ben was to read a portion of his book for the crowd at the height of the night's events and the room gathered around to hear the words spoken that were written about the warriors our country had sent forward to defend the freedoms we currently have the opportunity to enjoy. These were people that had some pull in DC with ties leading up to the presidential offices and staff. One of them told a story about one night as Obama's drinking buddy.

Mr. Kessling took the center of the room with a copy of his book and was introduced to the waiting crowd. He started with a few words on how the book came to be in the article that was published in the journal two years prior. He spoke about how Operation *Resiliency* had accomplished some good for this particular unit that had been through an incredible amount of resistance and continue to do so even now. It was not a story of pity or brokenness, but one of men that were incredibly strong in their character and abilities as they adapted to the ever-changing and evolving battle they were in.

He proceeded to read the chapter about Joey Caron's father's experience as the notification officers showed up on his doorstep. I don't know how he got through the passage and you could tell that he was struggling at times while reading. I would never be able to read that chapter aloud as I had tears in my eyes when I had read the book myself. We don't normally see that side of the situation and it provided a very different perspective to the reader. It was very real to him too and it was surreal to see a hushed and reverent the room as they hung on to every word.

This is why his book was written and I was fortunate enough to see it happen. It surpassed any free meal from Golden Corral or Applebee's I would have received that day, I'll tell you that. With the caliber of people that were there, who knows, maybe I will have witnessed the initiation of better care than what is currently being provided for US Military Veterans.

All of this brought to you with the best of intentions, by the book we loved to hate.

Times are Changing

Change can be painful and as wartime ended, so did the need for a lot of the combat arms guys that were produced during the war efforts. They are a different breed and will usually have a bit of baggage from the places they have been along with the instances they faced in order to survive. It can be rough to be under the command of one of these guys, but mark my words, they just want to keep you alive.

The Army is getting better at performing certain tasks but only because the upcoming generation is proving to be smarter and more well informed than those of times past. The progression has been staggering to see as technology and connection accelerate as we progress, but that comes at a price as well.

Numbers for recruitment in the military are at an all-time low. Even with slots wide open for jobs that need filling, no one is taking them up on it. A few reasons are the restrictions are fairly high and society is ushering its own way to ineligibility due to mental health reasons, physical limitations, drugs experimentation, or sometimes even something as minor as an incident with alcohol as a minor.

As Big Army starts to focus on "readiness" while making sure that all the boxes are checked among their troops, it's become a joke. Gone are the time slots and funding for real world training and in its place, it hosts sexual harassment awareness events that are coupled with online training that needs to be completed along with a day or two of a "death by PowerPoint" presentation that was delegated to some poor lieutenant or the unit chaplain. I remember the distinct difference between the commands I found myself caught between during that period of time.

The clash of culture and coming change was something that had been stirring up even while we had been deployed in the Arghandab. I am not going to go into the full picture of everything that happened, but it's noteworthy that not only were our battalion commander and command sergeant Major removed while we were mid deployment, other elements within the chain of command were removed from the echelons of command during those particular years.

Canadian General General David Menard was removed for inappropriate relations with a subordinate soldier. Basically, he had an affair with a soldier under his command, a trend that has caused more than a few to be put on the chopping block over the years. Our ISAF commander, 4-star General McCrystal, was removed by Obama for political reasons in 2010 after an article in *Rolling Stone* quoted some things he had said in passing. His successor was removed for an affair he was having during his career as well. The removal of our brigade commander, Colonel

Brian Drinkwine, came in 2012 as an investigation into his leadership and his wife's harassment of the troops found him relieved of command.

I delved into the situation during writing this book because these factors played another part in the frustration that tied into our deployment experience. Who is to say how all the cards fell, but one thing is for certain, there were large amounts of politics heaped onto some of the roughest fights we experienced in the war during those times. The fight was happening on all fronts, and in the end, no one really won.

There are always those who are willing to show up to do the right thing when the time comes and there will be those that sit on the sidelines and judge the actions of those who are really doing the work. You will find that anywhere but let's not prioritize the boxes. The people that comprise the military are where the focus is needed to be and the readiness to take a stand for what is right, and honest, and true.

Military service has begun to shift towards trying to be a standard "job" as opposed to a way of life. Instead of the men being forced into tough situations together, they all want to go home at night. Just punch a 9–5 clock and kiss the wife and kids at night. I don't blame them either. It's all I wanted to do when I was serving, but I didn't understand until later why that wasn't always possible, nor should it be. If you can't handle a few nights away from home, then how will you handle an extended combat situation for months on end? Your job is to win and part of that is to know your craft and your team. They should be family to you. You should be able to tell us as much about them as the rest of the people in your life.

That culture is one that our society, along with the military, is starting to lack. That was one of my biggest takes when I rotated back into the 82nd Airborne for my last eight months in service. I had spent a lot of time across the street, but here I was again. Back off of Longstreet in the very buildings where it all began. But this time was all different. No one knew the guys under their charge, the teams didn't even hang out in their off time. The nights for them consisted of going back to their barracks rooms to play video games on consoles or gaming computers that could heat a small barracks room in just 30 minutes.

Fort Bragg has always had its challenges as the brutal wartime rotation had been a constant mission for the units housed there for over a decade. There had been a removal of a lot of the "hard chargers" from earlier in the war and the remainder of them that existed were torn in picking and choosing their battles while successfully maintaining a career. I remember being called out by a sergeant major for remedial PT with my guys after one of the teams came up short by underperforming. I was right there pushing with them because it was my failure point as well, but the new push by command was for paperwork to be done on these guys.

The majority of the privates don't learn quickly from the new methods. It was no longer OK to issue physical punishment for an infraction. They wanted us to start building paper trails and writing people up for everything. There is a time for that, but for the most part, I would rather take the 20–30 minutes to make myself stronger while instilling a mental (and sometimes even physical) reaction that stops me from performing the error again.

I even asked the platoon plainly after I was told to "get on it" when I didn't have papers from my platoon coming across the 1SG's desk. "Would you guys rather me tackle the problem right then and there or would you like me to start hitting your paycheck and time off?" I even gave them the option of letting me know that they could request paperwork instead of physical training as punishment for an infraction and I would issue the corresponding punishment via a write-up… it never happened.

When only two platoons exist in the company and my section didn't have anyone going AWOL or causing problems, there might be an answer nestled within the shared struggle concept. I also reinstituted the old rule that had been nailed into my skull by now CSM Donald McAlister so many years ago. You always had to travel in buddy teams. I encouraged the squads to hang out together on the weekend. Sometimes, that bond is only accomplished by bringing them all out to the field for a month and letting them create their own influences as they camped at the ranges.

Involvement (Call to Action)

A lot of the guys are at this point these days and some are realizing that it's going to be up to us to attempt to bring change by being involved in the system that gave us both a lifetime's worth of experience to talk about in both excited and fond memories as well as the terror of reliving the past that creeps up to visit at the most inopportune times. We can't lean on the system that is currently in place, but we need to use our adaptability and ingenuity to find ways to adapt, integrate, and support each other, much how we did in the past.

One of such efforts was recognized in the value of a platform that David Huff put together using speaking points during a roundtable Zoom discussion that became known as the Veterans Peer Group project. Sometimes, guys will only open up to those who have been through the same struggle as them. They see those that haven't served as someone they can't relate to or an outsider. The Veterans' Affairs office is getting better about addressing the mental health challenges that are showing up in our veterans, but we are not there yet. There had been a trauma specialist, a female major, who was flown to COP Ware during one of the ceremonies for the deceased (it may have been after Brunk) but there had been few that wanted to talk to her. The ones that did go offered the excuse that they just wanted to sit and talk with a woman for a bit. Even if they did unload everything that was going on through their thought processes currently, they would never have admitted it. Breaking down wasn't looked on well and would be set aside to deal with later on, after the bombs and guns were silenced.

It's one of the rules of addressing trauma. Get to it as quickly as possible and try to have an immediate effect on how the subject will experience or view the situation down the road. It's a patch. These guys are much better off in a lot of instances if they have some kind of support network to decompress and have a safe place to discuss without feeling like others are looking down on them.

Hopefully, these type of projects are something that we can get off of the ground and we will continue to test and refine as the project has already been outlined, tested, initial framework laid out, and early budget requirements have been drafted. At least we are out there trying to do something. Maybe it's just a shift in battlespace and our sense of purpose lies within the struggle to bring forth a product that helps.

One of the problems we face stems from the negative or false portrayal of veterans within movies and other entertainment outlets. They always show the crazy uncle who fought in Vietnam or the grandpa that took on the "Japs" in the Pacific theater. Don't startle grandpa if he is snoozing in his chair, he will choke slam you without realizing what he's doing. Yes, these guys exist, but most react in a way you would never know the inner workings behind the situation in their head. A lot of them are your day-to-day tradesmen and small business owners. They do well in the situations that are rough and need someone with their determination and resilience to stick it out. Given a little bit of guidance, these people are the type that can help America navigate the rough patch we are in right now.

Most veterans have the ability inside of them to be a community leader. Even if they weren't in a leadership role within the military, they know what right looks like in that regard, and that is half the battle. Once you attach a purpose to their life, most will excel in ways never seen before because there is a focus involved and the winning mindset is something that has been ingrained. Finish the mission.

I think that's the approach one of the men has taken with his own life. During Operation *Resiliency*, he had admitted that he had contemplated suicide when he was contacted about the reunion event being held by the Independence Fund. He told us that he figured it would be nice to see the guys again before he moved on from this world. Thankfully, the situation changed for him during that retreat.

He is now heavily involved in a system that tries to place veterans with programs to help them through whatever crisis situation they might be going through. On a recent call, he confided in me that he has been contacted by a few of the other guys about their own thoughts of suicide. It's something he has been burdened with because he has always had a listening ear for the soldiers he served with. The voice of reason while going through a rough patch… but no one ever asks him how he is doing. It's part of the role he plays, but it's one that we need to be aware of and be there for these guys so they don't have to carry it alone.

That's why we are starting to see companies such as Black Rifle Coffee, founded by veterans, stand up, because they know what's required of them and they want to give back and bolster their community through an effort that can be an inspiration to everyone.

The founder, Evan Hafer, now hosts a "shark tank" style production that is based on veteran projects that can directly help their community. Once they make it through the initial stage, he helps them with framework and a plan to get their idea off the ground. He uses his own personal strengths as a multiplier within a community that can do more as a whole, rather than as our own separate entities. That's a CIA-learned trick of the trade, by the way. You don't have to be the smartest or the best operator... just the best case manager to handle or coordinate the assets that get the job done.

Change is coming for the veteran community. We as a society have never been more disconnected from one another in a world that holds the ability to connect all of us into a powerful voice if we choose to do so. We need to work on a way to coordinate our efforts in such a way that optimizes the value in joint coordinated efforts combined with force multiplier effects.

These lessons are ones that we should take forward and integrate into our civilian lives and businesses. The models for success are right in front of us, but a lot of us are too blind or stubborn to see them or listen. We need to learn from each other and not isolate ourselves from one another.

I hope that the guys within division get ahold of this book and realize that we need to not only honor our past but learn from it as well. We need to take the good with the bad, the athletic studs with the weirdo nerds, the men who lead from the front with gusto and those that choose to pull their strength from those gallant leaders that pave the way by example day in and day out. Just like Bravo Company learned those 10-plus years ago and exactly how the heritage of the 82nd was based on the name of being "All American." From every corner of the country, we need to take this band of multitalented misfits and adapt to the new challenges that are put out in front of us.

In closing, this was a book that was written for and with the men of Bravo Company 2/508 to establish a record of their deeds and actions on the battlefield over 10 years ago. It is a sensitive book for some and a chapter of some people's lives that they would rather forget than carry with them any further. Such is the way of war sometimes.

It isn't about medals, glory, or any sort of notoriety that people might attach to someone who fights in a war. Most that have seen the real face of war will tell you that they would never wish that hell upon anyone. If they tell you there is something grandiose behind the profession, they are either a liar or a recruiter. We don't seek the glory... most of us just do the job and move on. Some see a purpose in giving others purpose, others will use what they learned and enhance their profession and lethality as they take to it like a duck to water, and some make it a crutch or an excuse to float by in life as an "entitled war veteran." This is just how things shake out.

Something hit me a while back when reading an excerpt from Norm Hooten, one of the operators that was portrayed in the *Black Hawk Down* movie. It had to do with his perspective and experience during firefights. He offered the advice, "Keep your head. It's never as good as it seems and it's never as bad as it seems, but keep your head, and there's always a way out. That's the most important thing: Keep your head, don't panic. Never ever panic, it's the worst thing you can do."

We can all take a piece of advice from that wisdom and translate it into our everyday lives. Don't panic... slow down, measure your actions, and look for the way out as you fall back on your resilience to just keep moving forward. There have been times when guys will reach out to the others without making a big deal out of it or ever bringing it back up. They will help out, talk them off the ledge, or offer a listening ear or helping hand when no one else will give them the time of day. That's one thing that will never cease to amaze me about this group of guys. When it comes down to it, they are truly always there for each other no matter what. That's the type of brotherhood that's forged from a struggle like the one we faced in the valley and one that I'll always cherish being a part of no matter how any of us shake out.

Damn the Valley, Fury from the Sky, Airborne All the Way

Afterword

I had asked CSM Bert Puckett if he wanted to write something in letter format to the men of Bravo Company that were to be presented with copies during the launch of the book. He thought long and hard about it, but eventually relented to my nagging as some of the men had been aware there was a rumor of receiving some form of communication from their former CSM. After seeing the letter, I knew that although it had been intended for a select few, it should be shared. Enclosed with permission are his words.

When we deployed in 2009 as an "advise and assist battalion," I knew the Afghans were not ready. I had spent a year as the Afghan Army development sergeant major while assigned to the Combined Security transition Command to Afghanistan. I knew from that time what the Afghan Army's capabilities had been. Here we were, less than a year later, prepping to go and support the ANA. To allow them to work "by, with, and through" functioning as an "advise and assist" battalion.

I knew from recent experience that the Afghan National Army was not ready for independently led operations unless something changed dramatically in the less than a year I had been home. LTC Frank Jenio and I both knew that our "advise and assist" mission had the huge probability of becoming a kinetic environment extremely quickly. We pushed for training to be focused on as many squad- and team-level training events as allowed, specifically, live fires. We continually fought for assets from our higher HQ and were told that we were going overboard.

Our goal was to produce the most lethal and disciplined Battalion we possibly could in the time allotted. We achieved this goal through hard, realistic training; empowering leaders by underwriting mistakes and allowing growth; and being ruthless when it came to the standards of physical training and personal conduct.

The time spent in the pre-deployment work up was brutal with the extra stressors of a combative and unresponsive upper chain of command. In their mind, it was more important to dive deep into the pseudo intellectual gymnastics of the newest catch phrase captured within the doctrine of "COIN" (counter insurgency). We, as an Army and a nation, were trying to move at a rocket ship pace while the Afghans and the Afghan army were still using a horse and wagon.

Little did we know how correct our suspicions were when we were pulled back to FOB Walton to prepare to take the Arghandab valley, a valley that the Soviets were never able to secure. A valley that ate an entire Soviet motorized rifle regiment. A valley that had been a bastion of Taliban influence since the war began. A valley that will go down in the history next to other places infamous within military history, like the A Shau valley in Vietnam, the valley of death in Crimea, and the Shenandoah valley. Those men and women that moved into the valley and established themselves in a day, but then they were required to hold it. After a year of sustaining weekly casualties, they had succeeded, but no one that had entered that valley left unchanged. We all left a piece of ourselves there.

I had reached a goal that I had never known that I would when I was a young Ranger in 1986. I had become a Command Sergeant Major of an Airborne Infantry Battalion. In every Paratrooper within the battalion, I saw my own reflection. A young person who wanted to be part of something larger than themself. Someone who wanted to challenge themselves and rise to occasion. I attempted to treat them like the men and women that they were. Not kids to be coddled or babysat. In every difficult training event and mission, I had to be there. Not because it was my job, but because I was able to watch them accomplish amazing feats along with dealing with soul-crushing loss. I grew to love them as my own kids.

Then, I was forced to watch them come home in flag-draped coffins.

There isn't a day that I wake up and don't think of the men and women of Two Fury. Some have succumbed to the unseen wounds of combat after returning home. Too many. But more have gone onto amazing lives, both continuing in the service of our nation or as leaders within their communities and industry. They are still my sons and daughters.

This story is timeless. It is the story of soldiers on the pointy end of a nation's will. Stories like this have been part of the human condition ever since Hammurabi's men marched on the Elamites, or Caesar's legionaries surrounded Alesia. It is a "soldier's eye view" of what the ground looked like when the ground was exploding around them.

I consider myself fortunate to be in some way counted among them, even in some small part.

Fury from the sky
Airborne all the way
RLTW!

Bert Puckett
CSM USA (ret)

Glossary

117G — A manpack radio produced by Harris corporation that carried multiple capabilities and enhancements at the time of its operation.

18X — The program designed to prepare a new recruit for Special Forces selection and the follow-on qualification course. Because the pipeline starts with the 11X (infantry) train-up, soldiers will usually join the ranks of the infantry if they fail to make the full course requirements.

18E — A Special Forces communications sergeant.

30th AG — New trainee holding company that resembles purgatory in the scope of military life. A whole lot of sitting around and waiting with a lot of busy work to be performed by the recruits that are voluntold during the start of the day where they will be headed.

.50 cal — A .50 caliber M2 machine gun produced by Browning, affectionately called ma deuce, can fire multiple versions .50 ammunition rounds that range from ball to armor piercing incendiary rounds. These would be mounted in conjunction with M240 machine guns on the turrets of our vehicles to provide a better range of firepower capabilities while operating during a mounted capacity.

75th Ranger Regiment — A lethal, agile, and flexible force, capable of conducting many complex, joint special operations missions. Today's Ranger regiment is the Army's premier direct-action raid force.

A-10 — the A-10 Thunderbolt was designed to provide close air support for friendly troops on the ground with the ability to attack anything from ground troops to armored vehicles. The infantry hold a special place in their hearts for the A-10 as their capabilities will turn a bad situation into a winning one in a hurry when they arrive on station to go to work.

AAR — After-action review, a procedure that immediately debriefs everyone at the conclusion of a mission whether or not anything happened that anyone thought was of significance. Even if there wasn't an incident during the patrol, one could always find an area we needed to get better at performing.

ACU — Army Combat Uniform – uniform currently used within the United States Armed Services.

AC-130 — A C-130 airplane variant that has additional gunship capabilities including air-to-ground ordnance.

AK-47 — Primary weapon of choice for global uprisings due to its rugged nature and simplistic operation.

ANA — Afghan National Army

ANCD — the Automated Network Control Device serves as a Cryptology device for radios.

ANCOP — Afghan National Civil Order Police were and Afghan National Army force responsible for civil order and counterinsurgency type directives. Their function was to perform civil presence patrols, prevent violent public incidents, and provide a crisis/anti-terror response unit for the area it was assigned.

ANP — The Afghan National Police was the front line of defense against insurgency and organized crime within Afghanistan. Despite their efforts, the force was constantly plagued with Taliban insiders, corrupt policemen, and morally bankrupt personnel. Not all ANP were bad, but it was well known that you could never be sure who you were dealing with when you had to work with the ANP.

ASVAB — Armed Services Vocational Aptitude Battery, a multiple-aptitude battery that measures developed abilities and helps predict future academic and occupational success in the military. It is administered annually to more than one million military applicants, high school, and post-secondary students.

AWOL — Absent without leave or missing.

BAT — Biometrics Automated Toolset System is a biometric system used by multiple sources within Government Agencies to assist in finding insurgents and other wanted individuals.

BFT — Blue Force Tracker see Panasonic Toughbook.

C-17 — A strategic transport aircraft that is utilized by the United States Military.

CDC — The Centers for Disease Control is a government agency that deals with infectious diseases.

Chinook — A dual-rotor heavy-lift helicopter that remains one of the fastest helicopters within the US military arsenal and one of the most versatile as they are found in all sorts of variable configurations.

CIF — the Commanders In-extremis Force is a company within a Special Forces Group that focuses primarily on Direct Action and Counter Terrorism missions.

COIN — Counter Insurgency doctrine that has a total goal of creating strong and secure relations with the local populace to render insurgents' efforts ineffective and non-influential. There is an entire field manual written by General David Petraeus on the implementation of the doctrine in US operations abroad.

COIST — A Company Intelligence Support Team will collect and evaluate information to generate reports and courses of action to provide to the commander. They will usually provide the "red team" side of the picture as their job includes anticipating and learning the enemy's tactics.

COMSEC — Communications cryptology security key.

Connex — A shipping container.

COP — A combat outpost is a smaller military outpost usually found on the front lines and carrying a company of infantry soldiers plus any additional attachments.

Cougar — An MRAP variant that would normally be outfitted to carry light infantry in a larger capacity than the smaller crewed vehicles. You would see these with RPG cages being largely used by the British troops within Helmand. They were also heavily used by the EOD teams operating abroad as well.

CROWS — Common Remotely Operated Weapons Station is a weapons platform that allows troops to remotely engage targets without needing to leave the protection of their vehicle.

DFAC — Dining facility.

Dust-off — A term used to call for a medical casualty evacuation. These were typically an air lift as no one would dare drive into the valley because of the high IED threat.

E&E — Escape and Evade. Usually used when discussing a single individual stuck in a really bad situation where he needs to flee the scene and take minimal equipment with him.

ECP — An entry control point; the main (and usually only) entrance to the compound. These will usually include hard barriers, a forced serpentine pattern of travel, razor wire, armed guards, and a guard tower or position. The larger established FOBs would have vehicle control points you needed to pass through on the way in or out while the smaller COPs would stop foot traffic or small vehicles.

EFP — An Explosively Formed Penetrator is a version of an IED that is focused on penetration of armor.

EMP — An electromagnetic pulse that will render all electronic equipment that is operating within a specified vicinity inoperable. This pulse can be produced naturally from a lightning strike or artificially with an explosion.

EOD — Explosive Ordnance Disposal is an engineering profession that involves the study and process of disarming hazardous explosive devices.

FID — Foreign Internal Defense is a term that refers to an integrated approach to combating insurgencies by, with, and through host nation capabilities and forces.

FIST — Fire Support Team or forward observers are troops that specialize in providing the ability to call for fire in multiple capacities.

FOB — A forward operating base is slightly larger than a COP (combat outpost) and meant to play a supporting role in strategic goals and tactical objectives. Depending on the size of FOB, you would usually find a hard building chow hall and supporting units manning the guard towers which allowed you to get some sleep while on the way through. These would serve as jump points or refit areas for infantry units on the way to another posting within the combat zone.

Fobbit — Someone who camps out on the FOB all day and never goes out on missions. Generally, they talk loudly about what they would do in a combat situation but never let themselves near the possibility of ever being put in one.

FRG — the Family Readiness Group is a commanders program that is supposed to form a network of mutual support and assistance with a military family's deployment readiness.

FST — a Female Support Team was a specialized unit that used female troops in a capacity that allowed them to operate alongside combat arms units in an area and talk to the local women of the area. In most cases, the women were more willing to talk about the various problems the region was experiencing. The male soldiers in the infantry units could not talk to or approach the female populace as the reprisal from the males of the region would threaten their existence.

GP Medium — A medium-sized US Army tent that required tent poles, stakes, and multiple people to erect.

GPS — The Global Positioning System owned and operated by the United States government in conjunction with the United Stated Space Force.

Green Ramp — The Army's little hut of buildings off of the flightline at Pope Air Base that serves as shelter during preparation for an airborne operation or deployment.

Grunt — An infantry soldier.

Hesco — A rapidly deployable barrier that consists of a cage lined with a burlap type material to hold the environment-supplied materials of dirt, sand, and rocks that provide a ballistic barrier against enemy combatants who would try to attack the fortification.

HIIDE — The Handheld Interagency Identity Detection Equipment is a biometric system used by the US Military.

HiLux — Essentially a Toyota Tacoma with a slightly narrower body that is conducive to off-road portions driving.

HMMVW — A typical combat vehicle for infantry units at the time. The bombs were getting to be large enough to warrant the development of an updated and dedicated vehicle for troops in combat operations. These were largely replaced by the MRAP program.

IED — Improvised Explosive Devices were the major source of problems within the Arghandab River Valley at the time and the variety of devices we would find plagued our time moving around the region.

IOTV — The Improved Outer Tactical Vest is a body armor system that was designed to break away via a pull tab. This was to enhance first response battlefield care or in the event you needed to quickly ditch your body armor. You would practice getting out of the system in the event you ended up being pulled underwater or needed to squirm out of a vehicle roll over.

ISAF — the International Security Assistance Force was the largest coalition effort in the history of NATO. From 2001 to 2014, ISAF attempted to provide Afghan security forces with the equipment and training they would need to defeat the Taliban and other surrounding bad actors.

ITC — Intensive Training Cycle – just another name for field exercises that are focused on getting critical tasks trained before a deployment or operation.

Javelin — a single-man medium-range anti-tank weapon system that has an effective range of 1.5 miles.

Joe — a private, a "cherry" (only in the airborne), the lowest of the low. These are your grunts that perform most of the tasks that need doing within the military. The Marines will refer to them as "boots". I'm not really sure what the Navy calls them because we never hung around long enough to learn and the Air Force is too polite for that sort of thing.

JP8 — Jet propellent 8 is a jet fuel that is less toxic, has corrosion inhibitors, and is less flammable than its counterpart fuels.

JRTC — Joint Readiness Training Center in Fort Polk, Louisiana provides realistic training scenarios for units within the military and is considered the premier combat training center for enhancement of unit readiness in mission train-up.

KLE — a Key Leader Engagement was essentially just talking to locals that were suspected to have influence within the community. This was supposed to be a technique in getting to know the real issues in the areas we were trying to positively effect.

Lashkar Gah — LKG is the capital city in Helmand province but serves as the political center for the region. It is said that he who controls Lashkar Gah, controls the entire province. The city served as the operations center for British operations within Helmand and also housed large Afghan police training facilities.

LOC — Line of communication. This can also mean a road or passage when referring to war zone methods or lines of communication.

MaxxPro — A vehicle variant of the MRAP that is larger and can accommodate more troops and equipment. It also had configurations that allowed for the vehicle to be outfitted for specialty use, such as a dedicated medevac vehicle complete with ambulatory equipment.

MK19 — A belt-fed automatic grenade launcher that fires 40mm grenades up to 1,500 meters away. These would be vehicle mounted although we had one mounted in an alternate tower on a tripod to make short work of anything that might try come from the northern direction at COP Johnston.

M203 — A single-shot 40mm grenade launcher that attached as a modular enhancement to the M4 rifle.

M240 — A machine gun that fires 7.62 ammunition and is carried by an infantry platoon's Weapons squad. The gun will usually operate in a gun team capacity using two to three members due to the size and weight of the weapon.

M4 — The bread-and-butter rifle that is an updated version of the M16 and has been utilized by the United States Army since 1994. Improvements throughout the years have led to design changes that allowed for even greater versatility on the battlefield throughout its time in service.

Mullah — A religious leader who would usually hold a seat of power within the local government.

Multicam — A camouflage pattern that is designed for use within a wide range of environments and conditions. It was developed and produced by the American company Crye Precision and has been adopted for use widely in armed forces worldwide, particularly within special operations units.

MRAP — Mine Resistant Ambush Protected vehicle produced as an update due to the increase of the threat of IEDs during the Iraq War and War in Afghanistan. They fielded 12,000 vehicles from 2007 to 2012 until the JLTV (Joint Light Tactical Vehicle) replaced its role. One flaw found within the MRAP was the tendency to roll over easily which hastened its replacement.

MRE — A "meal ready to eat" that comes packaged in a tough brown plastic casing and comes in bulk via boxes of 24 separately packaged meals. They are usually handed out and whatever you get is the "luck of the draw" or up to whomever is handing out chow that night. Some of the meals weren't bad, but some were downright disgusting. However, it's better than starving.

Mystery Ranch — A civilian backpack company that pivoted to develop a line of specialty military bags in support of the need global operations had for better equipment. These were never officially issued but would be bought by the unit purchase agent after justification and allocation of funds for such equipment that was necessary.

NATO — The North Atlantic Treaty Organization is an intergovernmental military alliance between multiple nations that agree to protect one another in the event of attack from third parties.

ODA — An Operational Detachment Alpha is a Special Forces "A" team within the battle theater.

OP — An observation point will be an area where troops can have a broad overview of the battlefield below them and offer the commander additional overwatch from their position. A squad designated marksman with sniper rifle capabilities will generally be present.

OP4 — soldiers specifically designated to play the opposition or "bad guys".

Panasonic Toughbook — A laptop computer that was highly ruggedized for military-grade operations. They had a variety of applications and modules to enhance their capabilities such as GPS antennae, waterproof capability, and a Faraday cage for EMP protection.

Pedro — Callsign for United States Air Force combat search and rescue crews.

Platoon — A small group of soldiers consisting of two or more squads that is usually commanded by a lieutenant.

PLF — A parachute landing fall is the specific method of falling that they drum into your head via repetition and blunt force at jump school located at Fort Benning, Georgia. Armed with such knowledge, you gain the ability to jump from high heights without breaking your ankles if performed correctly. This is why you would occasionally see junior paratroopers jumping from the second and third stories of the barracks on Fort Bragg attempting to put their newfound knowledge to practical use. It was usually to impress a lady.

PNN — Private news network, a term to describe the underground rumor mill that would communicate mainly among the lower enlisted. Sometimes, the NCOs would jokingly play a game of telephone by letting something "slip" within earshot of the joes and see where the comment would come back and how fantastically different the story would be.

POG — Person other than grunt; anyone other than an infantry soldier.

PSD — Personal Security Detail.

QRF — A Quick Reaction Force is a dedicated squad or group that will be utilized if a situation or a mission goes wrong. There would always be a squad on standby with all of their equipment staged and ready to go at moment's notice as seconds count on the battlefield. In the event they were needed, they would be ready to go at the posting's entry control point in under five minutes. In some situations, they would sleep in their gear because they knew the possibility of being called out was extremely high.

RPG — a Rocket Propelled Grenade is a shoulder fired missile weapon that fires rockets with explosive warheads.

ROE — Rules of Engagement would be different depending on the area you were in to correspond with the threat level the area held. Different commanders had different expectations and sometimes they were biased to a non-lethal solution due to the blowback from the civilian populace that a mistaken shooting during a COIN fight could have.

RTO — The radio telephone operator is responsible for establishing, maintaining, and operating communication systems within the military. They use various communication devices such as radios, telephones, and other electronic equipment to relay information between units during military operations. In addition to this, they are also responsible for maintaining and troubleshooting communication equipment to ensure that it is in good working condition.

SAW — The Squad Automatic Weapon is a light machine gun that fires belt-fed 5.56 ammunition that can be carried in ammo "drums" or in belt form if necessary. The SAW is an excellent weapon when it doesn't malfunction which can be largely mitigated by the operator if they know the particulars of the individual SAW that was issued. Every machine gun has roughly the same operation, but with strange personality quirks that can be noticed given enough familiarity with the weapon. I personally hated the SAW, but easily saw its value in a firefight situation.

SATCOM — Satellite communications used in different capacities within the military. The main encounters for an infantry soldier would be the "soda can" antenna that would be placed on a tripod for a soldier on the ground to reach higher command even if that command element is back in the USA.

SOG — a highly classified, multi-service United States special operations unit which conducted covert unconventional warfare operations before and during the Vietnam War.

SOP — Standard Operating Procedure.

SOPC — The Special Operations Preparatory Class was a crash course in learning everything you needed to know to pass Special Forces assessment and selection.

Stryker — An armored vehicle that attempted to strike a balance between the infantry and armor capabilities of a Brigade Combat Team. With the ability to carry nine passengers in an armored platform, the Stryker was heavily used in Iraq where it saw marginal success. They have since received multiple updates including a V-shaped hull to mitigate the ever-present IED threat.

TOC — The tactical operations center was the hub for any of the battlefield operations that would be taking place at any given time. Each outpost would have a TOC that would need to maintain a constant posting to provide radio communications and command and control throughout the battlespace.

Toughbox — Exactly what it sounds like. A giant hard plastic box that the guys would overload with equipment to keep it secured while left in the tent areas of the outpost.

TTP — Tactics, techniques, and procedures.

UGR — Unitized group rations were the bane of existence while spending time at COP Ware. Sometimes you would have gotten supplies and would sit down to a wild meal of steaks and Alaskan crab legs, but most were spent pulling rations from a case full of MREs. On especially bad dinners though, the cooks would break out the UGR boxes. You wouldn't get the extras that were included in the MRE package that made the meal tolerable and the serving size that would be slopped on your plate would be half the portion an MRE would provide.

USASOC — United States Army Special Operations Command.

VBIED — A Vehicle-Borne Improvised Explosive Device is exactly what it sounds like. It's the high explosives of a homemade bomb packed into a mobile platform with an engine. This can be one of the worst forms of an IED threat due to the rate of travel and amount of explosive payload it can deliver.

Woobie — A poncho liner that serves as a warm blanket against the elements that one might come across. This is an infantryman's best friend when in the field and sometimes will find its way to replacing the typical throw blanket you might find on one's couch. A staple for a combat veteran as they will probably have one stashed within reach of their normal sitting places for whatever reason.

Army Ranks

Enlisted

E-1 — PVT — The lowest of the low.

E-2 — PV2 — You got a motivational promotion… you're still the lowest of the low.

E-3 — PFC — Finally getting somewhere… nope. Just another motivational promotion. Get to work.

E-4 — SPC — Hey, now you can take the lowest of the low to the detail yourself!

E-5 — Sgt — The manager of the supervisors. Now the new lowest of the low… in management.

E-6 — SSG — The middle ground where the management shams like an E-4 or are hard-charging beasts.

E-7 — SFC — Usually the platoon sergeant and well knowledgeable. Certifiable bi-polar at this point.

E-8 — MSG/1SG — These are the professional assholes.

E-9 — SGM/CSM — A sergeant major is a weird creature. They are usually open to hearing from the lower guys because it gives them an insight into what's happening behind the scenes and a good picture of the effectiveness of his command. However, they will snap on a dime once agitated.

E-9S — SMA — The Sergeant Major of the Army — a figurehead.

Officers

O-1 — 2Lt — The butter bar is the most dangerous of the officer ranks within the service. Essentially, he has the knowledge of a PVT, but commands an entire platoon of soldiers.

O-2 — 1Lt — Equivalent to the knowledge of a SPC at this point, they are on their way to commanding a company of soldiers after spending some time at this rank. Hopefully, the platoon sergeants have squared these guys away by now so they can focus on the job instead of learning on the fly.

O-3 — Cpt — In command of a company of soldiers in the last real position that will be very personal with the men under his command.

O-4 — MAJ — Found in the office a lot.

O-5 — LTC — First actual rank achieved by an officer. They can finally start implementing some good as long as they are allowed to and are liked by the higher command.

O-6 — COL — The in-between spot that determines whether they stay what is called an "Iron Eagle" or ascend into the ranks that include stars.

O-7 — BG — Happy to receive his affirmation for dedicating his life to the armed services, he is known for talking... a lot.

O-8 — MG — He has two stars on his chest now and may command a division of soldiers. Just look away.

O-9 — LTG — Did you not get the hint at the first two?

O-10 — GEN — You better pray that you don't say or do anything stupid around this guy. It'll end up in a book.

Index